The Principal's Hot Seat

The Principal's Hot Seat

Observing Real-World Dilemmas

Nicholas J. Pace
Shavonna L. Holman
Cailen M. O'Shea

ROWMAN & LITTLEFIELD
Lanham • Boulder • New York • London

Published by Rowman & Littlefield
An imprint of The Rowman & Littlefield Publishing Group, Inc.
4501 Forbes Boulevard, Suite 200, Lanham, Maryland 20706
www.rowman.com

86-90 Paul Street, London EC2A 4NE, United Kingdom

British Library Cataloguing in Publication Information Available

Library of Congress Cataloging-in-Publication Data

Names: Pace, Nicholas J., author. | Holman, Shavonna L., 1976– author. | O'Shea, Cailen
    M., 1988– author.
Title: The principal's hot seat : observing real-world dilemmas / Nicholas J. Pace,
    Shavonna L. Holman, Cailen M. O'Shea.
Description: Lanham, Maryland : Rowman & Littlefield, 2022. | Includes bibliographical
    references. | Summary: "This book moves beyond dry case studies to provide readers
    with a window into the ways principals seek to navigate challenging, unpredictable,
    and authentic school leadership dilemmas"— Provided by publisher.
Identifiers: LCCN 2021059271 (print) | LCCN 2021059272 (ebook) | ISBN
    9781475859843 (cloth) | ISBN 9781475859850 (paperback) | ISBN
    9781475859867 (epub)
Subjects: LCSH: High school principals—United States. | High schools—United
    States—Administration—Decision making. | Educational leadership—United States.
Classification: LCC LB2831.92 .P34 2022 (print) | LCC LB2831.92 (ebook) | DDC
    371.12/011—dc23
LC record available at https://lccn.loc.gov/2021059271
LC ebook record available at https://lccn.loc.gov/2021059272

For those with the heart for school leadership

Contents

Preface

It's no secret that expectations for school principals are increasing. Gone are the days when a good principal was viewed merely as a manager who kept the kids in line and the building clean. Today's principals find themselves in an increasingly complex, intense environment that requires far more than was expected even a few years ago.

School leadership knowledge isn't enough. Principals will be about as effective as their ability *to apply* the knowledge, skills, and dispositions they learn in graduate school. As one urban superintendent stressed to us recently, "If they can't lead, we're not interested. We need authentic leaders more than ever before."

Enter the second edition of *The Principal's Hot Seat*. As former teachers and principals turned professors who spend our lives working with school leaders, we are continually struck by the range of situations they face. In the span of a few moments, principals move from the routine to the hyperintense and unpredictable. Scenarios they share might seem bizarre or far-fetched, but only to those unfamiliar with today's principalship. We know from years of experience that the true life of a principal is often stranger than fiction.

A desire to capture this unpredictability and intensity in an authentic learning experience led me (Pace) to develop the Day in the Office Principal's Role Play at the University of Northern Iowa in 2007. Since its inception, Day in the Office has produced some potent, memorable, and dynamic moments of learning for more than 800 aspiring principals. The exercise has become a highlight of the principalship program at the University of Northern Iowa and has expanded to the University of Nebraska-Lincoln and North Dakota State University, where it is facilitated by Drs. Shavonna Holman and Cailen O'Shea, respectively.

The second edition of *The Principal's Hot Seat* features new and updated scenarios, often recreated by school leaders who experienced them firsthand. One by one, stakeholders share their concerns with the principal, from affluent donors who are alarmed by proposed changes to the health curriculum, to the father who thinks the charismatic young teacher is far too friendly with his daughter, to the teacher who has had it with the toxic atmosphere in her professional learning community, among others.

In today's school environment, the principal's ability to effectively handle these issues in an appropriate, ethical, standards-based, empathetic way is not just important. It is essential. This second edition provides aspiring and practicing principals alike with the unique opportunity to observe and critique the actions of principals, while considering essential questions, such as:

- What do the standards in my state and district require me to do in such a situation? Did the principal act in accordance with those standards? What might I have done differently?
- How might this case touch some of my experiences or biases? What equity issues are present?
- How will I feel when facing a similar situation? What scenarios would be more comfortable or challenging for me and how can I tailor my professional growth accordingly?

USING THE SCENARIOS

Each scenario begins with a concise introduction to the issue, background information, a sampling of relevant literature, and a transcript of the conversation. Scenario-specific questions are designed to facilitate a thorough consideration of the principal's actions. Each also includes overarching questions designed to help readers dig deeper, explore emotions and bias, apply standards, and consider potential variations to the scenarios. Each concludes with suggested extension or internship activities and resources for further study.

The scenarios are designed for flexibility and can be used in a number of ways, including:

1. Homework: Readers view particular scenarios and come together to share their assessment of the principal's performance.
2. Group Exercise: Readers view particular scenarios together and compare their assessments. Alternately, small groups might view the same scenario and then compare thoughts with others.
3. Reading vs. Seeing: Read the introduction and transcript and then answer the questions that follow. Next, view the video and see if judgments and impressions change.
4. Stop Action: While viewing a scenario for the first time, the facilitator pauses the video to solicit assessments of the principal's performance,

input on what the principal should say or do next, and/or predictions for what may happen next.
5. Focus on Body Language: Try viewing the scenarios without sound to focus on nonverbal communication and perceived levels of tension.
6. Other applications, as determined by the instructor/facilitator and students.

A FINAL COMMENT

We emphasize a particularly important point: The "principals" in these scenarios are committed educators of various backgrounds, talents, and experience levels. In this second edition, some are students of educational leadership, while others have some years of experience. Like all of us who aspire to lead, they have much to learn. Those assuming the role of principal in this project have put themselves on display in an extraordinarily public way, in front of peers, professors, and others whom they will never meet. Their efforts, vulnerability, courage, and desire to grow are worthy of respect. Rookies and veterans alike can learn from their actions.

In developing, observing, recording, and unpacking the scenarios, we have learned nearly as much as our students. We have learned from interpretations we didn't expect, perceptions we would have missed, and ideas we never would have tried. We are reminded that right actions and clear ways forward are often easy to come by from the relative safety of a classroom or online learning environment, but reality is more complicated. We are reminded that robust preparation of school leaders requires an intentional bridge between theory, practice, and personal authenticity. While the standards are heavy on the *science* of school leadership, the way leaders bring them to life is even more complicated. It's *art*.

Video footage from an unscripted role play can be found at https://textbooks. rowman.com/principals-hot-seat2e.

Acknowledgments

We are indebted to many for assistance and inspiration in this project. First and foremost, we thank the many principalship students, practicing educators, and volunteer actors who have courageously put themselves on display. Quite simply, this edition would not exist without their willingness to take the risks of publicly wading into the scenarios. The students and actors are recognized individually in the section entitled "About the Contributors" at the end of the book. We're grateful to Tom Koerner and Carlie Wall of Rowman & Littlefield for their enthusiasm, flexibility, and patience during delays and uncertainty brought about by the COVID-19 pandemic. They are the best in the business.

Many valued colleagues and friends have contributed mightily to this project. The first edition could not have evolved into the second without the generous assistance of University of Northern Iowa colleagues Stephen W. Taft, John K. Smith, and Deborah J. Gallagher, in addition to Lt. Marty Beckner of the Cedar Falls (IA) Police. As we worked to strengthen this second edition at the University of Nebraska-Lincoln, Haley Apel, Loren Rye, Dan Hartig, Ann Marie Pollard, and Donald Morrison of the Omaha Public Schools provided key behind-the-scenes support and expertise.

Seeing the power of this exercise and the learning it produces reminds us of how fortunate we are to do the work of building and supporting school leaders.

Hot Seat #1

Stop Picking at Kids!
(High School)

Willie Barney knows his son Trevor is no angel. Thus, he was unsurprised when the call came from school: Come and pick up Trevor, who has been suspended for swearing at a teacher. Willie presents himself as a plainspoken man who has raised his son to be respectful and do his work at school. But when he arrives in Principal Hefel-Busch's office, Willie found an all-too-familiar story: Teachers subtly antagonize students and push their buttons until they react and get suspended, while teachers' behaviors go unchecked. It's not his son's fault.

Since the tragedy at Columbine High School, bullying has captured the attention of educators, from classrooms to research studies. Although debates about how much of this behavior is simply a part of growing up versus when it becomes harmful and dangerous are ongoing, research frames bullying at epidemic proportions. Casper and Card (2017) concluded that as many as 75% of students had been victims at some point in school. Whether bullying comes in the schoolyard or cyberspace (Kowalski et al., 2019; Resett & Gámez-Guadix, 2017), it is usually based on ethnicity, body size, socioeconomic status, sexual orientation (Pace, 2009; Savage & Miller, 2011), or some other characteristic, and we know the results can be tragic (Graham, 2010).

While peer-to-peer bullying has occupied center stage (Swearer et al., 2009; Thomas et al., 2018), far less attention has been given to a disturbing aspect of life in schools: teachers who bully students. Researchers have identified this as an understudied and often unseen problem (Zerillo & Osterman, 2011). Acknowledging that we as educators simply enjoy some students more than others, many have taken Whitaker's (2004) advice that teachers "don't have to *like* the students; you just have to *act as if* like you like them" (italics in original) (p. 46). However, some researchers (McEvoy, 2005; Whitted & Dupper, 2008) have concluded that many teachers are unable to heed Whitaker's advice and instead engage in what McEvoy (2005) described as a "pattern of conduct, rooted in a power differential, that threatens, harms, humiliates, induces fear, or causes students substantial emotional distress" (p. 1).

While some teachers overtly mistreat students, Sylvester (2011) concluded that others bully students in more subtle, almost unnoticeable ways, such as the use of sarcasm, secret names, or arbitrary enforcement of particular policies. In many ways, privilege is invisible to those who have it or those who remain free from bullying by authority figures. Datta et al. (2017) found that students who reported being bullied by teachers were much more likely to be disengaged, have lower grades, view school discipline as unfair, and have a negative perception of their school's climate. Many see adults as generally unsupportive.

In a fascinating and extensive study of a rural Iowa high school, Carr and Kefalas (2009) examined how "teachers, parents, and other influential adults cherry-pick the young people" who seem destined for good things, offering them special treatment and frequent accolades (p. 19). "Those kids were placed on a different trajectory because the entire town was behind them, cheering for them to make it and supporting them in concrete ways" (p. 20). Students who are not seen as members of this group, argued Carr and Kefalas, received far less affirmation and investment and often "managed to internalize the judgments from teachers" who saw limited possibilities for them (p. 65). This "authority abuse" may be nearly invisible to many but is a key consideration for principals (McEvoy, 2005, p. 1).

In this scenario, Principal Hefel-Busch has an opportunity to hear a parent's side of the story, considering Trevor's actions and school policy. Knowing that all teachers want their administrators' support on discipline cases, she also faces the question of whether the problem lies with Trevor, the teacher, or both.

THE TRANSCRIPT

Dad: Well, I'm trying to figure out why my son is being suspended from school. I get a phone call saying that he cursed at a teacher. A teacher's pickin' at the kids every time I come up over here. And somebody's messin' with somebody all the time. All ya'll do is pick on people.

Principal: Can you tell me your student's name?

Dad: Uh, Trevor.

Principal: Trevor, okay. Will you tell me a little bit about what happened?

Dad: All I know is he cursed out the teacher. The teacher was pickin' at him, so he cursed at him. You tell me, you're the one that's here! You're supposed to know what's going on.

Principal: You're right. I am. That's why I want to hear, you know, there's always more than one side to the story. So I really appreciate that you came in.

Dad: The only side I got is a phone call saying I need to come pick him up.

Principal: And that was today?

Dad: That was today.

Principal: Well, the first thing I'm really glad you came in, I appreciate you coming in to talk about it. The other thing is, is the one thing we can't have is if Trevor did curse at the teachers, that's not acceptable. We can't have that.

Dad: Teachers shouldn't be picking at him. Every time I come up to this flippin' school that's all I hear.

Principal: Have you met with the teacher about it?

Dad: That's why I'm here!

Principal: Okay. Well, that would be what I would like to do. I would kind of, since I don't know much of the story—

Dad: What the—

Principal: It doesn't sound like—

Dad: Why would I want to meet with the teacher who's sitting here picking at my kids all the time?

Principal: Well, I think it'd be a good idea to maybe solve the problem.

Dad: What problem's going to be solved? What are you going to do differently?

Principal: That's why I would like to meet with the teacher down here and maybe Trevor to see what we can do.

Dad: Trevor is sitting out in the office. The teacher, like I said, every time I get a phone call . . . over and over again, ya'll continually picking at him.

Principal: M hmm, m hmm. And I understand you feeling that way. But if Trevor is cursing at teachers or getting himself—

Dad: Hey, I've told him not to curse at teachers. I've told him that regardless what to do. But the fact of the matter is that a bunch of adults around here that just continuously pick, pick, pick at kids! What do you expect them to do?!

Principal: Well, I appreciate you supporting us and telling him not to curse, you know curse at teachers and get upset. I appreciate that. And I would really like us to work it out. Because if someone is picking on Trevor. Ya know. If it is because people are human . . . and if there is that relationship isn't there between you and the teacher then I would like to get that worked out.

Dad: You guys don't have relationships with anybody!

Principal: Oh, yeah, I think we do. I think we do. I mean I'm really glad you came in. You know. That's a start. I'm glad you support us at home and tell Trevor not to, you know, that he shouldn't engage in those, you know, name-calling or disrespect towards the adults. I mean, we appreciate that.

Dad: But he's a kid. Kids are going to do those things. If the adult does it, the kid's gonna do it.

Principal: You're right.

Dad: So what do you do with a teacher who's picking at kids?

Principal: Well, that would be my responsibility.

Dad: And that's what I'm asking you. What do you do with kids? You're kicking him out of school. I know what's happening to my son. What's gonna happen to a teacher who is continuously picking at kids?

Principal: Well, the first thing I'm going to do is I'm going to meet with the teacher and I'm gonna try to find out what's happening. How things are going. I would like to talk to Trevor. We can do that together or we can do that, ya know, at a different time.

Dad: And then what?

Principal: Then we're going to get back together and we're going to come up with a plan.

Dad: So how does that fix the teacher's behavior that is continuously picking at my son?

Principal: Well hopefully it's not going to continuously happen. We're going to figure out what's going on and we're going to fix it.

Dad: So, what is the consequence for the teacher?

Principal: Right now, I'm going to meet with the teacher. And hopefully figure out what's going on. I want to meet with Trevor.

Dad: So, if you figure out the teacher's picking at my kid, what are you gonna do?

Principal: Well, if there is the relationship, if there is a problem with the relationship, my suggestion at that point is there are a few things we can do. We maybe move Trevor into a different classroom . . . maybe have a different teacher.

Dad: That's what I want. I want him moved to a different classroom because I'm tired of him picking on him. The fact of the matter is I don't know what difference it will make, because all of your teachers pick at people anyways.

Principal: Well, I would like for us to meet with Trevor and the teacher first before we make that decision. You know. Would you be willing to do that?

Dad: I've already talked to him; he's a fool!

Principal: The teacher?

Dad: Yes! And if he gets loud with me, I'm gonna whoop his butt across the street! I'm tired of dealing with him!

Principal: Right, right. And I understand that. We don't want that to happen. You know, this is what I would like to do. You know. If you don't want to meet with the teacher, then I'll meet with the teacher and then the two of us and Trevor can get back together and go from there. But if the relationship is this bad, if the bridge is burned this badly, then maybe it is in the best interest for Trevor to be moved to a different class.

Dad: All right. That's what I want. I want him moved.

Principal: Okay, so how about today you take Trevor home. Um, he's probably pretty upset, I can tell you are pretty upset. Again, I appreciate you coming in to talk to me. And then I'll do some talking with the teacher and maybe a couple of the other teachers too and see maybe where we can best put Trevor . . . for a different, for a different teacher.

Dad: Thank you.

Principal: You're welcome.

DISCUSSION AND REFLECTION QUESTIONS

1. Identify the primary and secondary issue(s).
2. Identify areas in which you believe the principal acted effectively.
3. Identify areas in which you believe the principal could have acted more effectively.
4. After thanking Dad for coming in, the principal explains (at 0:50) that Trevor using profanity toward the teacher is unacceptable. Dad responds by complaining that the teacher "shouldn't be picking at him." Given that many teachers identify issues related to respect as frequent reasons for office referrals, how should she respond? Is it possible that there is a cultural or generational issue between the teacher and students? Is it

possible that Dad is simply deflecting blame for the situation toward the teacher?

5. At 1:41 Dad explains that he has told Trevor not to curse at teachers but goes on to say, "Fact of the matter is that the adults around here that just continuously pick, pick, pick at kids! What do you expect them to do?!" How should she respond to the question? Have you known teachers who push students' buttons?

6. Principal Hefel-Busch discusses the importance of relationships. Dad counters that if kids see teachers drawing kids into verbal exchanges like this, kids will respond negatively, to which the principal agrees. Dad then asks (at 2:46) what she's going to do with "a teacher who is continuously picking at kids." How should the principal respond?

7. At 3:07 Dad is still pressing to know what the principal will do with the teacher's behavior. In saying that, "Hopefully it's not going to continuously happen. We're going to figure out what's going on and we're going to fix it," is Principal Hefel-Busch implying that she believes the teacher *is* picking at Trevor?

8. Dad continues to demand to know what will be done with the teacher if the principal determines that he is, in fact, picking at students. The principal floats the possibility of moving Trevor to another teacher's classroom. Is this a good idea? Does it effectively address the issue?

9. At 3:40 Dad jumps on the idea of moving Trevor to a different classroom, but also complains that it may not do any good "because all of your teachers pick at people anyways." Is that a sign of an impossible parent or a more pervasive problem among the faculty? How can Principal Hefel-Busch know?

10. Principal Hefel-Busch suggests a meeting to discuss the issue. Dad complains that he has already talked to him and "he's a fool." He goes on to say, (3:59) "If he gets loud with me I'm gonna whoop his butt across the street! I'm tired of dealing with him!" How should the principal respond? Do you interpret this as frustration or a threat?

11. At 4:19 the principal suggests that if the relationship between Trevor and the teacher is badly damaged, that perhaps Trevor should be moved to a different class. Is this an appropriate course of action or should she proceed with the meeting with Trevor and the teacher? Could moving Trevor trigger a rash of other parents wanting their children moved?

REFLECTION AND DISCUSSION QUESTIONS

Balcony View

Generally speaking, how did the principal perform in this scenario? What would you have done differently?

Standards in Action

Which standards do you see as relevant in the scenario? Does the principal effectively meet them? Are there standards and/or criteria left unmet by the principal's actions?

Peel the Onion

Like an onion, leadership challenges have multiple layers. The presenting issue may be singular or appear simple in nature. Often, however, it represents one part of an underlying, more complex issue. The best leaders address concerns in the moment, while not losing sight of root causes. What is/are the presenting issue(s)? Do you see potential nuanced factors that should be explored?

Self-Check

We all come to our roles with unique experiences, perspectives, and biases that influence our perceptions and actions. Picturing yourself in the principal's chair, describe your emotions.

Switch It Up

How might your thinking or approach change if the gender, ethnicity, language, age, sexual orientation, socioeconomic status, disability, or other descriptors of the players involved were different?

Equity Lens

Equity-driven leaders understand that diversity takes many forms. What equity- or diversity- related issues could be present in this scenario?

Power and Presence

In televised presidential debates, "looking presidential" is an important measure of a candidate's performance. The same is true for principals. Halpern and Lubar (2003, p. 3) define leadership presence as being more than "commanding attention" to include "the ability to connect authentically with the thoughts and feelings of others." Does the principal exert an effective presence? Describe the power balance between the principal and the visitor. Does positional or personal power between the principal and visitor seem uneven or problematic? What does body language say that words do not?

Principal's Priority

How serious is the situation? Are de-escalation techniques needed?
How *soon* should the principal address this situation?
Should the principal inform a supervisor about this issue and get them involved?

Reach Out?

Should the principal involve other individuals, professionals, resources, or organizations?

In a Word

Capture the principal's performance in the scenario using one word.

Collaborate

Collaborate with a classmate or colleague to rewrite or alter the case with a different set of circumstances. Share your new case with other colleagues to ascertain how they would approach it.

Extension and Internship Experiences

- What type of data does your building track regarding office referrals? Are there common definitions for concepts like "respect" or "insubordination?" Can the data be disaggregated by teacher, classroom, student demographics, etc.? What conclusions could be drawn?
- Does your building/district conduct surveys with students and stakeholders to ascertain their perception of issues like those raised by Willie?

If so, how is the data used? If not, should such a survey be constructed and administered?

- Are there teachers in your building who have a reputation for pushing kids' buttons or bullying? Interview an administrator to learn their perspective on how to address this issue.
- Are there some teachers who frequently have difficulty interacting with particular groups of students (related to gender, ethnicity, language, social class, sexual orientation, etc.)? Ask an experienced principal how they have addressed this. Has your building or district engaged in professional development related to cultural competency?

REFERENCES AND RESOURCES

Carr, P. J., & Kefalas, M. J. (2009). *Hollowing out the middle: The rural brain drain and what it means for America*. Beacon Press.

Casper, D. M., & Card, N. A. (2017). Overt and relational victimization: A meta-analytic review of their overlap and associations with social–psychological adjustment. *Child Development* 88(2): 466–483.

Datta, P., Cornell, D., & Huang, F. (2017). The toxicity of bullying by teachers and other school staff. *School Psychology Review* 46(4): 335–348. doi: 10.17105/SPR-2017-0001.V46-4.

Graham, S. (2010). What educators need to know about bullying behaviors. *Phi Delta Kappan* 92(1): 66–69. Retrieved from EBSCO*host*.

Halpern, B. L., & Lubar, K. (2003). *Leadership presence: Dramatic techniques to reach out, motivate, and inspire*. Penguin Group.

Kowalski, R. M., Limber, S. P., & McCord, A. (2019). A developmental approach to cyberbullying: Prevalence and protective factors. *Aggression and Violent Behavior* 45: 20–32.

McEvoy, A. (2005). *Teachers who bully students: Patterns and policy implications.* Paper presented at the Hamilton Fish Institute's Persistently Safe Schools Conference, Philadelphia, PA. Retrieved from http://www.stopbullyingnow.com/teachers%20who%20bully%20students%20McEvoy.pdf.

Pace, N. J. (2009). *The principal's challenge: Learning from gay and lesbian students.* Information Age.

Resett, S., & Gámez-Guadix, M. (2017). Traditional bullying and cyberbullying: Differences in emotional problems, and personality. Are cyberbullies more Machiavellians? *Journal of Adolescence* 61: 113–116.

Savage, D., & Miller, T. (Eds.). (2011). *It gets better: Coming out, overcoming bullying, and creating a life worth living.* Dutton Adult.

Swearer, S. M., Espelage, D. L., & Napolitano, S. A. (2009). *Bullying prevention and intervention: Realistic strategies for schools.* The Guilford Press.

Sylvester, R. (2011). Teacher as bully: Knowingly or unintentionally harming students. *The Delta Kappa Gamma Bulletin* 77(2): 42–45.

Thomas, H. J., Connor, J. P., & Scott, J. G. (2018). Why do children and adolescents bully their peers? A critical review of key theoretical frameworks. *Social Psychiatry and Psychiatric Epidemiology* 53(5): 437–451.

Whitaker, T. (2004). *What great teachers do differently: Fourteen things that matter most*. Eye on Education.

Whitted, K. S., & Dupper, D. R. (2008). Do teachers bully students? Findings from a survey of students in an alternative education setting. *Education and Urban Society* 40(3): 329–341.

Zerillo, C., & Osterman, K. F. (2011). Teacher perceptions of teacher bullying. *Improving Schools* 14(3): 239–257. doi:10.1177/1365480211419586.

Will You Hold Him Accountable? (Middle School)

Teacher aides and associates play a vitally important role in schools. From clerical duties like making copies to extra one-to-one assistance with students, they provide stretched teachers with essential assistance. When a teacher aide has a knack for building relationships with students, the entire classroom environment can change. The Bureau of Labor Statistics (2020) estimated that schools employ nearly 1.5 million teacher aides and assistants nationally, with the number more than doubling between 1996 and 2016 (Gottfried, 2016). Giangreco et al. (2010) estimated that on a given day we might expect to see teacher aides or paraprofessionals present in almost any classroom in the United States.

While their prevalence and importance are increasing, research indicates that adequate professional development and support for teacher aides is sorely lacking. In a special issue of *Psychology in the Schools* focused on training and support for teacher aides, Reddy et al. (2021, p. 644) observed, "Despite their increased presence and seminal role in the provision of student supports, paraprofessionals receive very limited training and inconsistent supervision to meet the needs of students."

Some principals thrive on the unpredictability and variability of the job. In this scenario, Megan, a teacher aide, reminds us of that unpredictability when she comes to Principal Neugebauer's office, with her agitated partner, Kyle, accompanying her not to talk about her need for professional development, but something far more alarming.

Megan explains that she recently ended an intimate relationship with Jim, a science teacher. In Principal Neugebauer's office, she shares that Jim has begun harassing her and spreading rumors about her at school. Megan says she loves working at the school and with the ever-present concern over budgets, fears that the things Jim is saying may make her a target for job cuts. While Megan explains her concerns, her new partner, Kyle, complains that the friendly relationship between Principal Neugebauer and Jim makes it unlikely that Megan will be treated fairly. Kyle has his own ideas about how the situation could be resolved.

Research suggests that what Megan describes is not uncommon across society. High-profile cases of sexual harassment and abuse have fueled the #MeToo movement, and new attention to what Bongiorno et al. (2020, p. 11) call a "pervasive and hidden social problem." Despite new awareness, women making reports often experience negative outcomes, stigma, backlash, and blame (Bergman et al., 2002; Solnit, 2018). Further, Goh et al. (2021) found that claims of sexual harassment were more often seen as credible when coming from women perceived to have "feminine features, interests, and characteristics" (p. 1).

In 2018, the Education Week Research Center launched a study of sexual harassment and assault in P-12 education. The findings paint a staggering picture of the way sexual harassment is addressed—or neglected—in schools:

- While educators may perceive sexual harassment and assault as less common in education than other fields, nearly a third report having witnessed sexual harassment or assault between educators, and one in five reported having personally experienced it. Females were more likely to experience sexual harassment or assault at school (25%), but males were more likely to report it.
- More than 40% who have witnessed harassment or assault felt that it produced a hostile work environment, but most who experience or observe it choose not to make a report.
- Approximately a third of administrators reported receiving sexual harassment or assault reports, but educators making such reports believed that inaction is the most frequent result.
- While two-thirds of educators recall training on sexual harassment at school, only 13% say it was useful, and less than a quarter indicated they were well familiar with their school's definition of sexual harassment and assault.

Hachiya et al. (2014) noted an essential bottom line: "every allegation of sexual harassment should be quickly and thoroughly investigated." (p. 336), knowing that schools are "liable for environmental harassment if senior management does not take immediate and appropriate steps to terminate harassing conduct and discipline the offending party" (p. 322). Understanding that "a false allegation of harassment may significantly damage an educator's reputation and destroy his or her career" (p. 336) underscores the importance of thorough investigations of any complaints. "If an accusation is proved to be true, then definitive action to punish must be demonstrated. If the accusation is proved false, then definitive action should be taken to punish the false accuser" (p. 336).

Brock and Grady (2004, p. 49) observed that "school leadership sometimes involves listening to the personal problems of staff members" and that the principal is often "viewed as a sympathetic listener or a trusted source of guidance." Megan is seeking such guidance as Principal Neugebauer stands at the starting point of determining what has happened between Jim and Megan, next steps, and what is required of a principal driven by standards, integrity, and the trust placed in him by the district.

THE TRANSCRIPT

Megan: Good morning.

Principal: Hi. Good morning.

Megan: I'm sure you remember me. Megan, one of your teacher's assistants.

Principal: Yes, of course. Good to see you. Thank you for coming in.

Megan: Thank you for taking some time today to talk with us. I hate to be a squeaky wheel, and I love working here and I don't want to cause any problems, but I'm sure you know that I had a relationship with Jim, our science teacher, and, you know, it just, it was a good relationship for a while and then it just kind of went off the rails a little bit. He became a little possessive and things and so I had to end that relationship and, you know, I don't want to cause any problems or anything but, he, I feel like he is just trying to ruin me. He's talking badly about me to other teachers, he's telling them that I cheated on him when I didn't.

Kyle: Show him the texts!

Megan: Kyle and I got together afterwards, he's just, he's harassing me. He's telling students bad things about me, he's making up lies about me. Last Saturday he called me 37 times in one hour. Here's some examples of texts that he's sent me. If you want to read those out.

Kyle: Oh, he's breaking the law, I mean it's straight- up harassment, is what it is. I mean, I know it is. I don't even know why we're here, because you guys have a tee time this afternoon, you and Jim do. I know you do, you guys golf together all the time.

Megan: I really don't want to cause any trouble but I just, I love working here and I really don't want to lose my job here and I know that he has power over me and I know that he's, you know, a teacher and I'm not. and I just, I just, I'm afraid because he says he's gonna make me pay and, you know, I, I just need help, I don't know what to do and I really want to keep working here.

Principal: First of all, let me, like, I appreciate that you brought this to my attention. I'm sorry that you are having to go through this, obviously very difficult breakup. Can I ask you first, some, what are some of the steps that you've already taken to resolve this issue? Have you spoken with him?

Kyle: It's gonna be me kicking his ass. That's what it's gonna be.

Megan: Well, I did speak with him and when I broke up with him, you know I, I told him that I wanted to have a good working relationship and obviously we have to work with each other and you know I, I didn't want this to impact it but, but I had to block his number, I mean, calling me that many times is just unacceptable. I didn't answer I just ignored him for a while, but he's getting more threatening and, and I just, I don't want to lose my job. I love working here.

Principal: Yeah, I can understand that, that would be really upsetting. Well, first of all, I do want to let you know that your, your position is not in jeopardy. We have appreciated all of the work you have done.

Kyle: He says that now. He says that now, but if it's between you and Jim. . . .

Principal: Uh, we appreciate all that you do, and the great work that you do with our students. And this should not have any impact on that. You said that you've already approached him about this and, and. . . .

Megan: I have. Yeah, I mean I did what I can, I don't know what else to do.

Principal: Okay.

Megan: Well, he's threatening me, you know he's talking to other teachers about me. He's slurring my name all over the school to other teachers and to students.

Principal: Okay. Well, one thing that I think is that if you do truly feel threatened, it would be important that you approach other authorities about this, you know, outside. And work towards, then seeing what other solutions there are legally for that, as well. As far as your time at work, it is important that all of our employees feel comfortable and safe when they enter our building. And I want to make sure that that's true for, for you, as well as for Jim and I haven't actually brought, Jim has not brought this up to me at all. So, I'm glad that you did. But I think that I need to have a—

Kyle: Are you gonna ask him on the golf course today?

Principal: Actually, I'm not a very good golfer, so I don't go there very often.

Kyle: That's not what we're hearing.

Principal: What, what I can do is have that conversation and make sure that he knows that our expectation for all of our staff is that we treat each other with mutual respect, and that this is a safe place.

Megan: So, will you hold him accountable to that, I mean if he's spreading lies to you about it and are you gonna, is there gonna be any consequences for the way that he's acting?

Principal: I will hold all of our staff accountable to those expectations. However, and I do need to listen to him and hear what he has to say. But I will hold him, and any staff to those expectations. As far as what comes out of that, just like this conversation is between you and I, outside of these doors, that's your story to tell, not mine. And I'd say the same thing to Jim also, so that's just the way to tell not mine, as well. However, everything that I do will be based on the best information. And if this continues to be an issue, I want you to bring that to my attention as well, so that we can ensure that you have that safe work environment and if other steps need to be taken, that's something that I can address at that point. But hopefully, we can find resolution before then. And I, again, I want to reiterate that if you do feel threatened, that there are other things, other authorities in the community that you should also be approaching. And of course, those things, should they impact the work environment we'll, we'll act on those as well.

Megan: So, can you assure that even with budget cuts this year that this won't affect my position?

Principal: As far as with that, I like I said, we really do really value your position. And I have no intention of letting any of my staff go. But this would not be a factor on that whatsoever.

Kyle: It's fine. I know where he works. So, if he doesn't take care of it, I will.

Megan: I don't want to see anything get violent. But I appreciate your support and, you know I'm happy for you to be here with me and support me through this.

Principal: And I appreciate that, you've been in here, you're supporting her as well. And, please let me know going forward if you need anything from me, on my end. As you navigate other options in terms of securing the boundaries that you're looking between you and Jim, and I will follow up on my end. As far as where my conversation with him goes, again that's, that's his story to tell. However, I do need to know if the issue was not resolved, and as these continue to impact your ability to best serve our students here at our school.

Megan: So, it is impacting me so far and if it does continue, what steps will be taken?

Principal: Well, at that point that would mean that my conversation with him has not had the result that it needs to. Because like I said, there is an expectation. And quite frankly, those expectations are laid out in our policies, both at the district and school level, and if those are not being followed there, there are actions that the district and I can take to make sure that it will. We'll keep that focus on the policy end and make sure that you are able to engage in your work in a safe environment. All right, so I will follow up with this and I will give you a call again, probably next, within a few days, by next week for sure to see how things are going and make sure that you're doing.

Megan: Thank you.

Principal: All right, thank you, and thank you again for coming in as well.

DISCUSSION AND REFLECTION QUESTIONS

1. Identify the primary and secondary issue(s).
2. Identify areas in which you believe the principal acted effectively.
3. Identify areas in which you believe the principal could have acted more effectively.
4. At 0:04, Megan introduces herself as a teacher's assistant in the building. Kyle, her partner, is accompanying her, but no introductions are made. Is it appropriate for Kyle to be involved? Should Principal Neugebauer continue the meeting with Kyle present? Would asking him to wait outside bring more tension to the environment?
5. Note Kyle's body language early in the meeting. Does it cause concern?
6. Principal Neugebauer looks to have decided to focus on the conversation, rather than taking notes. Would you approach the conversation in the same way? Are there specific questions you would suggest he ask?
7. At 1:44 Megan says she's afraid and that Jim "says he's gonna make me pay." Should this cause alarm? Should Principal Neugebauer explore the apparent threat specifically?
8. At 2:09, Principal Nuegebauer asks Megan to share any steps she has already taken to address the situation. Should he proceed with this line of questioning or are there other things you would want to know at this point?
9. After Principal Neugebauer asks Megan what steps she has taken to resolve the situation with Jim, Kyle says (2:12), "It's gonna be me kicking his ass. That's what it's gonna be." What should happen next?
10. At 2:24 Megan says she and Jim have to work with each other and didn't want the breakup to impact their work and later says "he's getting more threatening." How would you respond?
11. Kyle asserts that Principal Neugebauer and Jim have a personal relationship and often golf together. At 4:12, he asks if the principal will discuss the matter with Jim on the golf course that afternoon. At 4:15 Principal Neugebauer appears try to reduce the tension by saying he's not a good golfer and doesn't play often. Evaluate.

12. At 5:36 Principal Neugebauer advises Megan that if she continues to feel threatened that there are other resources available to her, but does not mention them by name. Should he be more specific? Are the alleged threats in need of definition?

13. After assuring Megan that her complaint will not put her position in jeopardy with potential budget cuts, at 6:12 Kyle says, "I know where he works. So, if he doesn't take care of it, I will." Does it matter if it is a real threat or just bluster? How should Principal Neugebauer respond?

14. At 6:28 Principal Neugebauer says he appreciates that Kyle has come to support Megan. Do you see this as an attempt to establish rapport? In saying this, is he indirectly or unintentionally affirming Kyle's veiled threats, perhaps encouraging them?

15. Does Principal Neugebauer meet what Brock and Grady (2004) described as a "sympathetic listener?" Explain. How might the level of perceived empathy impact the scenario?

16. Make a step-by-step list of what Principal Neugebauer should do when the meeting ends.

REFLECTION AND DISCUSSION QUESTIONS

Balcony View

Generally speaking, how did the principal perform in this scenario? What would you have done differently?

Standards in Action

Which standards do you see as relevant in the scenario? Does the principal effectively meet them? Are there standards and/or criteria left unmet by the principal's actions?

Peel the Onion

Like an onion, leadership challenges have multiple layers. The presenting issue may be singular or appear simple in nature. Often, however, it represents one part of an underlying, more complex issue. The best leaders address concerns in the moment, while not losing sight of root causes. What is/are the presenting issue(s)? Do you see potential nuanced factors that should be explored?

Self-Check

We all come to our roles with unique experiences, perspectives, and biases that influence our perceptions and actions. Picturing yourself in the principal's chair, describe your emotions.

Switch It Up

How might your thinking or approach change if the gender, ethnicity, language, age, sexual orientation, socioeconomic status, disability, or other descriptors of the players involved were different?

Equity Lens

Equity-driven leaders understand that diversity takes many forms. What equity- or diversity-related issues could be present in this scenario?

Power and Presence

In televised presidential debates, "looking presidential" is an important measure of a candidate's performance. The same is true for principals. Halpern and Lubar (2003, p. 3) define leadership presence as being more than "commanding attention" to include "the ability to connect authentically with the thoughts and feelings of others." Does the principal exert an effective "Principal's Presence?" Explain.

Principal's Priority

How *serious* is the situation?
How *soon* should the principal address this situation?
Should the principal inform a supervisor of this issue and get them involved?

Reach Out?

Should the principal involve other individuals, professionals, resources, or organizations?

In a Word

Capture the principal's performance in the scenario using one word.

Collaborate

Collaborate with a classmate or colleague to rewrite or alter the case with a different set of circumstances. Share your new case with other colleagues to ascertain how they would approach it.

Extension and Internship Experiences

- Does your building or district have a policy on relationship issues between staff members? To whom are employees supposed to report harassment in your school? What type of training do these officials receive? Interview the person(s) designated as investigators. Review the steps taken and forms used.
- Does your building/district offer professional development related to issues centered on harassment? Ask a group of teachers about their level of familiarity with mechanisms for reporting harassment.
- Friendships are different when one is a supervisor. Interview an experienced principal about navigating personal friendships and professional responsibilities.

REFERENCES AND RESOURCES

Alexander, K., & Alexander, D. M. (2019). *American public school law* (9th ed.). Wadsworth.

Bergman, M. E., Langhout, R. D., Palmieri, P. A., Cortina, L. M., & Fitzgerald, L. F. (2002). The unreasonableness of reporting: Antecedents and consequences of reporting sexual harassment. *Journal of Applied Psychology* 87: 230–242. Doi: 10.1037/0021-9010.87.2.230.

Bongiorno, R., Langbroek, C., Bain, P. G., Ting, M., & Ryan, M. K. (2020). Why women are blamed for being sexually harassed: The effects of empathy for female victims and male perpetrators. *Psychology of Women Quarterly* 44(1): 11–27. https://doi.org/10.1177/0361684319868730.

Brock, M. E., & Anderson, E. J. (2019). Training professionals who work with students with intellectual and developmental disabilities: What does the research say? *Psychology in the Schools* (58): 702–722.

Brock, M. E., & Carter, E. W. (2017). A meta-analysis of educator training to improve implementation of interventions for students with disabilities. *Remedial and Special Education* 38(3): 131–144. https://doi.org/10.1177/0741932516653477.

Brock, B. L., & Grady, M. L. (2004). *Launching your first principalship: A guide for beginning principals.* Corwin Press.

Bureau of Labor Statistics. (2020). *Community and social service occupations.* https://www.bls.gov/oes/current/oes_nat.htm#25-0000.

Education Week Research Center. (2018). *Sexual harassment and assault in the K-12 workplace.* https://epe.brightspotcdn.com/77/e4/ac43219b4a969719087d58fffaa8/sexual-harassment-survey-report-education-week.pdf.

Giangreco, M. F., Suter, J. C., & Doyle, M. (2010). Paraprofessionals in inclusive schools: A review of recent research. *Journal of Educational & Psychological Consultation* 20(1): 41–57. doi: 10.1080/10474410903535356.

Giangreco, M. F., Suter, J. C., & Hurley, S. M. (2013). Revisiting personnel utilization in inclusion-oriented schools. *Journal of Special Education* 47(2): 121–132.

Goh, J. X., Bandt-Law, B., Cheek, N. N., Sinclair, S., & Kaiser, C. R. (2021). Narrow prototypes and neglected victims: Understanding perceptions of sexual harassment. *Journal of Personality and Social Psychology.* Advance online publication. https://doi.org/10.1037/pspi0000260.

Gottfried, M. A. (2016). Teacher's aides in kindergarten: Effects on achievement for students with disabilities. *The Journal of Educational Research* 111(5): 620–630.

Hachiya, R. F., Schoop, R. J., & Dunklee, D. R. (2014). *The principal's quick reference guide to school law: Reducing liability, litigation, and other potential legal tangles* (3rd ed.). Corwin Press.

Halpern, B. L., & Lubar, K. (2003). *Leadership presence: Dramatic techniques to reach out, motivate, and inspire.* Penguin Group.

Meritor Savings Bank v. Vinson, 477 U.S. 57. (1986).

Meyer, E. J. (2008). Gendered harassment in secondary schools: Understanding teachers' (non) interventions. *Gender & Education* 20(6): 555–570. doi: 10.1080/09540250802213115

Miller, E. M., & Mondschein, E. S. (2017). Sexual harassment and bullying: Similar, but not the same. What school officials need to know. *The Clearinghouse: A Journal of Educational Strategies, Issues, and Ideas* 90(5/6): 191–197.

Reddy, L. A., Lewka, A. J. & Glover, T. A. (2021). Supporting paraprofessionals in schools: Current research and practice. *Psychology in the Schools* 58(4): 643–647. https://doi.org/10.1002/pits.22457.

Solnit, R. (2018). Rebecca Solnit on the #MeToo Backlash: Stop telling us how to confront an epidemic of violence and abuse. Retrieved from https://lithub.com/rebeccasolnit-on-the-metoo-backlash/.

She Has It Out for All the Athletes! (High School)

Coach Green, an energetic high school social studies teacher and popular basketball coach, has earned a reputation as a passionate advocate for his players. In just a few years at the school, he has increased participation and success in basketball, while at the same time demanding good behavior from players and carefully monitoring their grades and behavior. While some deride his style as abrasive at times, others respect the way he uses basketball to connect with struggling students and families.

Miss Washington, a high school English teacher and accomplished poet, has also acquired a reputation as a strong teacher who emphasizes student responsibility and accountability. Many of the school's graduates have noted that Miss Washington's classes are more difficult than their freshman English courses in college. Like Coach Green, however, she also has detractors who complain she's overly rigid and take issue with her assertion that, "America is obsessed with sports."

On this Thursday afternoon, Coach Green asks Principal McDonald for help with an eligibility problem. James, a star player and college prospect, received a grade on Miss Washington's English test that will render him ineligible to play in Friday's district championship game. Coach Green questions the timing of the test, the pressure Miss Washington put on James to pass, and what he describes as Miss Washington's unwillingness to help James. He sees the week's events as evidence of her bias against athletes.

Conventional thinking among many educators has long held that student involvement in school activities leads to improved student performance in many areas. Fredricks and Eccles (2006) noted a "growing body of research in leisure studies, sociology, sports psychology and adolescent development demonstrating the beneficial effects of participation in extracurricular activities" (p. 698). A number of scholars (Alexandrov et al., 2017; Eccles & Barber, 1999; Oberle et al., 2019; Wretman, 2017) have identified a connection between participation and improved educational outcomes, while others have identified desirable connections, such as improved self-esteem (Mahoney et al., 2002; Umeh et al., 2020) and decreased dropout rates (Mahoney & Cairns, 1997; Neely & Vaquera, 2017). Mahoney (2000) contended that the benefits of participation may be especially valuable for at-risk students.

Other researchers have argued that sports have come to occupy too large a role in schools and society. Eitzen and Sage (2009, p. 91) noted that high school athletics have become so important that many schools "appear to an outsider to be more concerned with athletics than with scholarly endeavors." Some have argued that assumed benefits of extracurricular involvement may be overstated or that involvement may be associated with negatives, such as increased alcohol use (Sznitman & Engel-Yeger, 2017) and higher levels of anxiety (Fredricks et al., 2002).

Coakley (2007, p. 485) noted that differences between athletes' and nonathletes' grade point averages, attitudes toward school, absenteeism, and other commonly identified factors associated with participation in sports "have been modest" and that "it has been difficult for researchers to separate the effects of sports participation from the effects of social class, family background, support from friends, identity issues, and other factors related to educational attitudes and achievement." Coakley also concluded that both sides "often exaggerate the benefits or the problems associated with interscholastic sports. Supporters emphasize glowing success stories, and critics emphasize shocking cases of abuse, but the most accurate descriptions probably lie somewhere in the middle" (p. 484).

Principal McDonald finds herself in the middle of a dilemma involving two respected teachers, a "good kid," and the role of athletics in high school. And the clock is running.

THE TRANSCRIPT

Principal: How're you doing?

Coach: Heather, I've been better, to be honest with you.

Principal: What's happening?

Coach: We've got a bit of a situation that you're probably not aware of. Our star basketball player, James Hill, and you may or may not be aware of this too. . . . We have a district championship game Friday night and you haven't been to a game all year, so you may not be aware of that. But Tuesday in Miss Washington's class, ah, she came to him and said "if you don't pass this test, get a C or better, you're gonna be ineligible for the game on Friday." Everybody knows Miss Washington has it out for athletes. You know, she's mad because nobody cares about the haiku or Ralph Waldo Emerson and everybody cares about how the football team does or how the basketball team does on Friday. Well, this is the biggest game we've had at this school in fifteen years. And without James, we're not gonna win the championship. So, he takes the test on Tuesday. She doesn't give him any warning other than right before the test, "Hey, you've gotta pass this test, get a C or better, or you're not gonna be eligible." James panics, doesn't do well on the test. He came to me in tears and we've got a couple other things that play in to this. . . . It's not just about the team and him not being able to play on Friday . . . certainly we need him to win. But it's about the fact that if he doesn't pass this class, he can't get that college scholarship. And the only way he's going to college . . . you know, cause as soon as I got done talking to James, Mom called me. Mom was in a panic and said, "Hey, James's only chance to go to college and get out of this situation we're in here as a family is through an athletic scholarship." And we've got two coaches coming in to watch the game Friday. We don't win the game; we don't get to play another game. So, the fact that James might be eligible on Monday doesn't do us any good. He needs to be eligible to play on Friday. And if he plays in the game on Friday and we win, his opportunities for college, his opportunities to get out of the situation he's in are right there in front of him. She doesn't care. And everybody knows she has it out for athletes. She's had it out for athletes all ten years I've been here. And she doesn't care. You know, I went to her directly and said, "Hey, can James do anything, can we get him a tutor, how can we help him through this process." "He's just like any other student to me." That's all she said. And it's really frustrating as not only a teacher but as a coach that I have to deal with this kind of stuff when we've got our biggest game of the year. You know, and I want to be at practice, which started five minutes ago and my assistant started it. I waited out there for ten minutes to get in here to see you. It's extremely frustrating. And I want to know what's going to be done now, so he's able to play on Friday.

Principal: So, he didn't do very well on the test and she told him if he did not get an A, what would happen?

Coach: If he didn't get a C or better. . . .

Principal: C or better. . . .

Coach: If he didn't get a C, he wouldn't be able to play on Friday. Because the school policy is, you know, you've gotta be eligible in all your classes when they do the grade checks in order to be eligible to play in the game. Well, he's eligible in all his other classes but he's not eligible in this class cause he's got an F right now in this class, okay? Ah, and so, you know, understanding that's school policy, I want to know what can we do to get him to be able to play in this game so that he doesn't miss out on all these opportunities. Without this scholarship, without him playing this game, those opportunities don't exist.

Principal: And you did say that you went to her and asked her to give him a tutor?

Coach: I did. I went to her, but it was a waste of time. I knew it would be. You know, she didn't have time for me. And it's not really my fight. It's James's fight, and I understand that . . . and his mom. And James went to her too, that's where he went to first, but she didn't want to deal with James either.

Principal: Well, I think we're kind of at an impasse, a little bit, because um, I mean, you did go and talk to her, but that's my question, I guess. Did James go and talk to her?

Coach: He talked to her. Yep, he did. Absolutely. The minute he got the test.

Principal: And how did that conversation go?

Coach: As I said, she's not gonna do anything. She said he's just like any other student . . . so he can't, I'm not gonna do anything to help him that I wouldn't do for any other student. So, what she's telling me is that she must not be willing to help anybody.

Principal: Is James over at practice . . . right now?

Coach: He's at practice but that's not going to do us any good, cause he can't play in the game. I gotta know what's gonna happen cause these college recruiters are flying to see the game and they fly in and say, "Where's James?" Ah, you know, he's not eligible. . . . Red flag, no scholarship. He's out of luck.

Principal: Um. . . .

Coach: James is pumping gas like his two older brothers who couldn't get eligible.

Principal: And I am concerned about that, I mean I feel like James has real potential . . . he can probably play ball in college and things like that, but I guess what I'm concerned about is that, um, first of all, well, let me ask this first, I guess, did the mom or the parents ask . . . find out about a tutor or did they contact the teacher or anything like that?

Coach: Ah, no. To my knowledge, because James just found out that he was worried . . . that he needed to pass this class on Tuesday when he took the test.

Principal: Oh, I'm sure James knew throughout the trimester or semester that he was not doing fine in the class. . . .

Coach: Well, I don't know how she communicates because this isn't a problem just with my athletes, it's a problem with all the athletes. She seems to have it out for them. So, whether or not they did or not, I guess I don't know that. My fear is what's going to happen to him in the next two days. And you know, Mom is panicked and I . . . I'm not gonna go to Mom and say "he can't play Friday." Somebody else has got to tell her. Cause I can't do that to them. She's gonna be outraged, and she's gonna want answers as to why this is the case.

Principal: Well, I think, um, maybe we need to talk to . . . or I need to talk to the teacher . . . um, and see. I'm not saying that I'm really delighted about the idea that a coach has come in here asking me to break a school rule for one student. I don't think that's something we want to open that door and set that precedent . . . and although I am concerned about James, I guess I just feel like, you know, where were his parents, you know, a couple weeks ago even, um, and I know you're telling me that you went and talked to the teacher and this is the first I've heard of it and unfortunately, if you would have come to me right after you talked to her and said, "look, this is my concern about James, she has not, I'm trying to get him a tutor, she has not even remotely interested in helping him out to pass English," I, you know, that would be something I needed to know a couple weeks ago and not right now. I'm just not sure. . . .

Coach: Didn't know about it a couple weeks ago, otherwise I would have come to you. You're absolutely right. If I'd have known about it two weeks ago, we wouldn't have this problem. But every week, we do these grade checks and he's fine, he's fine, he's fine. . . . Oh! District championship. Oh! James is ineligible.

Principal: Well, when did these conversations happen then about the tutor . . . is what I'm asking.

Coach: Wednesday. The test was Tuesday, got the results Wednesday, game is tomorrow which is Friday. I'm here right now. I mean, as quickly as I can act with still trying to coach my team, teach my classes and do everything else, you know . . . and. . . .

Principal: So, you were asking about a tutor after he had already failed the test?

Coach: What can I do, yeah. Tutor, make- up work, anything. I'm just trying to work with her to work with James.

Principal: Well then you know as well as I do that it's too late then.

Coach: Well, we've got . . . I understand your needing . . . can't change the rule . . . I'm not asking you to change the rule. I'm asking you to look at this situation and James. . . . He's been a model citizen, never been in trouble, you know, represented our school since he was a sophomore on the varsity basketball team and hasn't been in trouble in any of his classes. . . . Here he is, a chance to go to college and she's gonna blow it all up cause . . . she doesn't think he . . . you know, he didn't pass this test all of the sudden right before the district championship.

DISCUSSION AND REFLECTION QUESTIONS

1. Identify the primary and secondary issue(s).
2. Identify areas in which you believe the principal acted effectively.

3. Identify areas in which you believe the principal could have acted more effectively.

4. Early in the scenario (33:23), Coach Green notes that Principal McDonald has not been to a basketball game all year. Is this appropriate? Does he have a reason to expect the principal to attend basketball games? Is it appropriate to raise the issue in this way? Would you respond to his comment? As principal, what will be/are your intentions for attending extracurricular activities? Will you/have you communicated those intentions to sponsors, coaches, and students?

5. At 33:37 Coach Green says, "Everybody knows Miss Washington has it out for athletes . . . she's mad because nobody cares about the haiku or Ralph Waldo Emerson and everybody cares about how the football team does or the basketball team does on Friday." Is it appropriate for him to level this charge against Miss Washington? Do you interpret his comment about haiku and Emerson as disrespect of Miss Washington and her program or simply frustration? Should Principal McDonald respond?

6. Part of Coach Green's complaint seems to be that James found out just before taking the test on Tuesday that he needed a C or better on the test to be eligible to play on Friday. Does he have a reasonable argument that this impacted James's performance on the test and that his score making him ineligible so close to the championship game on Friday is unfair? Assuming Miss Washington refused to provide James assistance that was any different from what other students might receive, does Coach Green have a legitimate complaint? How should a principal decide between strict adherence to policy and exercising judgment and flexibility for the good of an individual?

7. At 37:25 Principal McDonald says she's sure James knew his grade in the class before the test. Coach Green counters that he does not know how Miss Washington communicates and what James knew, but insists that these issues are not unique to the players on his team. Most teachers are dedicated professionals with students' best interests in mind. They are also human. Assume that Miss Washington is perceived by some teachers, parents, and students to "have it in" for athletes. What might be done in a situation in which a teacher is perceived by some to have a vendetta against a particular group of students? What if Coach Green had come with a group of coaches and extracurricular sponsors who all expressed the same concern about Miss Washington?

8. At 38:30 Principal McDonald questions why issues surrounding James's grades weren't raised two weeks before and that this is the first she has heard of the situation. What is an appropriate role for the principal to play in matters like these? We know that involved families are very

important, yet levels of parental involvement differ. What if James's mother holds the view that her job is to provide a home for James and the school's job is to educate him?

9. Coach Green counters that weekly grade checks indicated that James's grade in English was fine and that he did not know about the issues until after the test on Tuesday. If Miss Washington has not entered or recorded grades for several weeks, is his claim more legitimate?

10. At 39:23 Principal McDonald says that since the tutor was not discussed until after the test on Tuesday "You know as well as I do, it's too late." In your opinion, is this an example of the principal enforcing the policy and allowing James to experience the consequences of becoming ineligible? Or is it a case of acting too rigidly and not looking closely enough for a way for James to be eligible to play? If Principal McDonald decides to find a way for James to become eligible to play, is she acting unethically? Or is she acting with the best interests of a student who stands to benefit from some flexibility and discretion on the part of the principal and teachers?

11. Principal McDonald said she is not comfortable with a coach asking her to break a school rule for one student. Coach Green counters that he understands the rule and is not asking her to break it, but rather look at James's situation. How should teachers address policies they believe are ill-conceived? How should principals deal with policies they believe are ill-conceived?

12. If Principal McDonald chose to investigate Coach Green's claim that Miss Washington has a bias against athletes, what data might she examine?

13. Regardless of the way Principal McDonald chooses to handle this situation, what might she do in the future to avoid a similar situation?

14. If James is held ineligible by the school, does he have any legal recourse? Would it be unethical for Coach Green to encourage James's family to pursue legal avenues? If he did, how should Principal McDonald respond?

15. Make a list of the steps Principal McDonald should take immediately following the meeting.

REFLECTION AND DISCUSSION QUESTIONS

Balcony View

Generally speaking, how did the principal perform in this scenario? What would you have done differently?

Standards in Action

Which standards do you see as relevant in the scenario? Does the principal effectively meet them? Are there standards and/or criteria left unmet by the principal's actions?

Peel Back the Onion

Like an onion, leadership challenges have multiple layers. The presenting issue may be singular or appear simple in nature. Often, however, it represents one part of an underlying, more complex issue. The best leaders address concerns in the moment, while not losing sight of root causes. What is/are the presenting issue(s)? Do you see potential nuanced factors that should be explored?

Self-Check

We all come to our roles with unique experiences, perspectives, and biases that influence our perceptions and actions. Picturing yourself in the principal's chair, describe your emotions.

Switch It Up

How might your thinking or approach change if the gender, ethnicity, language, age, sexual orientation, socioeconomic status, disability, or other descriptors of the players involved were different?

Equity Lens

Equity-driven leaders understand that diversity takes many forms. What equity- or diversity-related issues could be present in this scenario?

Power and Presence

In televised presidential debates, "looking presidential" is an important measure of a candidate's performance. The same is true for principals. Halpern and Lubar (2003, p. 3) define leadership presence as being more than "commanding attention" to include "the ability to connect authentically with the thoughts and feelings of others." Does the principal exert an effective presence? Describe the power balance between the principal and the visitor. Does positional or personal power between the principal and visitor seem uneven or problematic? What does body language say that words do not?

Principal's Priority

How *serious* is the situation? Are de-escalation techniques needed?
How *soon* should the principal address this situation?
Should the principal inform a supervisor of this issue and get them involved?

Reach Out?

Should the principal involve other individuals, professionals, resources, or organizations?

In a Word

Capture the principal's performance in the scenario using one word.

Collaborate

Collaborate with a classmate or colleague to rewrite or alter the case with a different set of circumstances. Share your new case with other colleagues to ascertain how they would approach it.

Extension and Internship Experiences

- Some would argue that the entire situation should be handled by the activities director rather than the principal. Yet these situations often find their way to the principal. What is the division of responsibility at your school or district?
- What is your school or district policy related to extracurricular eligibility? Are there also conference or state requirements? Who has the ultimate responsibility for checking grades and communicating about student progress? Interview a principal or activities director around these issues. Review the rules and determine if there are holes in the reporting procedures, timing, redress of concerns, etc. Are these communicated to parents and students through a handbook and/or meetings?
- In your school or district, are teachers required to maintain current grades for the purpose of determining eligibility? How does this work for teachers who collect few daily or weekly grades and instead employ large test or project grades periodically?

REFERENCES AND RESOURCES

Alexandrov, D., Tenisheva, K., & Savelyeva, S. (2017). The relationship between extracurricular activities and adolescents' academic performance and self-concept. *Educational Studies* 4: 217–241.

Coakley, J. (2007). *Sports in society: Issues and controversies* (9th ed.). McGraw Hill.

Cushman, K. (2006). Help us care enough to learn. *Educational Leadership* 63(5): 34–37.

Darling, N. (2004). Participation in extracurricular activities and adolescent adjustment: Cross-sectional and longitudinal findings. *Journal of Youth and Adolescence* 34(5): 493–505.

Eccles, J. S., & Barber, B. L. (1999). Student council, volunteering, basketball, or marching band: What kind of extracurricular involvement matters? *Journal of Adolescent Research* 10: 10–43.

Edwards, R., Smokowskia, P., Sowers, K, B., Dulmus, C. N., & Theriot, M. T. (2005). Abuse of power: When school personnel bully students. *Journal of Evidence-Based Social Work* 1(2–3): 111–129.

Eitzen, D. D., & Sage, G. H. (2009). *The sociology of North American sport* (8th ed.). Paradigm Publishers.

Fredricks, J. A., Alfeld-Liro, C., Eccles, J. S., Hruda, L. Z., Patrick, H., & Ryan, A. M. (2002). A qualitative exploration of adolescents' commitment to athletics and the arts. *Journal of Adolescent Research* 17: 68–97.

Fredricks, J. A., & Eccles, J. S. (2006). Is extracurricular participation associated with beneficial outcomes? Concurrent and longitudinal relations. *Developmental Psychology* 42: 698–713.

Halpern, B. L., & Lubar, K. (2003). *Leadership presence: Dramatic techniques to reach out, motivate, and inspire.* Penguin Group.

Mahoney, J. L. (2000). School extracurricular activity participation as a moderator in the development of antisocial patterns. *Child Development* 71: 502–516.

Mahoney, J., & Cairns, R. (1997). Do extracurricular activities protect against early school dropout? *Developmental Psychology* 33: 241–25.

Mahoney, J. L., Schweder, A. E., & Stattin, H. (2002). Structured afterschool activities as a moderator of depressed mood for adolescents with detached relations to their parents. *Journal of Community Psychology* 30: 69–86.

Marsh, H. W., & Kleitman, S. (2002). Extracurricular school activities: The good, the bad, and the non-linear. *Harvard Educational Review* 72: 464–514.

Neely, S. R., & Vaquera, E. (2017). Making it count: Breadth and intensity of extracurricular engagement and high school dropout. *Sociological Perspectives* 60(6): 1039–1062.

Oberle, E., Ji, X. R., Guhn, M., Schonert-Reichl, K. A., & Gadermann, A. M. (2019). Benefits of extracurricular participation in early adolescence: Associations with peer belonging and mental health. *Journal of Youth and Adolescence* 48(11): 2255–2270.

Reeves, D. R. (September 2008). The extracurricular advantage. *Educational Leadership* 66(1): 86–87.

Reis, S. M., Colbert, R. D., & Hebert, T. P. (2005). Understanding resilience in diverse, talented students in an urban high school. *Roeper Review* 27(2): 110–120.

Roberts, J. (December 2007). A sane island surrounded. *Phi Delta Kappan* 89(4): 278–282.

Sznitman, S., & Engel-Yeger, B. (2017). Sensation seeking and adolescent alcohol use: Exploring the mediating role of unstructured socializing with peers. *Alcohol and Alcoholism* 52(3): 396–401.

Umeh, Z., Bumpus, J. P., & Harris, A. L. (2020). The impact of suspension on participation in school-based extracurricular activities and out-of-school community service. *Social Science Research* 85: 102354.

Wretman, C. J. (2017). School sports participation and academic achievement in middle and high school. *Journal of the Society for Social Work and Research* 8(3): 399–420.

Hot Seat #4

It's Time for Them to Go (Middle School)

It is October of Principal O'Donnell's first year when Dr. Lindaman, the associate superintendent for human resources, stops by her office. Dr. Lindaman has earned a reputation as a serious administrator with high expectations and a direct style. Her intense focus on accountability has produced an enthusiastic group of followers, along with some detractors. Supporters sing her praises, noting they always know right where they stand, while others fear getting caught on her bad side. "Once you're in her crosshairs, it's over," they say.

Dr. Lindaman informs Principal O'Donnell that she has decided time has run out for three middle school teachers. She says their negative attitudes over several years have had a significant impact on the school's culture and climate and they show no signs of changing. While Dr. Lindaman never says the word "termination," she clearly does not want to see them continue as teachers in the district. Dr. Lindaman's position leaves Principal O'Donnell trying to find a balance between her own style, forming her own opinions about staff, and not alienating the associate superintendent.

Teacher quality debates have churned for years (Tucker, 1997). From educational journals and texts devoted exclusively to instructional leadership to popular media such as *Newsweek* and the evening news, demands for better teaching abound. Debate rages about whether the focus should be on improving current teachers and the systems in which they work or ferreting out underperformers.

In their controversial *Newsweek* cover story, Thomas and Wingert (2010) complained that "Many principals don't even try to weed out the poor performers (or they transfer them to other schools in what's been dubbed the 'dance of the lemons')" (para. 6). *Time* followed suit in 2014 with a searing indictment of the system in its "Rotten Apples" cover story.

Glass (2014, p. 13), coauthor of *50 Myths and Lies that Threaten America's Public Schools* pushed back, charging critics with "parroting an insult of a nation of hard-working educators." Whitaker (2020, p. 12) argued that "everyone wants to be good at what they do" and identified 20 behaviors that principals aspiring to greatness should practice. Among others, Whitaker challenged principals to "deliberately apply a range of strategies to improve teacher performance" (p. 156).

While the "dance of the lemons" has received considerable attention in both the literature and popular media, mistreatment of teachers by school administrators has flown largely under the radar. Sam (2020) identified six themes of unethical leadership practices experienced by teachers, including administrators being unavailable, breaches of confidentiality, undermining individual dignity, abuse of power, favoritism, and prioritizing personal gain. Blase (2009) noted that while workplace abuse across many fields has been widely studied, research into school administrator mistreatment of teachers is scant. A full 70% of teachers in a study by Blase et al. (2008) reported extended periods of abuse by school administrators. Jazzar and Algozzine (2007, p. 154) cautioned that "professional disagreements between educational leaders and those they lead do not constitute sole grounds for dismissal" and advised leaders to "avoid any actions regarding evaluation for dismissal that constitute harassment or intimidation."

When administrators have arrived at the decision to dismiss a teacher, Rebore (2012) emphasized a thoughtful and thorough process, including extensive documentation and consultation with the school's attorney to ensure the reasons are defensible and a list of valid reasons for termination:

> Physical or mental condition unfitting him or her to instruct or associate with children; immoral conduct; insubordination, inefficiency, or incompetency in the line of duty; willful or persistent violation of, or failure to obey, the state laws pertaining to schools; willful or persistent violation of the published policies and procedures of the school board; excessive or unreasonable absence from work; a conviction of a felony or a crime involving moral turpitude. (p. 131)

As Associate Superintendent Lindaman pushes, Principal O'Donnell finds herself in a landscape familiar to many principals—squarely in the middle. First, she faces the practical question of how to carry out teacher-evaluation policies in the real world (Donaldson & Woulfin, 2018), while occupying dual roles of instructional leader and evaluator (Kraft & Gilmour, 2016). While Dr. Lindaman wants the teachers gone because of what she sees as negative attitudes, Nixon et al. (2016) found that nearly 73% of principals identified *instructional skills* as the most important reason for not renewing teacher contracts. In examining implementation of teacher evaluation policies and practice, Derrington and Campbell (2015, p. 20) noted how superintendents "effectively support principals both technically and emotionally by serving as active listeners, acknowledging the stress they experience, followed by support specifically designed to mitigate these challenges and concerns." Donaldson and Mavrogordato (2018) stressed the importance of relational and organizational factors in principals' work with teachers and argued that principals would benefit from support from district level leadership, along with stronger pre-service experiences around teacher evaluation.

All told, Principal O'Donnell stands at the complex intersection of the law, ethics, and trust, among other things. She must determine if she is experiencing "toxic leadership" (Watt et al., 2016) from the associate superintendent, has inherited three longtime lemons, or is dancing to some shady music.

THE TRANSCRIPT

Associate Superintendent: Hi Emily. How are you doing?

Principal: Hi Dr. Lindaman, Good to see you again.

Associate Superintendent: Hi . . . good. Well, I'm gonna cut right to the chase here. Last week, once again, the three teachers that you and I've been talking about all along—John, Sue, Gary—um . . . raised all kinds of havoc in my office. They are questioning policies, they're questioning all kinds of things and they're . . . the climate that they create in the building is not good. And here's what I'm thinking. I'm thinking they need to go. I think it's time, and so I guess what I'm gonna ask you to do is to get them out. And I think this is the last year for them. I think it's, I think it's time. And so, you know we have the April 15th deadline, so I guess I need to know what you're thinking, because in my mind, they've gotta go.

Principal: Well, I've only, I've only been here a couple months and I really . . . obviously, I've heard some things about, ah, you know, what their behavior is and I know they've come to see you a couple of times. Ah, I would like a chance to get to know them first and kind of see what their strengths are and ah, their weaknesses and then, um, and maybe see if I can, you know, change the culture or something that I'm gonna do this year, ah, makes them more of a community in our building. Uh, obviously I want to listen to them and see their side, but ah, I guess just see what . . . see what the real issues are. . . .

Associate Superintendent: Right. Well, and I guess what I'd want you to understand is it's been . . . it's not just this year. It has been historically. You know, these are, two of them are veteran teachers, one of them is fairly new, about five years I think she's got five . . . six years. But, I think, I mean, I think if you look at everything that they've done over time, it's been a long time. And I think that they've worn out their welcome. I think it's about time that they go and I'm not sure that they would deserve . . . and I appreciate what you're thinking, but I'm thinking . . . they need to go. They need to go now.

Principal: Hmm. It's just really hard for me to dive into something like that when I'm not even really familiar with their teaching style, when I'm not familiar with, ah, with all of their history. I haven't been around long enough. Um, it's just, it's really hard for me to make judgments on people that I don't even really know right now. Um, obviously you have a longer history with them, but I'd still like to give them an opportunity to kind of prove themselves and see where they fit in my building and if we can find a place for them.

Associate Superintendent: Well, then what do you plan to do with them? I mean, how would you get to know them? I mean, what, what would you . . . want to do with them to get to know them and to try to find out what the pattern is? What's your plan?

Principal: Um, well a lot of times, ah, you know, I want to start to try to build a relationship with them and maybe see where they're coming from. Um, a lot of times, um, teachers . . . I've taught with teachers that have been teaching a long time and they just, they feel that they're not heard and they don't always have the same opinions. . . .

Associate Superintendent: Oh, they're heard. . . .

Principal: They don't always have the same, the same opinion, the same views, but sometimes we can work on that, you know, in professional leadership and um, I'd like to see my other teachers too and see their strengths and maybe we can do some things within the building and, um, you know, build some professional learning communities. Ah, we can structure our professional development around some of those concerns. Um, obviously, you know, if there are, if they're not a good fit, I'll be able to see that in a year or two, I would think, ah. . . .

Associate Superintendent: Well, and the negativity I think of the two are . . . is the biggest issue. The negativity and the negative climate that they bring to the building. And I guess, you know I just, in my mind, like I said, I know you haven't had the history that I have with them for years and years, but um, that negativity is the thing that's probably gonna have to be addressed the most. And if it can't be under control, it's time for them to go.

Principal: Well, and I appreciate the fact that you're looking out for me because I think you're trying to defuse any future situations. . . . Um, is there . . . I'm, I think all of them teach different subjects areas. . . .

Associate Superintendent: Right.

Principal: Is there a different, um, maybe school that they could go to where . . . if we split them up . . . I mean are they feeding off each other?

Associate Superintendent: Well, and I guess that would be what you have to figure out. I don't know. I mean I do think that there is some sense of the fact that they feed off of each other. There's kind of a little bit of a mob mentality with the three of them . . . that they've certainly been heard. . . . The squeaky wheel has been greased many times with them. The louder they get, the more attention they get and . . . so I'm just, I'm really concerned and it's not just for you, but it's for the whole building and I think, that's why I think, I mean I think this year has to be the end for them.

DISCUSSION AND REFLECTION QUESTIONS

1. Identify the primary and secondary issue(s).
2. Identify areas in which you believe the principal acted effectively.
3. Identify areas in which you believe the principal could have acted more effectively.
4. Dr. Lindaman gets right to the point and says she thinks it is time for three teachers to "go." How should Principal O'Donnell respond? Should the fact that Emily is a new principal impact her response? Critique the response Principal O'Donnell gives at 40:47.
5. Dr. Lindaman leaves little question that she would like to have the three teachers gone. Are her reasons well-established? As human resources is her main area of responsibility, how much deference should Principal O'Donnell give to Dr. Lindaman's opinion?
6. Dr. Lindaman communicates directly and cuts right to the chase in her conversation with Emily. Principal O'Donnell seems less direct in her communication. Should she be more direct in expressing herself? Or is her approach practical, given that she is new and is talking with the associate superintendent?
7. At 42:35 Dr. Lindaman asks Principal O'Donnell to spell out her plan for getting to know the teachers in question. Evaluate Principal O'Donnell's response. Is this a plausible course of action? Is anything missing?
8. At 43:37 Principal O'Donnell suggests that within a year or two she should be able to identify the most important issues with the teachers. Dr. Lindaman identifies negativity and its impact on the school climate. Given that Dr. Lindaman has said the problems have been ongoing and are not limited to this year, is it appropriate for Principal O'Donnell to ask for a couple of years to work with them on these issues? Is it appropriate for the associate superintendent to simply tell the new principal she thinks it is time for these teachers to go?
9. At 44:26 Principal O'Donnell asks if the teachers could be split up and sent to other schools. Is this a reasonable idea? Perhaps their negativity

would be lessened if they were not allowed to "feed off each other," as Dr. Lindman noted. On the other hand, if the teachers have had the negative impact she describes, is it ethical to send them to other buildings? Would Principal O'Donnell be engaged in the Dance of the Lemons? Is it ethical to hand off her problems to another school?

10. Principal O'Donnell says she appreciates the associate superintendent looking out for her. Of course any administrator wants to trust their supervisor. It is possible, of course, that the associate superintendent views the three teachers unfairly. Perhaps the teachers are raising legitimate issues that Dr. Lindaman simply doesn't want to hear. As a new leader, how can Principal O'Donnell:
    • Demonstrate her competence to her supervisors;
    • Respect the teachers in her building;
    • Form her own opinions on the quality of the staff in her building;
    • Act ethically and according to standards?

11. Is it possible that the associate superintendent is simply testing Principal O'Donnell? Perhaps she would like to see the three teachers go, but would be satisfied if their attitudes changed or they simply spent less time in her office complaining. Perhaps Principal O'Donnell's predecessor failed to provide instructional leadership and communication, and the associate superintendent wants to see if Emily can do so. In what ways can we expect to be challenged as new leaders? To what challenges do you look forward? What challenges are less appealing to you?

12. The scenario ends with the associate superintendent indicating some flexibility in terms of the way Principal O'Donnell might deal with the three teachers immediately but sticks to her belief that this year should be "the end for them." Despite this belief, student performance or previous evaluations have not been mentioned. Does the negativity Dr. Lindaman describes sound like a sufficient reason for them to go?

13. What if at the end of the scenario Dr. Lindaman had said, "Emily, I appreciate your desire to get to know them and see if you can help them grow or at least stop the negativity. But *I* want them out of your building. Out of the district. At the end of the year, period. Can you do that?" How should she respond?

14. Would it be ethical for Principal O'Donnell to attempt to remove the three teachers by "driving them out" (i.e., assigning them the least-desirable schedules, extra duties, and other things they would not like)? What is the difference between "counseling" and "driving" a teacher out? Would it be unethical if Principal O'Donnell told the three teachers directly that Dr. Lindaman wants them gone and that they must immediately work to improve their performance and change their attitudes or their contracts may be considered for termination?

15. Should Principal O'Donnell be concerned about Dr. Lindaman's approach and/or ethics? Or should she remember that, as a first-year principal, she needs strong guidance from experienced leaders like the associate superintendent?
16. Assume Principal O'Donnell determines that Dr. Lindaman is correct and that her building would be better off without these three teachers. Are there limits to what Principal O'Donnell should do to ensure that the teachers do not return? If so, what?
17. Would it be reasonable to argue that perhaps these three teachers simply need a new start and fresh leadership that Principal O'Donnell may be able to provide? Or is it unrealistic to think a school or district change will make a difference?

REFLECTION AND DISCUSSION QUESTIONS

Balcony View

Generally speaking, how did the principal perform in this scenario? What would you have done differently?

Standards in Action

Which standards do you see as relevant in the scenario? Does the principal effectively meet them? Are there standards and/or criteria left unmet by the principal's actions?

Peel the Onion

Like an onion, leadership challenges have multiple layers. The presenting issue may be singular or appear simple in nature. Often, however, it represents one part of an underlying, more complex issue. The best leaders address concerns in the moment, while not losing sight of root causes. What is/are the presenting issue(s)? Do you see potential nuanced factors that should be explored?

Self-Check

We all come to our roles with unique experiences, perspectives, and biases that influence our perceptions and actions. Picturing yourself in the principal's chair, describe your emotions.

Switch It Up

How might your thinking or approach change if the gender, ethnicity, language, age, sexual orientation, socioeconomic status, disability, or other descriptors of the players involved were different?

Equity Lens

Equity-driven leaders understand that diversity takes many forms. What equity- or diversity-related issues could be present in this scenario?

Principal's Presence

In televised presidential debates, "looking presidential" is an important measure of a candidate's performance. The same is true for principals. Halpern and Lubar (2003, p. 3) define leadership presence as being more than "commanding attention" to include "the ability to connect authentically with the thoughts and feelings of others." Does the principal exert an effective presence? Describe the power balance between the principal and the visitor. Does positional or personal power between the principal and visitor seem uneven or problematic? What does body language say that words do not?

Principal's Priority

How *serious* is the situation?
How *soon* should the principal address this situation?
Should the principal inform/involve a *supervisor* on this issue?

Reach Out?

Should the principal involve other individuals, professionals, resources, or organizations?

In a Word

Capture the principal's performance in the scenario using one word.

Collaborate

Collaborate with a classmate or colleague to rewrite or alter the case with a different set of circumstances. Share your new case with other colleagues to ascertain how they would approach it.

Extension and Internship Experiences

- Discuss the conditions under which an experienced principal, superintendent, or central office administrator believes a teacher should be removed from the classroom. What are key decision points? What criteria make a teacher a candidate for counseling out versus a more overt termination process? When might a teacher simply need a "new start" in a different building?
- What specific standards, laws, or guidelines exist to help principals in your district or state determine when a teacher can and should be "counseled out" or terminated? License revocation?
- Interview an experienced principal or central office administrator about "counseling" teachers out versus the ethics of "driving" a teacher out. Has the administrator ever been in a situation like Principal O'Donnell?

REFERENCES AND RESOURCES

Almy, S. (2011). *Fair to everyone: Building the balanced teacher evaluations that educators and students deserve.* Education Trust.

Blase, J. (2009). School administrator mistreatment of teachers. *International Handbook of Research on Teachers and Teaching: Springer International Handbooks of Education* 21(5): 433–448. doi: 10.1007/978-0-387-73317-3_28.

Blase, J., & Blase, J. (2002). The dark side of leadership: Teacher perspectives of principal mistreatment. *Education Administration Quarterly* 38(5): 671–727.

Blase, J., & Blase, J. (2003a). *Breaking the silence: Overcoming the problem of principal mistreatment of teachers.* Corwin Press.

Blase, J., & Blase, J. (2003b). The phenomenology of principal mistreatment: Teachers' perspectives. *Journal of Educational Administration* 41(4): 367–422.

Blase, J., Blase, J., & Du, F. (2008). The mistreated teacher: A national study. *Journal of Educational Administration* 46(3): 263–301.

Derrington, M. L., & Campbell, J. W. (2015). Principal concerns and superintendent support during teacher evaluation changes. *AASA Journal of Scholarship and Practice* 12(3).

Donaldson, M., & Mavrogordato, M. (2018). Principals and teacher evaluation: The cognitive, relational, and organizational dimensions of working with low-performing teachers. *Journal of Educational Administration* 56(6): 586–601. https://doi.org/10.1108/JEA-08-2017-0100.

Donaldson, M. L., & Woulfin, S. (2018). From tinkering to going "rogue": How principals use agency when enacting new teacher evaluation systems. *Educational Evaluation and Policy Analysis* 40(4): 531–556. https://doi.org/10.3102/0162373718784205.

Edwards, H. Sweetland (2014, November). The war on teacher tenure. *Time* 184(17).

Futernick, K. (2010). Incompetent teachers or dysfunctional systems? *Phi Delta Kappan* 92(2): 59–64.

Glass, G. V. (2014). Myth: Incompetent staff can't be fired. *School Administrator* 71(11): 13.

Glass, G. V., & Berliner, D. C. (2014). *50 Myths and lies that threaten America's public schools: The real crisis in education.* Teachers College Press.

Halpern, B. L., & Lubar, K. (2003). *Leadership presence: Dramatic techniques to reach out, motivate, and inspire.* Penguin Group.

Jazzar, M., & Algozzine, B. (2007). *Keys to 21st century educational leadership.* Pearson.

Kraft, M. A., & Gilmour, A. F. (2016). Can principals promote teacher development as evaluators? A case study of principals' views and experiences. *Educational Administration Quarterly* 52: 711–753.

Nixon, A., & Packard, A., & Dam, M. (2016). Teacher contract non-renewal: What matters to principals? *NCPEA International Journal of Educational Leadership Preparation* 11(1): 19. https://files.eric.ed.gov/fulltext/EJ1103656.pdf.

Nolan, J. F., & Hoover, L. A. (2008). *Teacher supervision and evaluation: Theory into practice.* John Wiley & Sons.

Rebore, R. W. (2012). *The essentials of human resources administration in education.* Pearson.

Sam, C. H. (2020). What are the practices of unethical leaders? Exploring how teachers experience the "dark side" of administrative leadership. *Educational Management Administration, and Leadership* 49(2): 303–320.

Thomas, E., & Wingert, P. (2010, March). Why we can't get rid of failing teachers. *Newsweek* 24. Retrieved from http://www.newsweek.com.

Tucker, P. D. (1997). Lake Wobegon: Where all teachers are competent (or, have we come to terms with the problem of incompetent teachers?). *Journal of Personnel Evaluation in Education* 11: 103–126.

Watt, S. R., Javidi, M., & Normore, A. H. (2016). Increasing darkness: Combining toxic leadership and volatility, uncertainty, complexity, and ambiguity (VUCA). *The dark side of leadership: Identifying and overcoming unethical practice in organizations* (Advances in Educational Administration, Vol. 26, pp. 195–206). Emerald Group Publishing Limited, Bingley. https://doi.org/10.1108/S1479-366020160000026015.

Webb, L. D., & Norton, M. S. (2009). *Human resources administration: Personnel issues and needs in education.* Pearson.

Whitaker, T. (2015). *Dealing with difficult teachers* (3rd ed.). Eye on Education.

Whitaker, T. (2013). *What great teachers do differently: Seventeen things that matter most.* Eye on Education.

Whitaker, T. (2020). *What great principals do differently: Twenty things that matter most* (3rd ed.). Eye on Education.

Zepeda, S. J. (2007). *Instructional supervision: Applying tools and concepts* (4th ed.). Eye on Education.

Hot Seat #5

Do You Support My Program? (Middle School)

Mr. Cox has taught Spanish at Hoover Junior High School for 20 years. His energy and passion has helped the program grow to more than 150 students, many of whom actively participate in the Spanish Club. In recent years, the group's Cinco de Mayo celebration has become a staple of springtime festivities at Hoover.

On the afternoon of May 4, Mr. Cox catches Principal Dan Scannell in his office with a complaint. Mr. Cox has gotten wind of a rumor that a number of students are planning to protest the Cinco de Mayo celebration. Mr. Cox believes three other teachers bent on sabotage are promoting the protest out of personal or professional jealousy. With little time to spare before the end of the day, Principal Scannell pieces together the story and tries to formulate a plan.

Teaching can feel like a lonely endeavor. Schedules, class size and a tradition of working alone produce what amounts to a culture of isolation in many schools. Where isolation flourishes, relationships are hard to nurture. Payne (2008, p. 35) cited work by the Consortium on Chicago School Research that concluded "the quality of relationships among adults determined much of what did or did not happen in schools." Hoy et al. (2006), Hoy et al. (1992), and others have pointed to the importance of trust among teachers and principals.

As pointed out by Mr. Cox, professional jealousy could be the nexus of this issue. Jealousy has been conceptualized as a multidimensional construct with cognitive, emotional, and behavioral components and is familiar experience in human relationships (Dammani, 2019). Jealous individuals may resort to aggressive behaviors (DeSteno et al., 2006) including sabotage, competitiveness, and attempts to discredit or discourage their rival's work (Dogan & Vecchio, 2001). Comparably, individuals experiencing malicious envy may be tempted to harm their rival (Cohen-Charash & Mueller, 2007), engage in unethical behaviors against their rival (Gino & Pierce, 2009), and attempt to socially undermine this individual (Tai et al., 2012), as Mr. Cox believes is happening to him.

Those with a supervisor perceived as favoring another subordinate may ruminate about their own worth in the organization ("Am I not a valuable employee?"). Similarly, an employee who prefers another supervisor can call into question the supervisor's self-esteem and workplace identity ("Am I a bad manager?") (Andiappan & Dufour, 2018). The authors also suggest that value be placed on shared knowledge, shared goals, and mutual respect. Since knowledge is a critical resource in organizations (Lecuona & Reitzig, 2014), sharing access to information should reduce jealousy. Identification of shared goals can also reduce the drive for exclusivity in relationships that often leads to jealousy (Ritchie & Van Anders, 2015).

One way to encourage the practice of shared knowledge and goals would be through implementation of professional learning communities (PLCs). As cited by Antinluoma et al. (2021), the construct of professional learning communities has become a prevailing framework for teachers' professional learning and development (Watson, 2014; Turner et al., 2018). Evidence suggests that teachers' work within successful PLCs improves instruction, which may lead to improved student achievement (Lomos et al., 2011 & Jones et al., 2013) and contribute to the effectiveness of schools (Louis et al., 2010; Hofman et al., 2015). Evidence also suggests that teachers' collaborative practices, like reflective professional dialogue, positively influence the collective learning of new practices (Weissenrieder et al., 2015), teachers' professionalization (McLaughlin & Talbert, 2006), teachers' participation in professional development (Skerrett, 2010), and school reform and change (Sleegers et al., 2014). This research suggests that, through PLCs, Mr. Cox and his colleagues could engage in comprehensive conversations about ideas, thoughts, and any insights that would promote student learning, growth and opportunities such as the Cinco de Mayo celebration. Cross-curricular activities relative to this celebration could also be planned and implemented throughout the entire school, impacting all students instead of just those in the Spanish Club.

On the eve of the annual Cinco de Mayo celebration, Mr. Cox has Principal Scannell wondering if this type of collaboration and sharing is possible in the long term in his school. With the protest and walkout rumored to be happening tomorrow, he needs to determine an immediate course of action.

Teacher: Dan, you got a second?

Principal: Yeah, Mr. Cox. How are you doing?

Teacher: I've been better.

Principal: You wanna have a seat someplace . . . here or over there?

Teacher: I don't know. I'm kind of mad. I don't know if I wanna sit just yet.

Principal: Okay.

Teacher: You've heard . . . you know about my big Cinco de Mayo celebration picnic that we do every year.

Principal: Yeah, definitely.

Teacher: Well, you know, we talked about that at team leaders. . . .

Principal: Okay.

Teacher: And no one ever said a word and now today, ah, you know the thing's gonna be tomorrow and today I start finding out from kids that there's some teachers trying to sabotage this.

Principal: Oh, wow.

Teacher: So, I . . . I am gonna sit.

Principal: Okay, that'd be great and we can sit over here or if you want something to write on.

Teacher: Ah, I'll sit here.

Principal: That's fine. Alrighty. Well, I, ah, that's frustrating. That's frustrating.

Teacher: It is frustrating! And I guess first of all, I've gotta know do you support my program here?

Principal: The Cinco de Mayo celebration?

Teacher: The Cinco de Mayo and the Spanish program, 'cause . . .

Principal: I think, ah, I think that Cinco de Mayo culturally is a really important event in that, ah, in your program and it's important to recognize and pursue and see how that might play into our curriculum. Um, tell me a little bit more about where you feel you're getting resistance.

Teacher: Well, because there's ah, three teachers trying to stage a walkout tomorrow because they're pissed.

Principal: All right.

Teacher: Jealous . . . I don't know what they are. But they're mad that ah, you know, 20 years I've been here at Hoover and we've done this every year and haven't had any issues. . . . Five principals, they've all been supportive and now, ah, a couple of newer teachers and some ones that are just cranky and suddenly this is a big issue . . . So I. . . .

Principal: Okay.

Teacher: Sorry, I had to jot down some notes 'cause I was too mad and I was sure I'd miss something.

Principal: Okay.

Teacher: Ah, I even hesitated. I didn't know if I should tell you who they were but I'm just irritated enough that I think you need to know who they are.

Principal: Well, I'll tell you. You know what, kind a walking in, I'd be frustrated with the information that I got that somebody was trying to, ah, maybe dismember one of the activities I was doing. . . .

Teacher: Darn right!

Principal: But I would like to know the names of those teachers so that we can talk to them and kind of see where they're coming from and maybe what their concerns are and see where we can get with that.

Teacher: All right. Ah, the first one's Mrs. Johnson.

Principal: Okay.

Teacher: Math teacher.

Principal: Do you mind if I . . .?

Teacher: No go ahead. You need my pen?

Principal: And I can even take that when you're done with it, if that's possible.

Teacher: Yep, that'd be fine.

Principal: All right, well let's just lead with that.

Teacher: Well, she's mad, first of all, that you put her on that plan of assistance two months ago.

Principal: Okay.

Teacher: And you know, kids just run wild in that classroom as it is and everybody knows it and she just cries or yells, or I don't know. . . .

Principal: And do you know, her mentor is. . . .

Teacher: Mrs. Jordan. . . .

Principal: Okay, all right, well. . . .

Teacher: But, it's a lost cause. You know that, you're in and out of there every day as it is. But she's mad because it's gonna make kids miss math supplemental time to be part of this picnic tomorrow and she's afraid that that's just one more reason you're gonna fire her 'cause they're gonna miss more math time and she won't put up with that. So, that's something that you're gonna have to deal with and then there's Mr. Williams, the band director.

Principal: Okay.

Teacher: And, ah, he's irritated that kids are gonna miss some band lessons. . . .

Principal: Okay.

Teacher: You know, like that's the end of the world. Ah, doesn't agree with your new arrangement that, you know, they can't get pulled out of math and reading to go to band lessons and. . . .

Principal: Yeah.

Teacher: I sure would like to only have to teach, you know, a little bit during the day with one group of kids and then have three or four the rest of the day, but that's not how it works.

Principal: Yeah.

Teacher: Ah, Mrs. Smith, she's the other one and this is a shocker because she's our ELL teacher.

Principal: Yeah.

Teacher: But, she's got a bee in her bonnet because she thinks we should have a Bosnian celebration instead of a Spanish one. Now I know there's a hundred and fifty Bosnian kids here and there's fifty Spanish kids, but we don't teach Bosnian. We teach Spanish.

Principal: Yeah, I agree and but at the same time, you know, we can always explore the possibility. . . .

Teacher: Okay.

Principal: We have a lot of different ethnicities that come through our building and I think you being a Spanish teacher would really empathize with wanting to, you know, see those students have their faces and cultures represented. . . .

Teacher: Oh, of course! But . . . I would think so.

Principal: In our curriculum and you may be even able to give some pointers into some kind of a celebration of their culture because of your familiarity with doing that with Cinco de Mayo.

Teacher: I don't want her sabotaging this big event that we've got going on.

Principal: Oh, no. We don't want that.

Teacher: Well here's what I think you need to do. I think you need to get on the PA and make an all-school announcement.

Principal: Okay.

Teacher: And I even wrote one for you as a sample. . . .

Principal: I do certainly appreciate that. Do you mind if I take a look at it and kind of. . . .

Teacher: No, and I put it in all caps because I think you should talk loud when you make this announcement.

Principal: Well, I usually do. The kids think I'm nuts. . . .

Teacher: Well, I know but I think you really need to talk loud 'cause, you know, if they're up in Mrs. Johnson's room they aren't gonna hear it unless they are talking loud. But you need to do that and you need to do this today because the picnic is tomorrow. . . .

Principal: Okay.

Teacher: So you think you might do that at the end of this period or at the end of the day, or. . . .

Principal: We've still got some time to kind of. . . . What I . . . I'll be honest with you. You know, I'm equally concerned that there may be some conflict among staff members about an event that we've got planned and is on the schedule. . . .

Teacher: Right.

Principal: And so I do want to pursue that a little bit . . . we've been working with her to see what kinds of supports we can provide in there . . . and so I'd like to talk with some of those teachers and kind of see where they're coming from and. . . .

Teacher: Well, I've got two more things I want you to do.

Principal: Oh, definitely. I can hear those.

Teacher: I want you to write up those teachers, 'cause they can't be trying to wreck this event. That's like insubordination or something. I know you'll find something somewhere to write them up.

Principal: Yeah.

Teacher: And, ah, I think that your two assistant principals and the SRO should patrol the hallways tomorrow to make sure no kids walk out of class to try to stage this, you know, big protest.

Principal: Well. . . .

Teacher: And, so if they're out in the hallways, you know, if you're not in eighth grade you don't come out to go to the party during any other time and you just keep some control here. I think that's what we need to do. . . . So there's my notes.

Principal: Well, you know, I do, ah, I appreciate you stopping in and sharing that with me and coming here rather than, so, you know, we can approach this maybe together and see how we can resolve that.

Teacher: So when am I gonna know when you're gonna do this stuff?

Principal: Well, again, I want to have some conversations with people and. . . .

Teacher: Okay, but it's tomorrow.

Principal: Yeah, I recognize that. And we've got the afternoon to kind of explore what's happening and see what's going on. I don't know that there's a problem with an announcement that kind of lets them know that the celebration is tomorrow and that we're supportive. . . .

Teacher: And that you support it. . . . 'Cause I want to make sure that . . . teachers understand that.

Principal: I can get behind it and be supportive of it, yeah. . . . We'll enjoy that celebration with the kids too.

Teacher: All right

Principal: But I do. I wanna hear what our other teachers are concerned with and see if there's a way to maybe help with their understanding or see how they can be participating in it or, you know, I really like the idea of a Bosnian celebration. I think that that's a group of kids that needs to see themselves represented so they can be engaged more in school and it's early on, I know you're frustrated. . . .

DISCUSSION AND REFLECTION QUESTIONS

1. Identify the primary and secondary issue(s).
2. Identify areas in which you believe the principal acted effectively.
3. Identify areas in which you believe the principal could have acted more effectively.
4. At 1:11 Mr. Cox asks the principal if he supports the Spanish program and Cinco de Mayo Celebration. Evaluate Principal Scannell's answer.
5. At 1:12 Principal Scannell says he would be frustrated to hear that a colleague might be trying to "*dismember* one of the activities I was doing." Evaluate.
6. At 1:12 Mr. Cox accuses three other teachers of trying to sabotage the Cinco de Mayo celebration. Evaluate Principal Scannell's response.

7. As Mr. Cox explains what he believes to be the reasons the three teachers object to the celebration, it becomes clear that he has his own issues with the teachers. Evaluate the principal's response to what Mr. Cox says are their reasons. Is it inappropriate for Mr. Cox to say what he says about his colleagues? Should Principal Scannell have addressed these comments with Mr. Cox or simply listened to try and get a full picture?

8. What do you think of Principal Scannell's suggestion that a Bosnian celebration might be a good idea? Should he raise this with Mr. Cox or wait until he has talked with the other teachers? Explain.

9. Anticipate Mrs. Johnson's reaction if she learns that Principal Scannell and Mr. Cox discussed her classroom, her plan of assistance, and the principal's assertion that "she struggles a bit." How would you respond if you were Mrs. Johnson? How should Principal Scannell respond when confronted by Mrs. Johnson?

10. Mr. Cox identifies a number of actions he wants the principal to take, including reading the announcement he wrote over the intercom and having patrols in the hallway. Evaluate Principal Scannell's response to the things Mr. Cox wants done. How would you respond to a teacher asking, suggesting, or telling you what to do in a case like this? Is Mr. Cox out of line in asking when Principal Scannell will take action? Or is he simply concerned because the celebration is tomorrow?

11. Does Principal Scannell adequately address the possibility of a walkout or disruption tomorrow? If he learns that the three teachers have overtly (or implicitly) encouraged some kind of student protest or walkout, what action should he take with students? With teachers?

REFLECTION AND DISCUSSION QUESTIONS

Balcony View

Generally speaking, how did the principal perform in this scenario? What would you have done differently?

Standards in Action

Which standards do you see as relevant in the scenario? Does the principal effectively meet them? Are there standards and/or criteria left unmet by the principal's actions?

Peel the Onion

Like an onion, leadership challenges have multiple layers. The presenting issue may be singular or appear simple in nature. Often, however, it represents one part of an underlying, more complex issue. The best leaders address concerns in the moment, while not losing sight of root causes. What is/are the presenting issue(s)? Do you see potential nuanced factors that should be explored?

Self-Check

We all come to our roles with unique experiences, perspectives, and biases that influence our perceptions and actions. Picturing yourself in the principal's chair, describe your emotions.

Switch It Up

How might your thinking or approach change if the gender, ethnicity, language, age, sexual orientation, socioeconomic status, disability, or other descriptors of the players involved were different?

Equity Lens

Equity-driven leaders understand that diversity takes many forms. What equity- or diversity-related issues could be present in this scenario?

Principal's Presence

In televised presidential debates, "looking presidential" is an important measure of a candidate's performance. The same is true for principals. Halpern and Lubar (2003, p. 3) define leadership presence as being more than "commanding attention" to include "the ability to connect authentically with the thoughts and feelings of others." Does the principal exert an effective presence? Describe the power balance between the principal and the visitor. Does positional or personal power between the principal and visitor seem uneven or problematic? What does body language say that words do not?

Principal's Priority

How *serious* is the situation?
How *soon* should the principal address this situation?
Should the principal inform/involve a *supervisor* on this issue?

Reach Out?

Should the principal involve other individuals, professionals, resources, or organizations?

In a Word

Capture the principal's performance in the scenario using one word.

Collaborate

Collaborate with a classmate or colleague to rewrite or alter the case with a different set of circumstances. Share your new case with other colleagues to ascertain how they would approach it.

Extension and Internship Experiences

- Examine your school or district policy on curriculum-related celebrations, such as the Cinco de Mayo picnic described by Mr. Cox. What is the process for proposing a similar event, such as the Bosnian celebration discussed in the case? What are the standards by which such activities are judged to be educationally relevant?
- Discuss with a mentor the most effective techniques for managing conflict between teachers and any lessons learned the hard way.

REFERENCES AND RESOURCES

Andiapan, M., & Dufour, L. (2018). Jealousy at work: A tripartite model. *Academy of Management Review* 45(1): 1–75. doi:10.5465/amr.2016.0299.

Antinluoma, M., Ilomäki, L., Lahti-Nuuttila, P., & Toom, A. (2018). Schools as professional learning communities. *Journal of Education and Learning* 7(5): 76–91.

Cohen-Charash, Y., & Mueller, J. (2007). Does perceived unfairness exacerbate or mitigate interpersonal counterproductive work behaviors related to envy? *Journal of Applied Psychology* 92: 666–680.

Dammani, K. (2019). *A study of the professional jealousy among teachers.* Munich: GRIN Verlag. Retrieved from http://www.grin.com/document/499063.

DeSteno, D., Valdesolo, P., & Bartlett, M. (2006). Jealousy and the threatened self: Getting to the heart of the green-eyed monster. *Journal of Personality and Social Psychology* 91: 626–641.

Dogan, K., & Vecchio, R. P. (2001). Managing envy and jealousy in the workplace. *Compensation & Benefits Review* 33: 57–64.

Gino, F., & Pierce, L. (2009). Dishonesty in the name of equity. *Psychological Science* 20: 1153–1160.

Halpern, B. L., & Lubar, K. (2003). *Leadership presence: Dramatic techniques to reach out, motivate, and inspire.* Penguin Group.

Hoy, W. K., Gage III, C., & Tarter, C. (2006). School mindfulness and faculty trust: Necessary conditions for each other? *Educational Administration Quarterly* 42(2): 236–255. doi: 10.1177/0013161X04273844.

Hoy, W. K., Tarter, C., & Witkoskie, L. (1992). Faculty trust in colleagues: Linking the principal with school effectiveness. *Journal of Research & Development in Education* 38. Retrieved from EBSCO*host*.

Jones, L., Stall, G., & Yarbrough, D. (2013). The importance of professional learning communities for school improvement. *Creative Education* 4(5): 357–361. doi: 10.4236/ce.2013.45052.

Lecuona, J. R., & Reitzig, M. (2014). Knowledge worth having in "excess": The value of tacit and firm specific human resource slack. *Strategic Management Journal* 35: 954–973.

Lomos, C., Hofman, R. H., & Bosker, R. J. (2011). Professional communities and student achievement—a meta-analysis. *School Effectiveness and School Improvement* 22(2): 121–148. doi: 10.1080/09243453.2010.550467.

Louis, K. S., Dretzke, B., & Wahlstrom, K. (2010). How does leadership affect student achievement? Results from a national US Survey. *School Effectiveness and School Improvement* 21(3): 315–336. doi: 10.1080/09243453.2010.486586.

McLaughlin, M. W., & Talbert, J. E. (2006). *Building school-based teacher learning communities: Professional strategies to improve student achievement.* Teachers College Press.

Payne, C. M. (2008). *So much reform, so little change: The persistence of failure in urban schools.* Harvard Education Press.

Ritchie, L. L., & van Anders, S. M. (2015). There's jealousy . . . and then there's jealousy: Differential effects of jealousy on testosterone. *Adaptive Human Behavior and Physiology* 1: 231–246.

Sleegers, P., den Brok, P., Verbiest, E., Moolenaar, N. M., & Daly, A. J. (2013). Toward conceptual clarity: A multidimensional, multilevel model of professional learning communities in Dutch elementary schools. *Elementary School Journal* 114(1): 118–137. doi: 10.1086/671063.

Skerrett, A. (2010). There's going to be community. There's going to be knowledge: Designs for learning in a standardised age. *Teaching and Teacher Education* 26(3): 648–655. doi: 10.1016/j.tate.2009.09.017.

Tai, K., Narayanan, J., & McAllister, D. (2012). Envy as pain: Rethinking the natures of envy and its implications for employees and organizations. *Academy of Management Review* 37: 107–129.

Turner, J. C., Christensen, A., Kackar-Cam, H. Z., Fulmer, S. M., & Trucano, M. (2018). The development of professional learning communities and their teacher leaders: An activity systems analysis. *Journal of the Learning Sciences* 27(1): 49–88. doi: 10.1080/10508406.2017.1381962.

Watson, C. (2014). Effective professional learning communities? The possibilities for teachers as agents of change in schools. *British Educational Research Journal* 40(1): 18–29. doi: 10.1002/berj.3025.

Weissenrieder, J., Roesken-Winter, B., Schueler, S., Binner, E., & Blömeke, S. (2015). Scaling CPD through professional learning communities: development of teachers' self-efficacy in relation to collaboration. *ZDM Mathematics Education* 47: 27–38. doi: 10.1007/s11858-015-0673-8.

Stick a Fork in It (Middle School)

Workplace climate and culture has a deep impact on an organization's environment and effectiveness. A positive workplace culture and climate improves teamwork, raises the morale, increases productivity and efficiency, and enhances retention of the workforce. Job satisfaction, collaboration, and work performance are all enhanced. And, most important, a positive workplace environment reduces stress in employees (Agarwal, 2018). On the flip side, a negative workplace environment can cause employees to become irritable, anxious, and defensive. This can lead to poor productivity, a lack of motivation and morale, poor communication, and the creation of gossip and small talk in the workplace (Murphy, 2018).

Ms. Snyder, an English teacher visits Principal Roby's office, a jumble of nerves. As she sits at Ms. Roby's desk, she shares her appreciation of the principal's open-door policy and appreciative of her always taking the time to listen to faculty concerns. With trepidation, Ms. Snyder expresses concern about Bob, a fellow teacher's disruption of the professional learning community (PLC) though negative comments, brash demeanor, and aggressive tone. While she is concerned enough to talk with Principal Roby, Ms. Snyder fears retribution and how Bob might react if he finds out she has shared her concerns with the principal.

The phrase *professional learning community* appeared in the 1990s after Senge's book *The Fifth Discipline* (1990) popularized the idea of learning organizations, related to the idea of reflective practice (Lieberman, 1995). Although definitions vary, consensus exists that PLCs can provide opportunities to focus collaboratively on learning rather than teaching and accountability for results that fuel continual improvement, and promote careful and persistent attention to learning, reflection, and problem solving, and transformations of school cultures and the systems within which they operate (DuFour, 2004; Fullan, 2006; Hord, 1997).

Bracket and Cipriano's (2020) research suggests that emotions drive effective teaching and learning, the decisions educators make, classroom and school climate, and educator well-being. They assert that educators' emotions matter for five primary reasons:

- for attention, memory, and learning;
- decision-making;
- relationships;
- health and well-being; and
- performance.

Amid these complicated emotions, anxiety, and group dynamics, Principal Roby must decide how to navigate the tension-filled gulf between one teacher's stated desire to be a part of a positive, collaborative, and reflective team and another who, by Ms. Snyder's account, is anything but interested.

THE TRANSCRIPT

Principal: Good morning, can we [elbow bump]?

Ms. Snyder: Absolutely. [elbow bumps]

Principal: Good morning, how are you?

Ms. Snyder: Good.

Principal: Thank you for coming in.

Ms. Snyder: Yes, well I always so appreciate your open-door policy, I mean, I've been here for six years, and I've always felt like anytime I come in, you just—I always come in with questions, and you ask such good questions back to me. You just make me such a good teacher and such a good learner, and I just really appreciate everything you always do.

Principal: Thank you, and I appreciate you as well.

Ms. Snyder: Thank you and I'm just kind of shaking a little bit because this is kind of an awkward conversation for me. I don't want to be that person but I'm having a real struggle with another staff member, and I just don't know what to do about it. It's, it's awful. I mean it's, when I go to lunch with you know how English teachers can be. But when I go to lunch, it's like, I call the lunchroom a viper pit, I mean because it's like, there's such negativity, all the time. And gosh I'm just shaking.

Principal: Just calm down, so, relax it's just me.

Ms. Snyder: Thank you. I really hope that you don't tell anybody.

Principal: I'm going to take notes. Okay, just for my sake. Because of where this conversation goes and what I need to do next step . . .

Ms. Snyder: Okay so if Bob knows—Okay there is that, his name. If Bob knows that I talked to you about this, like they'd come after me, and I'm so nervous about that. So, like we go to those PLCs, and I like PLC time because I get to see my friends, you know, we talk about students and stuff but he—the hateful things that he says, like he said one time that he wanted to stick a fork in somebody's eye and twist it, and it wasn't a student, but and then you know those learning objectives that you expect us to put on the board so students see them every day. Did you know that he taped his to the floor, right when the kids walk in?Just so well he says "Well now the kids are seeing them because they have to walk on them when they come in the room." I can't, I can't be a part of that negativity, and it takes over the whole PLC and we've tried, and pretty much me has tried to get him to be engaged but he just wants, so I feel bad, I feel like a rat. But I don't want to do.

Principal: Yeah, nope, so thank you for coming in to let me know what's going on. Nobody else has come and addressed any concerns with Bob with the PLC so I appreciate that you came in. I will have a conversation with Bob and will not let—

Ms. Snyder: That makes me so nervous.

Principal: Don't feel nervous. I will do it in a way that will not, he will not know who has talked to me. I will go in, and I've been in his room, and I actually liked that he had his learning objectives on the floor—

Ms. Snyder: Gord, there's Bob. Okay, let's act like we're talking about something else maybe so.

Principal: Yeah. How was your day, last night?

Ms. Snyder: Well, I knew I was coming in here, so I was little nervous but I'm, you know, okay, he's gone.

Principal: Okay yeah, don't worry with Bob. Okay, I won't even address about today because he's seen you in my office, I will address it with him later this week. Okay, I will not let you know the conversation that I've had with Bob but I will let you know that I have spoken with Bob. So I will just send you an email and say, I have had a conversation with Bob. I will check back with you in a week to make sure you don't still see the same things, or feel nervous when you're around Bob. I will just talk to Bob about our school and the culture we want to create a positive environment. I've been in Bob's room, and I actually like his learning objective on the floor because he has them on his board as well. And he mentions them, he references them, when he's in class and so I don't know if he's telling you guys one thing and doing a different thing when admin comes through because it has not been a problem.

Ms. Snyder: I'm just really nervous because I'm gonna be honest with you, it was you that he said he was gonna stick a fork in your eye and twist it.

Principal: I don't want you to be concerned about that because I'm not concerned about Bob sticking a fork in my eye.

Ms. Snyder: I think what he's going to do though, is tell you everything he knows you want to hear. And then he's going to come right back to that PLC and tank it. I'm not getting the experience that I need from this PLC, and I feel like it's impacting my students. And so, I want to know what's going to happen with that PLC and what's gonna happen at the viper's pit teacher's lounge.

Principal: So, I will talk with other people in your PLC and see if they feel the same way and then maybe there's some things that we can change for next year, with the PLC. We're at the end of the school year so there's no need to change with two weeks left in the school year but trust me when I tell you, I will talk with Bob, we will talk about the positive culture in our school, not the negativity, and I don't want you to be concerned that Bob is going to stick a fork in my eye.

Ms. Snyder: Yeah, I yeah, I'm pretty sure was a joke but still. I am really nervous now you said that you're going to talk to other teachers—

Principal: Ms. Snyder, look at me. I am going to do it in a way where they will not know that I have talked to anybody else. I'm just going to ask not just your PLC, everyone, I'm going to go to everyone and just ask, how have PLCs worked for us this year. What are some things you would like to keep and what are some things you would like to change? So it's just a blanket, they don't know that Ms. Snyder hasn't been in my office to address these concerns.

Ms. Snyder: So, do you think next year I have to be with him?

Principal: Well, we're gonna try not to, we're gonna see how the next two weeks ago, and how Bob changes his personality—

Ms. Snyder: Yeah, he needs to change.

Principal: And maybe he gets more positive after he's made aware of it. Okay, so if he has changed then we'll see about next year but let's just get through the next two weeks this year. And I want you just to relax, relax.

Ms. Snyder: Well, I'm an English teacher, we don't relax well.

Principal: I know, I know English is my forte. Ask Bob, I mean, I want you to if Bob asked you what you were doing it here, say we were talking about fundraising activities for next year. How about that? Because Bob has seen you in here.

Ms. Snyder: Okay, okay, okay.

Principal: All right. Does that sound good?

Ms. Snyder: Okay, yes, thank you.

Principal: I'm just gonna email you at the end of the week just to say, I've had the conversation, and that's it. I'm not gonna tell you what the conversation was, I'm just gonna let you know, I've had the conversation with Bob.

Ms. Snyder: All right, I really appreciate it. Thank you. Is anybody out there? Can I leave now?

Principal: You can leave now; the coast is clear.

DISCUSSION AND REFLECTION QUESTIONS

1. Identify the primary and secondary issue(s).
2. Identify areas in which you believe the principal acted effectively.
3. Identify areas in which you believe the principal could have acted more effectively.
4. When Ms. Snyder begins sharing how appreciative she is for the principal having an open-door policy and for helping her be a good teacher and learner, it is obvious she likes and feels comfortable with the principal. However, her demeanor quickly changes when she begins stating her reason for the meeting. What would be your initial thoughts witnessing Ms. Snyder's apparent nervousness?
5. Ms. Snyder is clearly afraid of potential repercussions if Bob knows she was in the principal's office. At (1:19) she even mentioned "they'd" come after me. The principal did not address this concern. Should Principal Roby ignore the comment or probe? Why or why not?
6. At (1:41) Ms. Snyder mentions "hateful" things Bob said, such as, "he wanted to stick a fork in somebody's eye and twist it." She later says the comment was directed at the principal. As principal, would you take this threat seriously? Would you ask Bob about the comment? Why or why not?
7. During their conversation, Ms. Snyder says Bob displays his learning objectives on the floor so the kids can walk on them, insinuating disrespect. However, Principal Roby shares that she has visited Bob's classroom and actually likes his learning objectives on the floor, noting they are also posted on the bulletin board. Is it problematic for the principal to share anything relative to Bob's teaching performance? Could this be a violation of Bob's privacy and confidential information, even though it was positive information about Bob's teaching?
8. At about (4:17) Ms. Snyder says she is not getting the experience she should be getting during in the PLC and it is impacting her students. Principal Roby indicates that she will talk with others in the PLC to

consider future changes. Evaluate her response. How should the principal respond, given Ms. Snyder's concern about negative impacts on students and the current school year coming to an end?

9. At 5:55, Principal Roby says she'll tell Bob that she and Ms. Snyder were in the office discussing fundraising, which is of course, not the topic of the conversation. How does this fit within ethical leadership? Do you consider this a lie or merely providing necessary cover for Ms. Snyder?

REFLECTION AND DISCUSSION QUESTIONS

Balcony View

Generally speaking, how did the principal perform in this scenario? What would you have done differently?

Standards in Action

Which standards do you see as relevant in the scenario? Does the principal effectively meet them? Are there standards and/or criteria left unmet by the principal's actions?

Peel the Onion

Like an onion, leadership challenges have multiple layers. The presenting issue may be singular or appear simple in nature. Often, however, it represents one part of an underlying, more complex issue. The best leaders address concerns in the moment, while not losing sight of root causes. What is/are the presenting issue(s)? Do you see potential nuanced factors that should be explored?

Self-Check

We all come to our roles with unique experiences, perspectives, and biases that influence our perceptions and actions. Picturing yourself in the principal's chair, describe your emotions.

Switch It Up

How might your thinking or approach change if the gender, ethnicity, language, age, sexual orientation, socioeconomic status, disability, or other descriptors of the players involved were different?

Equity Lens

Equity-driven leaders understand that diversity takes many forms. What equity- or diversity-related issues could be present in this scenario?

Power and Presence

In televised presidential debates, "looking presidential" is an important measure of a candidate's performance. The same is true for principals. Halpern and Lubar (2003, p. 3) define leadership presence as being more than "commanding attention" to include "the ability to connect authentically with the thoughts and feelings of others." Does the principal exert an effective presence? Describe the power balance between the principal and the visitor. Does positional or personal power between the principal and visitor seem uneven or problematic? What does body language say that words do not?

Principal's Priority

1. How *serious* is the situation? Are de-escalation techniques needed?
2. How *soon* should the principal address this situation?
3. Should the principal inform a supervisor of this issue and get them involved?

Reach Out?

Should the principal involve other individuals, professionals, resources, or organizations?

In a Word

Capture the principal's performance in the scenario using one word.

Collaborate

Collaborate with a classmate or colleague to rewrite or alter the case with a different set of circumstances. Share your new case with other colleagues to ascertain how they would approach it.

Extension and Internship Experiences

- Summarize this scenario to your mentor or building principal. Ask how they would have handled the situation or approached it differently (if anything). Discuss your perceptions and how you would have handled in comparison.
- Research the functioning of an effective PLC. If your school incorporates PLCs, compare your structure and processes to the research. How close does your PLC come to the ideal state?
- Review your school climate inventory. For any items that received a lower-than-expected rating, discuss with your principal how the items might be addressed. Or, if your school does not conduct a climate inventory, prepare one for your school and ask to implement it. Discuss the results and implications with your principal and/or leadership team.
- Interview a principal about problem solving when two teachers can't (or won't) get along. What tips can the principal share?

REFERENCES AND RESOURCES

Agarwal, P. (August 29, 2018). How to create a positive workplace culture. *Forbes*. Retrieved from https://www.forbes.com/sites/pragyaagarwaleurope/2018/08/29/how-to-create-a-positive-work-place-culture/?sh=7607f4654272.

Bracket, M., & Cipriano, C. (April 7, 2020). Teachers are anxious and overwhelmed. They need SEL now more than ever. *EdSurge*. https://www.edsurge.com/news/2020-04-07-teachers-are-anxious-and-overwhelmed-they-need-sel-now-more-than-ever.

DuFour, R. (2004). What is a professional learning community? *Educational Leadership* 61: 6–11.

Fullan, M. (2006). Leading professional learning. *The School Administrator*. Retrieved from http://michaelfullan.ca/wpcontent/uploads/2016/06/13396072310.pdf.

Halpern, B. L., & Lubar, K. (2003). *Leadership presence: Dramatic techniques to reach out, motivate, and inspire*. Penguin Group.

Hord, S. M. (1997). *Professional learning communities: Communities of continuous inquiry and improvement*. Southwest Educational Development Laboratory. Retrieved from https://sedl.org/pubs/change34/plc-cha34.pdf.

Lieberman, A. (1995). Practices that support teacher development: Transforming conceptions of professional learning. *Phi Delta Kappan* 76(8): 591–596.

Murphy, M. (2018). *How to deal with a negative work environment.* Retrieved from https://www.collinsmcnicholas.ie/how-to-deal-with-a-negative-work-environment.

I Get Him Here, You Send Him Home (Middle School)

Many educators have stated that the people they really hope to see often don't (or can't) attend conferences. Despite the bias and judgment present in the statement, it reflects the complexity many educators feel in building meaningful relationships with some parents and families. Today presents a rare and unexpected opportunity for Principal Robinson to have a much-needed conversation about young John Coulter's attendance and school performance.

On this unplanned visit, the frustrated Mr. Coulter acknowledges his son's attendance problems and how he struggles to get John to school. He says the school's policy has his son locked in a senseless cycle of unexcused absences followed by suspension. When Mr. Coulter gets John to school, he's promptly suspended for excessive absences, while his grades and motivation decline further. And so it goes.

Truancy is often a gateway to negative student outcomes. Research by the Robert Wood Johnson Foundation (2016) estimated that more than 6.5 million students encounter far-reaching negative outcomes related to truancy, including falling behind in school, an increased likelihood of dropping out, and future financial and health risks. Others point to lower self-esteem, isolation from peers, poor academic performance, mental health challenges (Dahl, 2016), elevated concerns around risky sexual behaviors, substance abuse, and depression (Dembo et al., 2017), future arrest (Mittleman, 2018), and even heightened risks for auto accidents (McCartt et al., 2003) as dangers for frequently absent students.

Dangers are more pronounced for non-white students, sexual minority youth, and students with disabilities. According to Brigeland et al. (2006), as many as half of Black, Latinx, and Indigenous students will not reach graduation. Gottfried et al. (2019) and Gee (2018) reported that students with disabilities are truant at higher rates than other students. Intersectionality of student race, ethnicity, and sexual orientation prompted GLSEN (Truong et al., 2020a, 2020b, 2020c, 2020d) to publish a powerful four-part series entitled *Erasure and Resilience,* examining the starkly troubling experiences of LGBTQ students of color. GLSEN (Kosciw et al., 2019) also reported that one third of students who identify as LGBTQ miss at least one day of school per month because of feeling unsafe.

Research also suggests that "get tough" and zero-tolerance policies may do more harm than good (Anderson, 2020; Curran, 2016; Freeman et al., 2016; Steinburg, 2018). Mireles-Rios et al. (2020) explored how such policies effectively "push out" Black and Latinx students. Newer efforts, including multitiered systems of support (MTSS) and positive behavior interventions and support have shown promise (Freeman et al., 2018), as have efforts to engage families and the larger community (Childs & Grooms, 2018; Huck, 2010; McConnell & Kubina, 2014; Murphy & Tobin, 2010).

As the scenario unfolds, Mr. Coulter paints a familiar picture. His son, a student with multiple needs, is falling through the cracks of a perhaps well-intended but illogical and ineffective policy. Principal Robinson finds herself trying to dispense parenting advice without offending a frustrated and disgruntled father, and come up with a new, workable solution.

THE TRANSCRIPT

Dad: Why, if my son won't come to school, when he does come to school you turn around and put him right back out . . . tell me how that makes sense. You want him there. When he gets there you send him home. Why?

Principal: Okay, I totally understand your concern. What is your son's name?

Dad: You do?

Principal: From what I hear, yes I do. What is your son's name, sir?

Dad: John.

Principal: John, okay, yep, I'm familiar with John. From what I can, um, remember about the situation, and actually I know your son. He's very pleasant . . . a couple of concerns that we talked about. . . . Some of the concerns, we have a couple of policies in place. Um. . . .

Dad: I don't care what your policy says. He's not coming to school. When he comes to school you send him home. Explain! It doesn't make sense.

Principal: And you know what, sir, I understand your concerns. And as a parent myself, that would be frustrating for me. But in school we have rules that are required. We have behavioral policies, we have attendance policies, and those are all rules that we have to follow. And, um, if you have a specific concern, our concern could be a number of things. And again, I totally understand your frustration.

Dad: But I can't get him out of bed, and when I get him out of bed, because he's missed so much school and I finally get his little lazy butt to school, and then you turn around a half hour later and call me and tell me he's suspended because he's skipped school.

Principal: Okay.

Dad: I don't care what your policy says it doesn't make sense, because that's what's happened. I'm trying to get him out of bed. I get him out of bed, I get him there and you send him back home.

Principal: If skipping school is the issue, and clearly in this situation it is, we have policies that state you need to be in school a certain number of days, a certain number of times. Unless he has an excuse from you, an excuse that says. . . .

Dad: He's lazy! He doesn't have an excuse!

Principal: Okay. And in that case we may need to look at some other options. We have a home school worker here in our building that would be more than happy to accommodate you if. . . .

Dad: She's been over there. She can't get him out of bed either.

Principal: Okay. And so then we may need to explore some more options together.

Dad: We even called one time to get a ride and nobody would come to get him.

Principal: Our home school worker's job is to be, kind of a liaison between the school and yourself, and we'd be more than happy to accommodate you.

Dad: Can she pick him up every morning?

Principal: If that's the need, then yes we would be more than happy, we want John at school. We need him here. He has to be here in order to be successful. We want him here. And I also want it to be a partnership between myself, the school, and you. It doesn't only need to be your responsibility, or only my responsibility. We need to be able to work together.

Dad: Then why are you sending him back home?

Principal: What we need to do. . . .

Dad: He's flunking. He's gonna do eighth grade again.

Principal: And I understand that. We have a couple of programs that may interest and accommodate his need. We have the Echoes program. We have extended day program. We have, um, some teachers that are willing to give up their lunchtime to work with your student. We have all of these things.

Dad: If he won't come to school during a regular school day, what makes you think that he's going to stay after school and then he's not going to come back after school when you sent him home for skipping?

Principal: Okay. And I understand that sir. You have some very valid concerns. I just want to talk about how we can work together to get your son here.

Dad: It's not working.

Principal: That much is true. I agree. I agree. If the issue is getting up, not being able to get up in the morning, maybe we should consider what time he's going to bed, some of the activities he's a part of.

Dad: All the boy does is sleep.

Principal: Okay. Well then you know what, maybe we can have our school psychologist just have a conversation with him.

Dad: Can she come to the house? Because I can't get him to school, and when I get him to school you turn him right back around.

Principal: Okay and if that's the. . . .

Dad: She make home visits?

Principal: Yes, we all make home visits. We all are more than happy to . . . whatever you need done, sir. Again, we want John at school. It's important for him to be in school. He has to be in school to be successful. So whatever it takes, whatever we need to do, I'm more than happy to do that. What I want to do is sit down with the team, the school psychologist, the home school worker, and our school counselor. . . .

Dad: That sounds great, but you're going to have to come get him.

Principal: Okay.

Dad: You're going to have to bring the whole crew to the house.

Principal: And you know what, again, whatever we need to do. We can make that happen. I'll be more than happy to do that.

Dad: What about the teachers who won't give him any homework?

Principal: What I want to do is meet with that team first and then I think the second step. . . .

Dad: It's out of sight, out of mind. If he's not there, they don't mind if he's not there. And when he gets to school, which is a struggle, you turn around and send him home.

Principal: And I apologize that you feel that way. . . .

Dad: I try. I burn up their phone lines, I fill up their email boxes. I get nothing.

Principal: Let me have that conversation with my first team. And then I will talk to my teachers. Because if that is happening, that is a valid concern and that needs to be addressed. So, let me speak with the first team and then my team of teachers and then let's say three days from now, Wednesday about 3:00 I can give you a call and update you on the situation.

Dad: Do I gotta bring him with me?

Principal: Actually, you know what, we can have a phone conversation first and then at that time we'll talk about the best time to meet.

Dad: He needs to be here. I wanna bring him in.

Principal: Okay, yep. That sounds good. Okay.

Dad: If I can find him. If you haven't put him out of school yet again.

Principal: Sir, I understand your concern. I do. And you know what? I just want to thank you for coming to see me. I appreciate you not just kind of letting it go and you wanting to address the situation.

Dad: I got that letter from that stinking computer and that phone system keeps calling me wanting to know where my kid's at.

Principal: Yeah, it's a pretty nice system.

Dad: No. It's getting old.

Principal: Ok. And I understand again sir. I really understand your concerns. But I really, really wanna, um, address the issue. I want to get it taken care of.

DISCUSSION AND REFLECTION QUESTIONS

1. Identify the primary and secondary issue(s).
2. Identify areas in which you believe the principal acted effectively.
3. Identify areas in which you believe the principal could have acted more effectively.
4. At 7:15 Dad asks if the home school worker will pick John up for school every morning. Does Principal Robinson overpromise in her response? Can she make this commitment? If your school has an employee of this type, what are the person's responsibilities? If not, who most often deals with these issues? Would picking John up for school, perhaps even waking him up, remove too much of the family's responsibility? On the other hand, Dad and Principal Robinson seem to agree that things are not working as they are now.
5. At 7:25 she speaks of a partnership and shared responsibility for John's success in school. Dad responds by asking why the school consistently

sends him back home. In your opinion, is Dad seeking help, venting, looking for a fight, making excuses, or something else? What should Principal Robinson say to Dad's pointed question?

6. At 7:40 the principal identifies a number of school programs designed to help struggling students like John. Again, Dad responds by asking, "What makes you think that he's going to stay after school and then he's not going to come back after school when you sent him home for skipping?" How should she respond?

7. At 9:25 Dad complains that he gets no response from messages he leaves with teachers. How should she respond?

8. At 9:50 Principal Robinson and Dad are discussing next steps. The principal suggests that it is not necessary to have John at the next meeting. Dad disagrees and says he wants to bring John, and the principal quickly switches positions and agrees. Is this a good decision or is she allowing Dad too much control over the situation?

REFLECTION AND DISCUSSION QUESTIONS

Balcony View

Generally speaking, how did the principal perform in this scenario? What would you have done differently?

Standards in Action

Which standards do you see as relevant in the scenario? Does the principal effectively meet them? Are there standards and/or criteria left unmet by the principal's actions?

Peel the Onion

Like an onion, leadership challenges have multiple layers. The presenting issue may be singular or appear simple in nature. Often, however, it represents one part of an underlying, more complex issue. The best leaders address concerns in the moment, while not losing sight of root causes. What is/are the presenting issue(s)? Do you see potential nuanced factors that should be explored?

Self-Check

We all come to our roles with unique experiences, perspectives, and biases that influence our perceptions and actions. Picturing yourself in the principal's chair, describe your emotions.

Switch It Up

How might your thinking or approach change if the gender, ethnicity, language, age, sexual orientation, socioeconomic status, disability, or other descriptors of the players involved were different?

Equity Lens

Equity-driven leaders understand that diversity takes many forms. What equity- or diversity-related issues could be present in this scenario?

Power and Presence

In televised presidential debates, "looking presidential" is an important measure of a candidate's performance. The same is true for principals. Halpern and Lubar (2003, p. 3) define leadership presence as being more than "commanding attention" to include "the ability to connect authentically with the thoughts and feelings of others." Does the principal exert an effective presence? Describe the power balance between the principal and the visitor. Does positional or personal power between the principal and visitor seem uneven or problematic? What does body language say that words do not?

Principal's Priority

How *serious* is the situation?
How *soon* should the principal address this situation?
Should the principal inform a supervisor of this issue and get them involved?

Reach Out?

Should the principal involve other individuals, professionals, resources, or organizations?

In a Word

Capture the principal's performance in the scenario using one word.

Collaborate

Collaborate with a classmate or colleague to rewrite or alter the case with a different set of circumstances. Share your new case with other colleagues to ascertain how they would approach it.

Extension and Internship Experiences

- Interview the building or district official responsible for school attendance, truancy, and parent liaison duties. What policies or programs are in place? Have these efforts increased or become a higher priority in recent years?
- Ask a mentor to describe successful and unsuccessful efforts aimed at improving attendance.
- Examine your building's suspension and attendance data. What trends emerge? What action, if any, is being taken related to the trends?
- Reasons for poor school attendance are many. Explore common and unexpected reasons for infrequent student attendance with an experienced principal, counselor, or other leader.

REFERENCES AND RESOURCES

Anderson, K. P. (2020). Academic, attendance, and behavioral outcomes of a suspension reduction policy: Lessons for school leaders and policy makers. *Educational Administration Quarterly* 56(3): 435–471. doi:http://dx.doi.org.libproxy.unl.edu/10.1177/0013161X19861138.

Bridgeland, J., Dilulio Jr., J., & Morison, K. (2006). *The silent epidemic: Perspectives of high school dropouts.* Civic Enterprises and Peter D. Hart Research Associates for the Bill and Melinda Gates Foundation. Retrieved from https://files.eric.ed.gov/fulltext/ED513444.pdf.

Bye, L., Alvarez, M. E., Haynes, J., & Sweigart, C. E. (2010). *Truancy prevention and intervention: A practical guide.* Oxford University Press.

Childs, J., & Grooms, A. A. (2018). Improving school attendance through collaboration: A catalyst for community involvement and change. *Journal of Education for Students Placed at Risk* 23(1–2), 122–138. doi: http://dx.doi.org.libproxy.unl.edu/10.1080/10824669.2018.1439751.

Curran, F. (2016). Estimating the effect of state zero tolerance laws on exclusionary discipline, racial discipline gaps, and student behavior. *Educational Evaluation and Policy Analysis* 38(4): 647–668. https://doi.org/10.3102/0162373716652728.

Dahl, P. (2016). Factors associated with truancy: Emerging adults' recollections of skipping school. *Journal of Adolescent Research* 31(1): 119–138. doi: http://dx.doi.org.libproxy.unl.edu/10.1177/0743558415587324.

Dembo, R., Krupa, J. M., Wareham, J., Schmeidler, J., & DiClemente, R. J. (2017). A multigroup, longitudinal study of truant youths, marijuana use, depression, and STD-associated sexual risk behavior. *Journal of Child & Adolescent Substance Abuse* 26(3): 192–204. doi: http://dx.doi.org.libproxy.unl.edu/10.1080/10678 28X.2016.1260510.

Freeman, J., Simonsen, B., McCoach, D. B., Sugai, G., Lombardi, A., & Horner, R. (2016). Relationship between school-wide positive behavior interventions and supports and academic, attendance, and behavior outcomes in high schools. *Journal of Positive Behavior Interventions* 18(1): 41–51. doi: http://dx.doi.org.libproxy.unl.edu/10.1177/1098300715580992.

Freeman, J., Wilkinson, S., Kowitt, J., Kittelman, A., & Brigid Flannery, K. (2018). Research-supported practices for improving attendance in high schools: A review of the literature. *Educational Research and Evaluation* 24(8): 481–503. doi: http://dx.doi.org.libproxy.unl.edu/10.1080/13803611.2019.1602546.

Gee, K. A. (2018). Minding the gaps in absenteeism: Disparities in absenteeism by Race/Ethnicity, poverty and disability. *Journal of Education for Students Placed at Risk* 23(1–2), 204–208. doi: http://dx.doi.org.libproxy.unl.edu/10.1080/108246 69.2018.1428610.

Goss, C. L., & Andren, K. J. (2014). *Dropout prevention.* Guilford Press.

Gottfried, M. A., Stiefel, L., Schwartz, A. E., & Hopkins, B. (2019). Showing up: Disparities in chronic absenteeism between students with and without disabilities in traditional public schools. *Teachers College Record* 121(8): 1–34. Retrieved from http://libproxy.unl.edu/login?url=https://www-proquest-com.libproxy.unl.edu/scholarly-journals/showing-up-disparities-chronic-absenteeism/docview/2461136679/se-2?accountid=8116

Halpern, B. L., & Lubar, K. (2003). *Leadership presence: Dramatic techniques to reach out, motivate, and inspire.* Penguin Group.

Huck, J. L. (2010, October 31). Truancy programs: Are the effects too easily washed away? *Education and Urban Society.* doi: 10.1177/001312451038071

Kearney, C. A. (2008). *Helping school refusing students and their parents: A guide for school-based professionals.* Oxford University Press.

Kosciw, J. G., Clark, C. M., Truong, N. L., & Zongrone, A. D. (2019). The 2019 National School Climate Survey: The experience of lesbian, gay, bisexual, transgender, and queer youth in our nation's schools. Gay, Lesbian, Straight Education Network (GLSEN). Retrieved from https://www.glsen.org/sites/default/files/2020-11/NSCS19-111820.pdf.

McCartt, A. T., Shabanova, V. I., & Leaf, W. A. (2003). Driving experience, crashes and traffic citations of teenage beginning drivers. *Accident Analysis and Prevention* 35: 311–320.

McConnell, B. M., & Kubina Jr., R. M. (2014). Connecting with families to improve students' school attendance: A review of the literature. *Preventing School Failure* 58 (4): 249–256. Retrieved from http://libproxy.unl.edu/login?url=https://www-proquest-com.libproxy.unl.edu/scholarly-journals/connecting-with-families-improve-students-school/docview/1651854553/se-2?accountid=8116

Mireles-Rios, R., Rios, V. M., & Reyes, A. (2020). Pushed out for missing school: The role of social disparities and school truancy in dropping out. *Education Sciences* 10: 1–15. Retrieved from http://libproxy.unl.edu/login?url=https://www-proquest-com.libproxy.unl.edu/scholarly-journals/pushed-out-missing-school-role-social-disparities/docview/2459012315/se-2?accountid=8116

Mittleman, J. (2018). A downward spiral? Childhood suspension and the path to juvenile arrest. *Sociology of Education* 91(3): 183–204. doi: http://dx.doi.org.libproxy.unl.edu/10.1177/0038040718784603.

Murphy, J., & Tobin, K. (2010). *Homelessness comes to school.* Corwin Press.

National Dropout Prevention Center. (August 22, 2021). *National Dropout Prevention Center.* https://dropoutprevention.org/.

Robert Wood Johnson Foundation. (2016). *The relationship between school attendance and health: Health policy snapshot.* Retrieved from http://libproxy.unl.edu/login?url=https://www-proquest-com.libproxy.unl.edu/reports/relationship-between-school-attendance-health/docview/2228676388/se-2?accountid=8116.

Rodriguez, L. F., & Conchas, G. Q. (2009). Preventing truancy and dropout among urban middle school youth: Understanding community-based action from the student's perspective. *Education and Urban Society* 41(2): 216–247.

Steinberg, M. (2018). Rolling back zero tolerance: The effect of discipline policy reform on suspension usage and student outcomes. *Peabody Journal of Education* 93(2): 207–227. https://doi.org/10.1080/0161956X.2018.1435047.

Truong, N. L., Zongrone, A. D., & Kosciw, J. G. (2020a). *Erasure and resilience: The experiences of LGBTQ students of color: Asian American and Pacific Islander LGBTQ youth in U.S. schools.* Gay, Lesbian, Straight Education Network (GLSEN). Retrieved from https://www.glsen.org/research/aapi-lgbtq-students.

Truong, N. L., Zongrone, A. D., & Kosciw, J. G. (2020b). *Erasure and resilience: The experiences of LGBTQ students of color: Black LGBTQ youth in U.S. schools.* Gay, Lesbian, Straight Education Network (GLSEN). Retrieved from https://www.glsen.org/research/black-lgbtq-students.

Truong, N. L., Zongrone, A. D., & Kosciw, J. G. (2020c). *Erasure and resilience: The experiences of LGBTQ students of color: Latinx LGBTQ youth in U.S. schools.* Gay, Lesbian, Straight Education Network (GLSEN). Retrieved from https://www.glsen.org/research/latinx-lgbtq-students.

Truong, N. L., Zongrone, A. D., & Kosciw, J. G. (2020d). *Erasure and resilience: The experiences of LGBTQ students of color: Native and Indigenous LGBTQ youth in U.S. schools.* Gay, Lesbian, Straight Education Network (GLSEN). Retrieved from https://www.glsen.org/research/native-and-indigenous-lgbtq-students.

Hot Seat #8

Who Called DHS?
(Elementary School)

Mr. Cox, the father of an elementary boy, extends a pleasant greeting to Principal Donlea when he arrives at her office unannounced. The pleasantries fade quickly, however, as he demands to know who placed a call to the state Department of Human Services (DHS) about a possible case of child abuse involving his son. As Mr. Cox demands to know who made the call, he unleashes a barrage of profanity. In the midst of Mr. Cox's anger, Principal Donlea faces difficult questions involving culture, parenting techniques and the school's role to protect children.

Perhaps no professional responsibility is greater than an educator's role as a mandatory reporter of possible child abuse. The key federal legislation addressing child abuse and neglect is the 1974 Child Abuse Prevention and Treatment Act (CAPTA), which has been expanded a number of times. CAPTA sets forth a federal definition of child abuse and neglect and sexual abuse requiring each state to have procedures requiring certain individuals to report known or suspected instances of child abuse and neglect. It also provides funding and guidance for the prevention, investigation, and prosecution of child abuse and neglect (Child Welfare Information Gateway, 2019a).

States, as well as the District of Columbia, American Samoa, Guam, the Northern Mariana Islands, Puerto Rico, and the U.S. Virgin Islands designate professions whose members are mandated to report child maltreatment. Individuals designated as mandatory reporters typically have frequent contact with children (Child Welfare Information Gateway, 2019b). While specific policies and procedures, such as which school officials are made aware of reports differ across schools differ, protection of children is paramount across systems.

Further, Dunklee and Shoop (2006, p. 292) noted legal differences in states requiring educators to report cases in which they have "reason to believe" or "reason to suspect" abuse. Though these definitions can be slippery, best practice is to focus on what a reasonable person in a similar situation would likely conclude. Commonly cited signs of neglect or abuse may include sadness, hostility, frequent fighting and reluctance to go home. While these signs have been *associated* with abuse, they cannot be viewed as *indicators* or absolute evidence. Rather, they are *cues* that should trigger the application of common sense and school policy.

Parental use of corporal punishment has generated intense debate and research for many years. What was once considered by some as an integral part of discipline, corporal punishment has been viewed by others as a violation of children's basic human rights (Durrant, 2008). Yet, more than 70% of Americans agreed in 2012 that it is sometimes necessary to discipline a child through spanking (Smith et al., 2013), with forms of corporal punishment permitted in 19 states. It is also worth noting that the United States is somewhat unique in terms of the attitudes, frequency, and legal issues around corporal punishment, as it is more culturally acceptable in America than many other nations—not only by parents, but by teachers. Conversely, in many nations, physical punishment of children has now been outlawed, even for parents (Cuddy & Reeves, 2014).

Some research has found that parents in rural areas and the Southern United States are more likely to employ corporal punishment and that boys are more frequently spanked than girls (Giles-Sims et al., 1995). Though some associate spanking with lower-socioeconomic-status families, Grogan-Kaylor and Otis (2007) pointed out that the connection between socioeconomic status and corporal punishment has been inconsistent. McLoyd and Smith (2002) and Grogan-Kaylor and Otis (2007) have found that, in comparison to white families, African American families are more likely to use corporal punishment.

Others have examined the way schools communicate with families of color. For all the talk about educators' efforts to effectively engage parents, Cooper (2009) noted that, when it comes to low-income families and families of color, "educators typically do not welcome, expect, or cultivate power sharing practices with students' families" (p. 380). Cooper further concluded that "middle-class, White parents are more likely to be perceived as caring parents. African American parents, however, are not cast in such a positive light, nor do they enjoy as much racial privilege" (p. 381).

As Mr. Cox continues to press Principal Donlea, we see the complicated intersection of race/ethnicity, class, culture, speech, and perception. Wilson et al. (2017) found that people have a tendency to perceive Black men as larger and more threatening than similarly sized white men. Citing Kochman (1982), Hecht et al. (2004, p. 106) noted that "contrary to the assumption that Afro-Americans and Whites share identical speech and cultural conventions, Kochman described differing norms and social styles, pointing to divergent patterns of intonation, expressive intensity, spontaneity, aggressiveness, and argument." According to Baugh (2004), many Black Americans face a frequent Catch-22 related to speaking and communication noting, "although they grew up around peers who value the dialect, when they enter professional society, another style of speaking is demanded" (p. 90).

Ostensibly, Mr. Cox came to school demanding to know who called DHS. As Principal Donlea works through Mr. Cox's outrage, she finds herself wrestling with a web of issues including confidentiality, culture and language, emotion, the law, and office decorum.

THE TRANSCRIPT

Principal: Good morning.

Dad: How're ya doing?

Principal: I'm Deb Donlea. Nice to meet you.

Dad: Deb Donlea, right?

Principal: Yes.

Dad: Are you the one who called DHS?

Principal: I'm sorry. . . .

Dad: Who in the hell called DHS?

Principal: Would you like to sit down so we can. . . .

Dad: Someone called DHS on me. They've been around my house and snooping around . . . and it's full of shit, you know?

Principal: Okay.

Dad: It's full of shit. This is full of shit.

Principal: Okay, well, I tell you what, Mr. Cox

Dad: You know my son, right?

Principal: Yes, I do. A wonderful child, wonderful child.

Dad: Uh huh, uh huh. And everyone's been talking to him and everything about, you know, what's going on and this and that. No one has contacted me. You know he had, I guess a little mark, or said, you know, he's been getting whoopings or whatever, this and that. I believe in whoopings, but you know what? You guys don't need to call DHS. That's bullshit.

Principal: Okay. Well, let me first, would you care to sit down and we can discuss this?

Dad: Why should I sit down? It's bullshit.

Principal: Well, I think if we sit down we can calmly talk about it as adults. . . .

Dad: Calmly talk about it? Oh! DHS is not at your fucking house. They're at my house. They're not at your house, ok?

Principal: Okay. All right. Well. . . .

Dad: My son is happy. Don't you think so?

Principal: Yes, he's a wonderful boy. He is a very happy young man.

Dad: Okay, okay, okay, so what's the problem?

Principal: Well, I tell you, I'm not exactly sure about. . . .

Dad: So who called?

Principal: You know, and let me tell you this, Mr. Cox, in a situation like this, ah, we are mandatory reporters as a school. . . .

Dad: I understand that shit . . . I read the fucking rules! I read them, but at the end of the day, you guys don't need to call DHS. I didn't get no call. Why didn't you call and say "is there something wrong?" You make me look like I'm a damn monster. I'm no fucking monster. I'm pissed.

Principal: I understand that, sir. And no, we don't think that you are a monster.

Dad: Oh yes you do. Well, DHS is around my house, not yours.

Principal: As mandatory reporters, we do have to . . . even if there is. . . .

Dad: Oh, there goes the fucking rule again, there goes the fucking rule again. I understand that fucking rule, you need to move on. Who called DHS?

Principal: That is something that is confidential, and DHS has to talk with about you about that.

Dad: Well, why don't you call them up? Call them up. Call them up right now. I want you to call them up and I want you . . . we can all sit down and see if I'm this abuser.

Principal: Okay, sir. I am not going to call DHS at this point. And we've got a couple choices here.

Dad: What are the choices?

Principal: The choices could be that you and I could sit down and calmly talk about this or we could make. . . .

Dad: I haven't invaded your space. Have I invaded your space?

Principal: No, you have not. But the tone that you're using with me is not. . . .

Dad: The tone? Is your secretary . . . am I talking a little too loud?

Principal: But you are using profanity and I do not wish for the students and the other people in this building to hear this. We are a school and we do have to set a good example for the children . . . so I would be more than happy to . . .

Dad: This is A and B. Don't you think this is a A and B conversation? This is an adult situation.

Principal: Yes it is.

Dad: If you was in my situation, what would you do?

Principal: I would probably talk with the DHS person that has been in contact with you and I understand that you are upset. I do understand that, but please understand that we have to go with suspicion. And in this situation, I'm sure and knowing your child and he is a wonderful young man and you seem like a very nice gentleman yourself. . . .

Dad: Huh. Not now.

Principal: But we have to. . . .

Dad: What I mean, you still, you know what? Here goes, this is the thing that bugs me. You're a mandatory reporter, correct? All right. Anything leading up to this point, I'm not getting no phone calls. He's getting good grades. Everything is working fine. He's not acting like he's some abused kid. But you know what? DHS is around my house asking questions, and you know what? Excuse my language, it's bullshit.

Principal: If I don't do my job and if my teachers don't do their job and do report any sort of suspicion, any sort of abuse, whether it's . . . we are liable and we could lose our job. We are here for the children. We want to do what's in the best interest for them. And you know there are times I'm sure when they don't find anything . . . anything that is wrong. But we have to look out for the kids. They are with us seven to eight hours a day.

Dad: That's all about interpretation, isn't it?

Principal: Well, we have to. . . .

Dad: Isn't it?

Principal: We have to. . . .

Dad: I would like to sit down with all the teachers, counselor and whatever. Let's ask to see who called DHS, because it's all about interpretation. Don't you think so?

Principal: Could be, but we're . . . at this point it doesn't really matter who called DHS. What matters is we need to get it solved. . . .

Dad: You're right about that. You're right about that one. You're right about that. It doesn't matter. You know why? Cause I'm the one going through hell. I'm the one going through the shit but you know what? You guys are off on your little ivory mountain there and you know what? I have to answer to some allegations that are false. I was raised with a few little whoopings. And you know what? I'm gonna raise my son the same damn way. And if you guys think it's abuse, you know what? You guys don't get it. You really don't get it.

DISCUSSION AND REFLECTION QUESTIONS

1. Identify the primary and secondary issue(s).
2. Identify areas in which you believe the principal acted effectively.
3. Identify areas in which you believe the principal could have acted more effectively.
4. Mr. Cox sets an aggressive tone in this scenario, asking immediately (15:57) "Who in the hell called (the Department of Human Services) DHS" adding that "it's full of shit." Should Principal Donlea immediately move to redirect his language? Should she advise Mr. Cox that he will be asked to leave if he continues to use profanity? Or should she simply listen and explore the issues he raises? Justify your position.
5. Mr. Cox acknowledges that he uses "whoopings" to discipline his son. He also says his son is happy and the principal agrees, noting that he is "a wonderful boy and a very happy young man." Mr. Cox then asks, (17:04) "So what's the problem?" Given that the school has reported a possible case of child abuse, how should the principal respond? Principal Donlea explains the school's role as a mandatory reporter for possible child abuse. Mr. Cox says he understands that policy and asks why the school didn't call him directly and inquire if there was a problem (17:39). Is this a reasonable question? How should the principal respond?
6. After demanding to know who placed the call and more profanity from Mr. Cox, Principal Donlea begins to offer Mr. Cox two choices for how to proceed. The (18:44) first is to sit down and "calmly talk about this." She never quite gets to the second option, because she addresses Mr. Cox's use of profanity and the level of his voice. Has she waited too long to explain that she does not want other employees or students to hear Mr. Cox's language? Or, by allowing him to express his frustration, has she shown herself as being willing to listen?
7. At 19:30 Principal Donlea asks Mr. Cox to "please understand that we have to go with suspicion," trying to get Mr. Cox to understand the

school's legal and ethical responsibility to protect children. Since she has previously said that Mr. Cox's son appears to be a wonderful happy boy, does her use of the word "suspicion" seem problematic? Does this send the message that she believes Mr. Cox has abused his son?

8. At 19:39 the principal again notes that Mr. Cox's son is a wonderful young man and that Mr. Cox seems like "a very nice gentleman." Evaluate.

9. Mr. Cox complains that he has received no communication from the school regarding potential concerns about his son or possible abuse until a formal call to DHS was made. Is this a valid complaint?

10. At 20:45 Mr. Cox suggests that the issue is related to different interpretations of discipline, corporal punishment, etc. He asks the principal, "It's all about interpretation, isn't it?" Given that some research has concluded that some racial/ethnic and socioeconomic groups are more likely to use corporal punishment than others, does Mr. Cox have a valid point? How should the principal respond?

11. When the principal tells Mr. Cox that it doesn't matter who called DHS, he argues that the investigation allows the school to go on about its business, while he is left to "answer to some allegations that are false." What are the practical implications for a parent/family under investigation for possible child abuse?

12. At 21:38 Mr. Cox notes that he was raised with "a few little whoopings" and that he intends to raise his son the same way. He says that if school officials view this as abuse, they "just don't get it." How should the principal respond? Is there a way Principal Donlea can understand Mr. Cox's rights as a parent while helping him understand the school's legal responsibilities?

REFLECTION AND DISCUSSION QUESTIONS

Balcony View

Generally speaking, how did the principal perform in this scenario? What would you have done differently?

Standards in Action

Which standards do you see as relevant in the scenario? Does the principal effectively meet them? Are there standards and/or criteria left unmet by the principal's actions?

Peel the Onion

Like an onion, leadership challenges have multiple layers. The presenting issue may be singular or appear simple in nature. Often, however, it represents one part of an underlying, more complex issue. The best leaders address concerns in the moment, while not losing sight of root causes. What is/are the presenting issue(s)? Do you see potential nuanced factors that should be explored?

Self-Check

We all come to our roles with unique experiences, perspectives, and biases that influence our perceptions and actions. Picturing yourself in the principal's chair, describe your emotions.

Switch It Up

How might your thinking or approach change if the gender, ethnicity, language, age, sexual orientation, socioeconomic status, disability, or other descriptors of the players involved were different?

Equity Lens

Equity-driven leaders understand that diversity takes many forms. What equity- or diversity-related issues could be present in this scenario?

Power and Presence

In televised presidential debates, "looking presidential" is an important measure of a candidate's performance. The same is true for principals. Halpern and Lubar (2003, p. 3) define leadership presence as being more than "commanding attention" to include "the ability to connect authentically with the thoughts and feelings of others." Does the principal exert an effective presence? Describe the power balance between the principal and the visitor. Does positional or personal power between the principal and visitor seem uneven or problematic? What does body language say that words do not?

Principal's Priority

How *serious* is the situation?
How *soon* should the principal address this situation?

Should the principal inform a supervisor of this issue and get them involved?

Reach Out?

Should the principal involve other individuals, professionals, resources, or organizations?

In a Word

Capture the principal's performance in the scenario using one word.

Collaborate

Collaborate with a classmate or colleague to rewrite or alter the case with a different set of circumstances. Share your new case with other colleagues to ascertain how they would approach it.

Extension and Internship Experiences

- What is your school or district policy related to potential or suspected child abuse? Do teachers, administrators, counselors, and support staff receive training on how to handle concerns, reporting protocol, etc.? Mr. Cox raises the issue of child abuse and interpretation. What do mandatory reporting laws in your state require of educators?
- Does your building designate a particular person to make such reports to the responsible agency in your state? Interview the official charged with responding to issues of this type.
- No principal likes to be caught off guard, especially with an irate stakeholder like Mr. Cox. Does your school or district have an established protocol for informing administrators that a concern has been reported? What school officials will be aware that reports have been made?
- Regardless of the outcome of the investigation, the school's relationship with Mr. Cox will be severely strained. Interview a principal or school-family liaison about effective practice for rebuilding.

REFERENCES AND RESOURCES

Baugh, J. (2004). Black street speech: Its history, structure, and survival. In R. L. Jackson II (Ed.), *African American communication and identities: Essential readings* (pp. 89–101). Sage. (Reprinted from *Black street speech: Its history, structure, and survival*, pp. 1–22, by J. Baugh, 1983, Austin, TX: University of Texas Press.)

Child Welfare Information Gateway. (2019a). *About CAPTA: A legislative history.* U.S. Department of Health and Human Services and Children's Bureau. Retrieved from https://www.childwelfare.gov/pubs/factsheets/about/.

Child Welfare Information Gateway. (2019b). *Mandatory reporters of child abuse and neglect.* U.S. Department of Health and Human Services and Children's Bureau. Retrieved from https://www.childwelfare.gov/pubPDFs/cw_educators.pdf.

Cooper, C. W. (2009). Parent involvement, African American mothers and the politics of educational care. *Equity and Excellence in Education* 42(4): 379–394.

Cuddy, E., & Reeves, R. V. (2014). *Hitting kids: American parenting and physical punishment.* Brookings Institute. Retrieved from https://www.brookings.edu/research/hitting-kids-american-parenting-and-physical-punishment/

Dunklee, D. R., & Shoop, R. J. (2006). *The principal's quick-reference guide to school law: Reducing liability, litigation, and other potential legal tangles* (2nd ed.). Corwin Press.

Durrant, J. (2008). Physical punishment, culture, and rights: Current issues for professionals. *Journal of Developmental and Behavioral Pediatrics* 29(1): 55–66.

Giles-Sims, J., Straus, M. A., & Sugarman, D. B. (1995). Child, maternal, and family characteristics associated with spanking. *Family Relations* 44(2): 70–176.

Grogan-Kaylor, A., & Otis, M. D. (2007). The predictors of parental use of corporal punishment. *Family Relations* 56(1): 80–91. doi: 10.1111/j.1741-3729.2007.00441.x.

Halpern, B. L., & Lubar, K. (2003). *Leadership presence: Dramatic techniques to reach out, motivate, and inspire.* Penguin Group.

Hecht, M. L., Ribeau, S., & Alberts, J. K. (2004). An Afro-American perspective on interethnic communication. In R. L. Jackson II (Ed.), *African American communication and identities: Essential readings* (pp.105–124). Sage. (Reprinted from *An Afro-American perspective on interethnic communication*, pp. 385–410, by M. L. Hecht, S. Ribeau, & J. K. Alberts, 1989, *Communication Monographs* 56.)

Kochman, T. (1982). *Black and white: Styles in conflict.* University of Chicago Press.

McLoyd, V. C., & Smith, J. (2002). Physical discipline and behavior problems in African American, European American, and Hispanic children: Emotional support as a moderator. *Journal of Marriage and Family* 64(1): 40–53.

Smith, T. W., Marsden, P. V., & Hout, M. (2013). *General social survey, 1972-2012.* (ICPSR 34802) [Cumulative file]. Inter-university Consortium for Political and Social Research. http://people.wku.edu/douglas.smith/GSS%201972_2012%20 Codebook.pdf.

Wilson, J. P., Hugenberg, K., & Rule, N. O. (2017). Racial bias in judgments of physical size and formidability: From size to threat. *Journal of Personality and Social Psychology.* doi:10.1037/pspi0000092.

Look What I Found!
(Elementary School)

Ms. Garza serves as the school district's first-ever Latinx principal. Recruited because of her expertise in reading instruction, dual language programs, and communication skill, the district was proud of its aggressive and successful recruiting efforts. Heather, an intense mother of four young children, appears unannounced in Principal Garza's office intent on sharing her displeasure with several aspects of the playground.

Sitting in Principal Garza's office with a large bag of dangerous items she claims to have found on the playground, Heather begins quizzing Principal Garza about the playground and recess. She peppers Principal Garza with questions on topics ranging from policy and equipment maintenance to records of injuries. She also informs Principal Garza that she has conducted her own research into playground safety. Her visit presents an opportunity for Principal Garza to address an issue that was far from the reasons she was recruited into her job: the role of recess and the outdoor environment.

There is a growing body of research stressing the critical need for active play for students. Playgrounds are an integral part of the school day, especially during recess. While recess offers opportunities for students to be physically and socially active, school nurses are well aware that unintentional injuries and incidents on the playground are common occurrences in the school setting (Olsen & Kennedy, 2019). Playground injuries remain as one of the most frequently observed sources of injury leading to hospital emergency room treatments (Adelson et al., 2018; Tuckel et al., 2017). Nabavizadeh et al. (2021) counted nearly 5.5 million hospital emergency room visits from playground injuries between 1995 and 2019, with more than 200,000 annually.

Research by the National Program for Playground Safety (NPPS) gave most playgrounds a C+ for supervision, maintenance, and safety (Olsen et al., 2002). These frequent shortcomings account for a staggering amount of playground-related injuries and are a common source of litigation against school districts (Frost & Sweeney, 1996; Olsen et al., 2008). To address these risks, NPPS developed the S.A.F.E. model for playgrounds, consisting of four key components of playground safety: supervision, appropriate environments, fall surfacing, and equipment maintenance (Thompson et al., 2007). Olsen and Kennedy's (2019) research further identified a need to improve playground safety conditions that would foster the well-being of students by minimizing risk hazards associated with the environment, equipment, and protective surfacing as well as routine inspection and repair. In addition to principals and maintenance staff, "school nurses play a vital role in the advocacy of playground safety" (p. 370).

Whether interested in playgrounds or helping with copying and field trips, volunteers can offer valuable help to schools. Beyond the active nature of recess, injuries may be due in part to recess policies and practices not receiving thorough enough consideration and untrained staff supervising one of the most dangerous parts of the school day (Bossenmeyer, 2012). Given that recess is one of the most dangerous parts of the school day (Posner, 2000), all recess supervisors should be adequately trained (Minnesota Department of Education & Minnesota Department of Health, 2013).

While volunteers can provide essential support to short-staffed schools, wise principals know that some would-be volunteers can create more problems than they solve, through disruption, meddling, or failing to understand their role. The task for principals then becomes how (or whether) to utilize, train, and supervise them. Heather's passion for the elementary school playground and desire to be involved leads Ms. Garza to invite Heather to become involved in the school's safety committee. As the scenario plays out, Principal Garza wonders if inviting Heather to be involved will be a wonderful part of the solution or an unfortunate mistake.

THE TRANSCRIPT

Mom: Hi, Miss Garza?

Principal: Hi Heather. How are you?

Mom: Nice to meet you.

Principal: Nice to meet you too. Why don't you sit down?

Mom: Thank you, thank you. Thanks for taking the time . . . the five minutes. . . .

Principal: Sure. How can I help you?

Mom: Well, first of all, I gotta ask do you know why I'm dressed like this?

Principal: You . . . are on a safety committee . . .?

Mom: Very, yeah, close, yeah. Well, any other thoughts?

Principal: Uh, you were helping out with crosswalks maybe somewhere?

Mom: Actually, I'm demonstrating because I've kind of had some concerns . . . what's going on outside your school. . . .

Principal: Uh huh. . . .

Mom: Just let me take this off cause I don't wanna. . . .You know I'm a parent . . . and I have four children under the age of five that . . . my kindergartner will be starting this year and I'm a little concerned about what's happening outside . . . we live right across the school and I know you have three recesses a day and I see your teachers, uh, they're out there in their stilettos, they have their flip-flops on, and I'm just disappointed in the behavior that's happening out there. . . . They're just on their cell phones texting—talking about laws, I have documentation . . . and I just wanted to know what your thoughts were on the outdoor environment.

Principal: Well, first of all, I'm glad you're here and talking about these concerns you have and I can validate your concerns because your child will be coming to our school next year.

Mom: Well that's a relief!

Principal: But I would like to share some thoughts of how we are coming together and wanting to improve our behaviors outside, not only with staff but with students as well. Currently we are having staff development on the safety issues. We're gathering a safety committee together and I would love for you to be involved. You could be a part of that committee and you could show us some examples of. . . .

Mom: Well, I just don't think that's . . . you know . . . I found this last week, okay, a jump rope, right . . . I found this hanging. Do you know each year seventeen children die on playgrounds? And strangulation is the leading cause. So just recently here in our community we just had a strangulation death. This is a major problem. This is just laying out there. I found this on the weekend. And then, wine! I don't know who's drinking out there but there's wine bottles out there. Have you ever stepped on a broken bottle? Because if this thing would be . . . yeah and my condom, I found a condom out there in my bag. So I've been picking up, I've been collecting things . . . I have documentation of what I have found outside! What are you gonna do about this stuff?

Principal: Well that could be part of our safety committee as well . . . maybe. . . .

Mom: Isn't that a little late? I mean, come on, this is four . . . evidence right here. These are all things I found on your playground. And in fact, I don't know if you were here when this happened but a kindergartner ran up to Mr. Olsen and said,

"Mr. Olsen, what is this?" A kindergartner! If my five-year-old found this . . . I mean, come on! What kind of school are you running here?

Principal: Well let me assure you that I will be out there to monitor more of this stuff. Now. . . .

Mom: When? Yesterday, today, tomorrow?

Principal: Well as soon as we can have our next recess, our next break . . . Uh, in the mornings when we have . . . the kids are arriving to school . . . I don't know if you do notice the parents who are out there helping us . . . Uh, and as long as once we get the safety committee rolling, uh, we can have all this presentation and show them the importance of elevating the safety of our school. As far as the jump rope is concerned, you know we do want to have our kids active out there and that's why we encourage them to use these kinds of equipment. In our school, we haven't had any issues as far as health or accidents or injuries that deal with any of the concerns that you have here. They're all. . . .

Mom: Do you know that for a fact?

Principal: Yes ma'am, we do. We haven't had any concerns . . . or any injuries or anything up to this point.

Mom: Well I read a statistic, I don't know . . . I should tell you. . . . And I'm so glad that you're coming into this school and you're excited and making changes, but I actually took it upon myself and I started doing research. For the past couple weeks I've been researching this topic and if you just google playgrounds, outdoor . . . go on the Google site. . . . You know, there are a lot of . . . good information out there. There's some certificate programs that are out there and so I've purchased these books and I've been reading and I'm actually certified as a playground supervisor by the National Program for Playground Safety, so I feel confident that I know my stuff and in fact there is a research study that was done about five years ago in the state of Iowa that not one school had the same injury report form. So I'm really shocked that you have not had any injuries out there. It just blows my mind because 80 percent of the injuries happen on the playground. You know, so I just . . . you know, I've heard this time and time again. . . .

Principal: Uh huh. . . .

Mom: In the research that I've done. . . .

Principal: Right . . . And maybe you can help us to do our own research here on our own campus. You know, I'm so pleased that you have done so much work and you're so involved. We need parents like you in our school. If I can hook you up with our counselor, we can get this committee started and I would be more than impressed if you could be part of that committee so we can resolve all of these issues that we have right now. . . .

Mom: I mean, but I want to ask you a serious question. Have you ever spent any time outside observing the children?

Principal: Yes, I have.

Mom: You have? How, how much?

Principal: Any time that I have a chance . . . that I'm not in a meeting or not pulled away by a parent, I am out there, yes.

Mom: Well, could you . . . I would like to see your files of your inspection reports of your documentation of . . . your staff. . . . Have they all . . . You said you have parents that are out there supervising. Have they been trained? Do they know what they're looking for? Or are you just assuming this is just easy, it's just the playground, anybody can watch children. Or do you really value the outdoor environment, the part of the curriculum?

Principal: Well, as far as the files are concerned, I don't want to share those with you because of the personal and private information that's in there. I wouldn't want any other parent coming in and asking about your child's information either, and I wouldn't share that with them also. Uh, but I. . . .

Mom: So you're telling me that . . . I'm so glad, but, I'm wonderful, I'm very happy that you're saying you look through them. But if I would go to your 12 staff, your 15 staff and I would ask them, you know, do you know what's going, you know, where are your boundaries, what are you playground rules, um, what should you be doing, you know. . . . If they're out there wearing their stilettos and their flip-flops and they don't have the right safety. . . . We think this is just first aid, but, you know, I have Kleenexes in here, it says to have Kleenexes. . . .

Principal: Right. . . .

Mom: Band-Aids, they should have this vest . . . um, clips, pooper scoopers, you know? What . . . I would like to check all your fanny packs in your school and see if there's a consistency with it.

DISCUSSION AND REFLECTION QUESTIONS

1. Identify the primary and secondary issue(s).
2. Identify areas in which you believe the principal acted effectively.
3. Identify areas in which you believe the principal could have acted more effectively.
4. Heather expresses a number of concerns related to the school's outdoor environment, ranging from the shoes teachers are wearing at recess to claiming that they are sending text messages during recess time. After thanking Heather for coming in to express her concerns, Principal Garza

begins to explain how the school is "coming together and wanting to improve behaviors outside" with students and staff alike. In doing this, does she effectively thank Heather for raising her concerns? Or does she imply to Heather that she agrees there is a problem? Should Principal Garza have asked to see the "documentation" Heather claims to have? By describing the staff development that is underway, does Principal Garza seem to empower Heather without knowing enough about her or the validity of her concerns?

5. At 23:58 Principal Garza describes the newly formed safety committee and says, "I would love for you to be involved." Is it a good idea to invite Heather to be involved in such a committee, given her apparent knowledge and interest in these issues? Perhaps it is a way to engage a potential critic as a partner. On the other hand, what if Heather has a reputation of being an impossible critic or simply a nuisance? Does Principal Garza run the risk of inviting every squeaky wheel onto a school committee by extending the invitation to Heather?

6. At 24:07 Heather begins showing a number of items she claims to have found on the playground, asking "What are you gonna do about this stuff?" How should Principal Garza respond? At 25:12 Principal Garza asserts that she "will be out there to monitor more of this stuff." Is she validating the importance of the playground or admitting that she has not provided effective oversight?

7. An experienced school administrator once said "the best public relations a school can have is a good band, winning football team, and a well-maintained building and grounds." Given this bit of folk wisdom, what is the role of the appearance in the school's playground and outdoor spaces?

8. At 25:14 Principal Garza commits to being "out there to monitor more of this stuff." Is that an admission that there are problems on the playground and that she and the school have not done an effective job of monitoring and maintaining the space? Or does it simply show that she takes Heather's concerns seriously? Assuming that Principal Garza's schedule is already highly demanding, is this a promise she should make? Is that additional time on the playground and outdoor space a wise use of her time? Why or why not?

9. At 26:40 Heather explains that she has conducted research into playground issues and has become certified as a Playground Supervisor by the National Program for Playground Safety. Does this make Principal Garza's invitation to serve on the school safety committee seem more or less appropriate?

10. After asking Principal Garza how much time she spends observing children on the playground, Heather asks to see the school's inspection

reports, etc. Is this a reasonable request? Is she entitled to see these documents? How should Principal Garza respond?

11. Heather further presses Principal Garza about the level of training, if any, that staff and/or parents on the playground receive. Are teachers, staff, and volunteers at your school provided training for playground supervision?

12. At 29:05 Heather says she would like to check the school's fanny packs to see if necessary, items are included. Is this asking for trouble or a potential way to turn Heather from a critic into part of the solution?

13. How should Principal Garza bring closure to the meeting?

REFLECTION AND DISCUSSION QUESTIONS

Balcony View

Generally speaking, how did the principal perform in this scenario? What would you have done differently?

Standards in Action

Which standards do you see as relevant in the scenario? Does the principal effectively meet them? Are there standards and/or criteria left unmet by the principal's actions?

Peel the Onion

Like an onion, leadership challenges have multiple layers. The presenting issue may be singular or appear simple in nature. Often, however, it represents one part of an underlying, more complex issue. The best leaders address concerns in the moment, while not losing sight of root causes. What is/are the presenting issue(s)? Do you see potential nuanced factors that should be explored?

Self-Check

We all come to our roles with unique experiences, perspectives, and biases that influence our perceptions and actions. Picturing yourself in the principal's chair, describe your emotions.

Switch It Up

How might your thinking or approach change if the gender, ethnicity, language, age, sexual orientation, socioeconomic status, disability, or other descriptors of the players involved were different?

Equity Lens

Equity-driven leaders understand that diversity takes many forms. What equity- or diversity-related issues could be present in this scenario?

Power and Presence

In televised presidential debates, "looking presidential" is an important measure of a candidate's performance. The same is true for principals. Halpern and Lubar (2003, p. 3) define leadership presence as being more than "commanding attention" to include "the ability to connect authentically with the thoughts and feelings of others." Does the principal exert an effective presence? Describe the power balance between the principal and the visitor. Does positional or personal power between the principal and visitor seem uneven or problematic? What does body language say that words do not?

Principal's Priority

How *serious* is the situation?
How *soon* should the principal address this situation?
Should the principal inform a supervisor of this issue and get them involved?

Reach Out?

Should the principal involve other individuals, professionals, resources, or organizations?

In a Word

Capture the principal's performance in the scenario using one word.

Collaborate

Collaborate with a classmate or colleague to rewrite or alter the case with a different set of circumstances. Share your new case with other colleagues to ascertain how they would approach it.

Extension and Internship Experiences

- What records does your school or district keep regarding playground maintenance and injuries? Conduct a review of those files, noting any action or concerns.
- Conduct a walk-through examination of your school's playground/outdoor space, noting any concerns.
- Does your school or district have a person designated to conduct safety and maintenance inspections of the playground and outdoor environment? Given increasing demands on principals' time, is this something that could/should be delegated to someone else? Or is this a key function of the principal? Why or why not? Interview a principal or director of elementary education on their view of the principal's role in this area.
- Research the laws in your state related to playground supervision.
- Recess and playgrounds are prime settings for injuries (and litigation), yet many supervisors receive little or no training. Research the process in your school or district and make recommendations.
- Visit the National Program for Playground Safety (playgroundsafety.org) to download and utilize key resources, such as the playground safety report card. Conduct an evaluation with the official responsible for playgrounds in your district.

REFERENCES AND RESOURCES

Adelson, S. L., Chounthirath, T., Hodges, N. L., Collins, C. L., & Smith, G. A. (2018). Pediatric playground-related injuries treated in hospital emergency departments in the United States. *Clinical Pediatrics* 57: 584–592.

Bossenmeyer, M. (2012). *Playground liability: Accident or injury.* Retrieved from https://peacefulplaygrounds.com/playground-liability-accident-or-injury.

Frost, J. L., & Sweeney, T. B. (1996). *Cause and prevention of playground injuries and litigation: Case studies.* Association for Childhood Education International.

Halpern, B. L., & Lubar, K. (2003). *Leadership presence: Dramatic techniques to reach out, motivate, and inspire.* Penguin Group.

Minnesota Department of Education & Minnesota Department of Health. (2013). *Moving matters! A school implementation toolkit.* Retrieved from http://www.health.state.mn.us/divs/hpcd/chp/cdrr/physicalactivity/movingmatters.html.

Nabavizadeh, B., Hakam, N., Holler, J. T., Namiri, N. K., Sadighian, M. J., Rios, N., Enriquez, A., Amend, G. M., & Breyer, B. N. (2021). Epidemiology of child playground equipment-related injuries in the USA: Emergency department visits, 1995–2019. *Journal of Pediatrics and Child Health* 1–8.

National Program for Playground Safety offers a host of resources related to playgrounds, safety, and recess. Their website is: playgroundsafety.org.

Olsen, H., Hudson, S. D., & Thompson, D. (August 2002). Child's play: What your school board should know about playground supervision and safety. *American School Board Journal* 189(8): 22–24.

Olsen, H., Hudson, S. D., & Thompson, D. (2008). Developing a playground injury prevention plan. *Journal of School Nursing* 24(3): 131–137.

Olsen, H., & Kennedy, E. (2019). Safety of school playgrounds: Field analysis from a randomized sample. *Journal of School Nursing* 36(5): 369–375.

Posner, M. (2000). *Preventing school injuries: A comprehensive guide for school administrators, teachers & staff.* Rutgers University Press. Retrieved from https://www-tandfonline-com.libproxy.unl.edu/doi/full/10.1080/08924562.2017.132024 7.

Thompson, D., Hudson, S. D., & Olsen, H. (2007). *S.A.F.E. play areas: Creation, maintenance, and renovation.* Human Kinetics.

Tuckel, P., Milczarski, W., & Silverman, D. G. (2017). Injuries caused by fall from playground equipment in the United States. *Clinical Pediatrics* 57: 563–573.

What Are They Doing in There? (Elementary School)

As an applicant for the elementary principalship, one of the first people Dameon Place met was Mr. Stamp, a popular, influential local banker and member of the interview committee. Dameon had been immediately impressed with Mr. Stamp's passion for the school and community and his gregarious communication style. After accepting the job, Principal Place appreciated Mr. Stamp's help in securing a mortgage from a local bank and meeting other influential community leaders. Mr. and Mrs. Stamp had gone out of their way to make Dameon and his family feel welcome, and it felt good to know some people not directly associated with the school district.

Mr. Stamp pops into Principal Place's office, concerned that his fifth-grade son is struggling in history. To Principal Place's surprise, his new friend believes the root of the problem lies not with his son, the curriculum, or the teacher. Mr. Stamp believes special education students in the class are distracting his son. And he wants his new friend, Principal Place, to fix it.

There are many dimensions to special education, including a wide array of services provided to qualifying students. According to Riser-Kositsky (2019), "special education encompasses the programs, which serve students with mental, physical, emotional, and behavioral disabilities" (para. 1). Under the guidance of the Individuals with Disabilities Education Act (IDEA) which became law in 1975, a "free and appropriate" education should be provided to children with disabilities. The law mandates that to the "maximum extent appropriate," special needs students are to educated with their nondisabled peers in the "least restrictive environment (LRE)" (Riser-Kositsky, 2019). According to Snyder et al. (2019), the number of students served by special education programs has grown from 6.5 million, or 13.4% in 2007–2008, to almost 7 million or 13.7% in 2017–2018.

As the number of students served has increased, so has the percentage of time special education students spend in regular education classrooms, although IDEA does not specify *how* school districts are to determine the LRE. As a result, variations and confusion, lack of cohesion, and different levels of professional development for general education teachers, are not uncommon. Often, general education teachers and special education teachers work separately with little cooperation or collaboration in curriculum planning and implementation (Nilsen, 2018). Collaborative teaching between general and special education teachers working together and combined experience to meet the needs of all pupils in the class, can therefore be a valuable model of teaching (Cook & Friend, 2010). Research indicates that joint discussion and reflection among teachers promotes an understanding that inclusion is a shared responsibility of all teachers and that it requires collaboration. It fosters the exchange of experiences and ideas and encourages mutual support and common follow-up practices among all teachers who teach students with special education needs (Bjoornsrud & Nilsen, 2018; Lyons et al., 2016).

Research suggests that inclusion is beneficial for all students—not just for those who receive special education services. In fact, research shows that inclusive education has positive short-term and long-term effects for all. Students with special education needs in inclusive classes are absent less often, develop stronger academic skills and are more likely to have jobs and pursue education after high school. The same research shows that special education students' general education peers also benefit. They are more comfortable with and more tolerant of differences. They also have increased positive self-esteem and diverse, caring friendships (Hehir et al., 2016).

For Principal Place, the precarious balance appears in the form of Mr. Stamp's call for Principal Place to "do something" about those special education kids who are distracting his son. His friend's demand leaves him needing to respond in a way that reflects the law, his philosophy, and educators' moral and ethical responsibilities to all students.

THE TRANSCRIPT

Principal: Hello, Mr. Stamp.

Dad: Dameon! How's it going, buddy?

Principal: Good to see you.

Dad: Good to see you too.

Principal: Let's have a seat here.

Dad: Okay.

Principal: I'll grab my paper.

Dad: Okay.

Principal: Thanks for coming in.

Dad: Yeah, you bet. Hey, Dameon, we've got a situation here. I was talking to Michael the other day, and he mentioned that in his history class. . . . Uh, with Mr. Peterson. . . . there's a couple kids in there that are distracting him from getting his work done. And so I kind of, ah, made an excuse to stop by the class-room the other day and I've gotta tell you, there are a couple of kids in there that shouldn't be in there, and I think we've gotta do something.

Principal: Okay. Ah, what's going on?

Dad: Well, I don't . . . for Michael, he's doing poorly in history.

Principal: Okay.

Dad: Uh, and ah, you know, it's a subject he shouldn't do poorly in, but there's a couple . . . the kids, I don't know their names, but they're those special educa-tion kids, okay? And they're, there's a couple of them and I was in there, you know, they're making noises and they're drooling and their wheelchairs are hit-ting other chairs and shit like that . . . I mean, they shouldn't be in there.

Principal: Okay.

Dad: I mean, don't you think . . . don't you gotta get them out of there?

Principal: No, I think they should be there. That's what we do here.

Dad: Seriously?

Principal: Yeah, it's, it's kind of a law. We need to include them as much as we can. I understand your concern. I understand Michael's having a hard time with the distractions going on. Ah, what period does he have history?

Dad: Seventh period, Mr. Peterson.

Principal: Seventh period. Ah. . . .

Dad: So that's your response? Is it's the law?

Principal: Well, it's part of my response.

Dad: Okay, what's the other part?

Principal: Well, I need to gather a little bit more information, to be honest with you. Ah, how has Michael done in history before? Has he done . . . or, you know, what. . . .

Dad: Well, mostly B's and he's getting a C right now, but you know, it's not just Michael. . . .

Principal: Okay.

Dad: It's all the kids. I mean, why do, I mean. . . .

Principal: Let's focus mainly on Michael, right now. . . .

Dad: Well, let's tell you this, if Michael were disrupting the class as much as those kids are disrupting the class, he'd be out of there. . . .

Principal: Okay.

Dad: What do you think about that?

Principal: I haven't seen the problem, so I don't know. You know, and that's the thing. I think that what I need to do, ah, Mr. Stamp, is I'd like to stop down, seventh period today actually. . . . I'll just, I'll go down and sit through the class with Mr. Peterson and gather a little bit more information. Is it okay if I call you after school today? Perhaps we can sit down with Michael and you and address the situation and get a look at, ah, some of the concerns that you both have regarding his grade and regarding the situation in the class.

Dad: Well, yeah, I suppose, I mean I would expect you're gonna at least do that, to see with your own eyes, and that's all well and good, but really, what are they doing in there?

Principal: They're learning.

Dad: Really?

Principal: Yeah.

Dad: You think they can learn?

Principal: I do.

Dad: Isn't it just a feel-good, everyone pretends they can learn, bullshit policy?

Principal: No, it's not. I understand that from the outside you may think that, but that's not what we're doing as public educators. We want to make sure that we try to get every student the best education possible and sometimes it's, and sometimes it's, ah, a difficult situation, but we're going to do the best we can for Michael. That's really the main concern here . . . for you.

Dad: Well, that is the main concern. So, how. . . .

Principal: And for me, the main concern is that all of my students in my building get an excellent education. And that's what I'm gonna do. I'm gonna go down and see Mr. Peterson's class today seventh hour. I'll give you a call after school.

Dad: But how is . . . I understand what you're saying, that everyone has to have a chance to learn. Fine. But, what about Michael? What about his chance? What about his rights? What about my money paying for him to go to this school? I mean, he can, I can go to another school.

Principal: Yes, you can. Yeah, and that's fine. If you'd like to do that, they'll have the same policies that we have regarding that. I'll talk to you after school today. I appreciate you coming in. Thanks a lot.

Dad: Okay. Talk to you then.

DISCUSSION AND REFLECTION QUESTIONS

1. Identify the primary and secondary issue(s).
2. Identify areas in which you believe the principal acted effectively.
3. Identify areas in which you believe the principal could have acted more effectively.
4. Judging from the start of this scenario, it appears that the two have met previously and may be on a first-name basis. Dameon, the principal, addresses the visitor as "Mr. Stamp." Mr. Stamp addresses Dameon less formally, with "Dameon, how's it going, buddy?"
5. Depending on the size of school and community, principals often live in "a fishbowl," being fairly well known in the community. At the same time, virtually every principal can describe the loneliness that comes with some aspects of school leadership. This can be made more complicated by stakeholders who may wish to leverage their relationship with the principal to their or their children's benefit. Practically speaking, how can a principal navigate the complicated path of acting professionally, respecting confidentiality, and telling stakeholders (and friends) things they don't want to hear all while maintaining friendships?
6. At 30:15 Mr. Stamp seems to assume that Principal Place will agree that the special education students in his son's history classroom are a distraction and should be moved. Evaluate Principal Place's response to Mr. Stamp.
7. Mr. Stamp seems unimpressed with Principal Place's response that the presence of special education students in his son's history class is the law. He seems to believe Principal Place is hiding behind the law and begins to discuss other students. At 30:57 Principal Place redirects the conversation to focus on Michael and his performance in history. Mr. Stamp counters and says, "If Michael were disrupting the class as much as those kids are disrupting the class, he'd be out of there. What do you think about that?" How should Principal Place respond? Principal Place's actual response is "I haven't seen the problem, so I don't know." Evaluate.

8. Mr. Stamp seems unsatisfied with the response to the situation, including Principal Place's plan to observe the class. He presses what may be a larger philosophical idea, asking what the special education students are doing in the class. Evaluate Principal Place's response.

9. At 32:28 Principal Place sets his notepad and pen on the table, signaling that the meeting is nearing an end. When Mr. Stamp raises Michael's rights and the possibility of them choosing to enroll in another school, Principal Place says, "Yes you can. And that's fine." Evaluate this statement. Does Principal Place seem to dismiss Mr. Stamp's concern or invite him to choose another school? Or is he simply acknowledging that Mr. Stamp understands his options and is free to enroll his son elsewhere?

10. Would a private school have the same policies?

11. Evaluate the way Principal Place brings closure to the meeting.

REFLECTION AND DISCUSSION QUESTIONS

Balcony View

Generally speaking, how did the principal perform in this scenario? What would you have done differently?

Standards in Action

Which standards do you see as relevant in the scenario? Does the principal effectively meet them? Are there standards and/or criteria left unmet by the principal's actions?

Peel the Onion

Like an onion, leadership challenges have multiple layers. The presenting issue may be singular or appear simple in nature. Often, however, it represents one part of an underlying, more complex issue. The best leaders address concerns in the moment, while not losing sight of root causes. What is/are the presenting issue(s)? Do you see potential nuanced factors that should be explored?

Self-Check

We all come to our roles with unique experiences, perspectives, and biases that influence our perceptions and actions. Picturing yourself in the principal's chair, describe your emotions.

Switch It Up

How might your thinking or approach change if the gender, ethnicity, language, age, sexual orientation, socioeconomic status, disability, or other descriptors of the players involved were different?

Equity Lens

Equity-driven leaders understand that diversity takes many forms. What equity- or diversity-related issues could be present in this scenario?

Power and Presence

In televised presidential debates, "looking presidential" is an important measure of a candidate's performance. The same is true for principals. Halpern and Lubar (2003, p. 3) define leadership presence as being more than "commanding attention" to include "the ability to connect authentically with the thoughts and feelings of others." Does the principal exert an effective presence? Describe the power balance between the principal and the visitor. Does positional or personal power between the principal and visitor seem uneven or problematic? What does body language say that words do not?

Principal's Priority

How *serious* is the situation?
How *soon* should the principal address this situation?
Should the principal inform a supervisor of this issue and get them involved?

Reach Out?

Should the principal involve other individuals, professionals, resources, or organizations?

In a Word

Capture the principal's performance in the scenario using one word.

Collaborate

Collaborate with a classmate or colleague to rewrite or alter the case with a different set of circumstances. Share your new case with other colleagues to ascertain how they would approach it.

Extension and Internship Experiences

- Principals are often in a position to tell others "no," whether the issue is legal, budgetary or involves judgment. Transitioning from the role of a classroom teacher, this often puts them in an unfamiliar position. How comfortable are you telling people no? Will it be more difficult for you say no to friends and acquaintances than strangers? Does your school or district have a stated policy with regard to mainstreaming special education students?
- Interview an experienced principal about the challenges present when friends lobby for a particular cause or decision to be made. How does the principal navigate decisions involving friends or their children?
- What are the applicable laws and policies related to LRE? Interview you principal, director of special education, or other appropriate official to gain insight into how they believe objections like Mr. Stamp's should be addressed.
- Many special educators and advocates have noted that special needs classrooms are often located in out of the way or undesirable corners of the building, amounting to an implicit message about the priority given to these students. Discuss real or potential bias and stigma issues with a special education leader in your district.
- Interview an experienced special educator or administrator about changes they have seen in special education over the years. What controversies have been navigated and how has the system evolved.
- Interview the parents of special needs students to explore their experiences with the special education program in your school, policies on LRE, etc. And identify implications for effective, equity-driven school leaders.

REFERENCES AND RESOURCES

Bjornsrud, H., & Nilsen, S. (2018). Joint reflection on action-a prerequisite for inclusive education? A qualitative study in one local primary/lower secondary school in Norway. *International Journal of Inclusive Education* 23(2): 158–173.

Cook, L. & Friend, M. (2010). The state of the art of collaboration on behalf of students with disabilities. *Journal of Educational and Psychological Consultation* 20: 1–8.

Halpern, B. L., & Lubar, K. (2003). *Leadership presence: Dramatic techniques to reach out, motivate, and inspire*. Penguin Group.

Hehir, T., Grindal, T., Freeman, B., Lamoreau, L., Borquaye, Y., & Burke, S. (2016). *A summary on the evidence of on inclusive education.* https://files.eric.ed.gov/fulltext/ED596134.pdf.

Lyons, W. E., Thompson, S. A., & Timmons, V. (2016). We are inclusive. We are a team. Let's just do it: Commitment, collective efficacy, and agency in four inclusive schools. *International Journal of Inclusive Education* 20(8): 889–907.

Nilsen, S. (2018). Inside but still on the outside? Teachers' experiences with the inclusion of pupils with special educational needs in general education. *International Journal of Inclusive Education* 24(9): 980–996.

Riser-Kositsky, M. (December 17, 2019). Special education: Definition, statistics, and trends. *Education Week*. Retrieved from https://www.edweek.org/teaching-learning/special-education-definition-statistics-and-trends/2019/12.

Snyder, T. D., de Bray, C., & Dillow, S. A. (2019). *Digest of education statistics 2017* (53rd ed.). Retrieved from https://files.eric.ed.gov/fulltext/ED592104.pdf.

Hot Seat #11

He Needs to Back Off!
(High School)

We all know the transformative impact teachers can have on students' lives. Many of us can describe teachers and coaches who have impacted our lives in immeasurable ways. We also know that sometimes, teacher-student relationships cross the line. At a time when massive teacher shortages permeate education, educator misconduct remains a serious concern. Teachers' sexual assault and harassment of students appear in isolated headlines, but it is an alarming and difficult-to-measure issue.

There's not much data on the subject—which encompasses a spectrum of behaviors ranging from inappropriate text messages to rape—and abusive teacher-student interactions aren't always reported to law enforcement (Blad, 2019). The number of investigations into inappropriate student-teacher relationships and/or teacher misconduct has increased significantly since the much-publicized 1990s case of Mary Kay Letourneau. Multiple high-profile cases have brought a spotlight to the dangers of teacher-student relationships that have crossed the line.

Clearly, such misconduct can result in dire lifelong consequences for students, including negative physical, psychological, and academic outcomes. To prevent incidents from occurring, school districts are tasked with complying with Title IX, a federal law that provides guidelines for prevention efforts and responses to school employee sexual misconduct in K–12 schools (Grant et al., 2017). Shakeshaft (2013) described common patterns of misconduct and ways to combat them in a must-read report in *Phi Delta Kappan* focused on hiring practices, monitoring environments, ongoing education and training, and attentive monitoring.

Shakeshaft (2004, p. 18) estimated that "more than 4.5 million students are subject to some form of sexual abuse by an employee of a school sometime between kindergarten and 12th grade." The same research estimated that nearly 10% of students may experience teacher misconduct other than physical touching. Blad (2019, para. 5) shares Shakeshaft's chief concern that schools don't always fully explore allegations of teacher sexual assault or they miscode them as consensual, as opposed to rape. Others may quietly dismiss employees without documenting concerns, only to leave them to be hired by other district—a pattern called "passing the trash."

While the actual number of abuse cases may never be known, some research has concluded that abuse by educators is likely underreported for a host of reasons, including a desire to avoid negative publicity and liability (Fauske et al., 2006). In many cases, as quoted by Stop Educator Sexual Abuse Misconduct and Exploitation (SESAME), other teachers "may have thought something was going on" but were afraid to report a fellow educator and be wrong. They didn't want to be responsible for "ruining a person's life" (SESAME, 2021, as quoted by the Children's Center for Psychiatry, Psychology and other Related Services, 2018). Shakeshaft (2013, p. 10) reached a similar conclusion, noting, "Most programs to stop sexual abuse are directed toward children, asking them to do what adults will not—report."

While experiencing sexual misconduct by a teacher can ruin a child's life, false allegations can destroy a career. In an article titled *Teach but Don't Touch*, the National Education Association (NEA) wrote "It's the worst thing that can happen to a school employee: being falsely accused of inappropriate behavior with students. Even if you're ultimately exonerated, the damage has already been done and the stigma can linger for years" (NEA, 2006, p. 1). The implications for all parties involved are formidable.

Mr. Coulter, the father of an eleventh-grade girl who serves as a manager for the varsity boys' basketball team, arrives in Principal Jones's office unannounced. He wastes no time in telling Principal Jones that the basketball coach, a handsome man in his early twenties, needs to leave his daughter alone. When Principal Jones probes for specifics, Mr. Coulter describes text messages, rides home from practice, and physical closeness between the coach and his daughter. While Principal Jones gives his word that he takes the situation seriously, Mr. Coulter wants to know exactly what action will be taken, by whom and when.

In this emotionally charged context, Principal Jones begins searching for answers.

THE TRANSCRIPT

Principal: Hi, Mr. Coulter.

Dad: How you doing?

Principal: Good, how are you?

Dad: Not real happy.

Principal: Okay, what can I do for you?

Dad: Your basketball coach needs to leave my daughter alone.

Principal: Can you tell me what he's doing?

Dad: Ah, let's see. . . . He's sent her a few text messages. She's a manager on the varsity basketball team, she's a junior, and ah, he sent her some text messages just saying hi, wondering what's going on. . . . He's given her a ride home from practice a couple times. I've put a stop to that. She's not getting anywhere near his car. Um, she told me that a couple times he's come up and put his arm around her shoulder . . . once or twice put his arm around her waist. He's being too close and needs to back the hell up. What are you gonna do?

Principal: Do you have copies of the text messages that I can take a look at?

Dad: I can get them.

Principal: Okay. I'd appreciate taking a look at those. I will definitely call your daughter in and have a conversation with her. . . . I'm gonna have a conversation with him as well.

Dad: What about your basketball coach? I'll get my daughter cleared up. That's not a problem. What about him?

Principal: I'd like to get the facts from all different sides. I hear your story now. I'd like to hear her story, and then I'd like to bring him in and find out what's going on from his perspective.

Dad: Because I know that one or two of the other players on the team that are her friends have also told me in a roundabout way that something looks funky. And if I keep hearing this stuff, then it might get a little bit ugly. He needs to stay away from her. I realize he's twenty-three, twenty-four, young guy, good-looking guy, whatever. He needs to leave my daughter alone, otherwise things are gonna get ugly.

Principal: I can assure you that I'm gonna get to the bottom of this . . . without a doubt. . . .

Dad: How?

Principal: Like I said, I'm gonna call everybody in and make sure that I understand the full side of the story . . . it sounds to me. . . .

Dad: And what if he kind of puts that little intimidation factor, "hey, shh, don't talk to him, nothing's wrong." Then what?

Principal: I'll make sure that I have a conversation with the young ladies before I call him in, before he knows that I'm conducting an investigation to find out what's going on. And I'll also call in the basketball players who are a part of the team who have observed the same behaviors that you're observing so that I can speak with them confidentially and privately before he. . . .

Dad: Then how are you gonna keep that, keep that from getting out?

Principal: A lot of behaviors. . . .

Dad: How are you gonna trust sixteen-, seventeen-year-old boys not to go, "Hey, coach is messing with Avery and now he's in trouble." How are you gonna keep that from getting out? 'Cause it will. I promise. And then all of the sudden you got a whole bunch of folks mad at her because they all like him. And she didn't do anything except wanting to help out.

Principal: Well, we'll call them in and try to make sure that it's as confidential as possible and we're gonna get to the bottom of it right away. Starting as soon as we're done with our conversation here, I'll begin calling people in to find out what's going on and to make sure that they have an opportunity to tell me what's going on honestly. I'm very concerned about the behaviors that you've explained to me. . . .

Dad: You better be. 'Cause very quickly, it's gonna go whoosh . . . right over the top of your head to somebody else and I'll keep going because. . . .

Principal: Sure

Dad: He needs to leave my daughter alone.

Principal: I agree. If the behavior is inappropriate, then, ah, there will be some consequences for the teacher. . . .

Dad: Such as?

Principal: Well. . . .

Dad: Like what?

Principal: We need to make sure of that, ah, what you're describing to me is accurate.

Dad: You gonna fire him?

Principal: Potentially, that could be something. . . .

Dad: Gonna have him charged?

Principal: We'll look at the evidence and find out what's going on and then we'll try to make a determination from there. Ah, it seems to me that obviously you're very concerned, I'm extremely concerned . . . about the situation, as well.

Dad: Concerned? Pissed off! Pissed off would be a better word because. . . .

Principal: I understand that, Mr. Coulter.

Dad: if it's me and him in the same room . . . I might be old, but I'll go down swinging.

Principal: Sure.

Dad: 'Cause if he keeps messing, it's not gonna be pretty. So you better, you better fix it.

Principal: We're gonna do everything in our power from preventing that situation from ever happening. And I can promise you that it will be handled appropriately. . . .

Dad: Don't make promises. . . .

Principal: It will be fixed. I'm making this promise to you because it's going to be a promise that's kept. That we're gonna, I'm gonna assure you that I'm gonna get to the bottom of this. I'm gonna find out what's going on. As a parent, I would be, if I were in your shoes I would be beyond concerned as well. I understand the concern, the anger and the frustration. . . .

Dad: You're lucky that my wife convinced me to come here instead of go straight there, because otherwise we'd have had a different type of situation on our hands, because I kind of put up with it, told her to stay away from him . . . this, that, and the other thing. She likes basketball, she can't play basketball herself so she wants to help out somehow. And this is not right. And you're lucky that my wife has a cooler head than me, bringing me here instead of going right to him, and it might have gotten weird.

Principal: I definitely appreciate you coming to me. . . .

Dad: So you have two days. Today is day one. By five o'clock tomorrow, I want some answers.

Principal: I can assure you, like I said before, I can assure you that I'm gonna get to the bottom of this as quickly as possible, and as soon as I find out all the facts, I'll contact you and be in contact with you right away.

Dad: And what if you find out that, yeah, he is doing all this stuff? Then what?

Principal: The consequences for the basketball coach will be appropriate to what's happened.

Dad: Is he gonna be done? 'Cause she's staying.

Principal: We need to find out what's going on first.

Dad: She's staying with the team.

Principal: We need to find out what's happening first, and then we'll go from there. So, right now, unless you have anything further that you can add to my understanding of what's happening, maybe we can just leave our conversation here and start to call people in. . . .

Dad: Have you gotten weird comments and things like that from other people?

Principal: I have not.

Dad: 'Cause, I, you know, you get your ear here and your ear here and you listen and you start to go, ah, naw, you dismiss it, dismiss it. But now all of the sudden it's come around to my daughter so I'm a little bit confused and a little bit confused and concerned that maybe . . . this ain't the first time.

Principal: I have not heard these concerns before. And had I heard concerns like this before, I can assure you that they would have been thoroughly investigated.

DISCUSSION AND REFLECTION QUESTIONS

1. Identify the primary and secondary issue(s).
2. Mr. Coulter gets quickly to the point with the implication that the basketball coach is behaving inappropriately toward his daughter. Principal Jones asks for specifics and if Mr. Coulter can produce the text messages that the coach allegedly sent to his daughter. Should Principal Jones immediately begin taking notes of the conversation? Or, does he effectively get Mr. Coulter talking about the situation and we can assume that Principal Jones takes detailed notes as soon as the conversation ends? Would the principal taking notes possibly interrupt the flow of the conversation?
3. Does your district have a stated policy regarding communication between employees and students? Does the policy address electronic communication such as text messages or social media? Does the policy address students riding in employees' vehicles?
4. Some would argue that school employees should take a vigilant stance on physical contact with students, transporting students in personal vehicles, and so on. Others, including some parents, say things such as, "if my child needs a hug, I hope someone at the school will give them a hug." Imagine that a coach has come to you asking for advice on whether to provide a student manager like Mr. Coulter's daughter a ride home after an away basketball game. What would you suggest?
5. At numerous points in the conversation, Mr. Coulter suggests that the situation with the coach could get "weird" or "ugly" and implies that he might react physically toward the coach. Does Principal Jones adequately address this? Explain. If not, how would you respond?
6. At 1:18:43 Mr. Coulter asks the principal what can be done to prevent the basketball coach from intimidating his daughter into keeping quiet. Evaluate Principal Jones's response. Would you respond to the question

in the same way? How could a principal address the possibility that the coach might try to use his influence in this way?

7. At 1:19:05 Mr. Coulter asks Principal Jones how he intends to keep the investigation "from getting out" as he believes it inevitably will. Evaluate the response to this concern. How would you respond? Not surprisingly, Mr. Coulter then presses Principal Jones to say whether the basketball coach will be fired if the allegations are shown to be true. Evaluate Principal Jones's response.

8. At 1:20:25 Mr. Coulter again mentions the possibility of a physical conflict with the basketball coach. Does Principal Jones effectively address this? Explain.

9. At 1:21:49 Mr. Coulter says that his daughter is "staying." What do you think Mr. Coulter means? That his daughter is staying at the school, continuing as a manager for the basketball team? Is it appropriate for her to continue as a manager of the basketball team? Should Principal Jones have suggested that Mr. Coulter's daughter cease her involvement with the team, pending the investigation? Would doing so potentially punish and/or ostracize her?

10. Mr. Coulter demands answers by "five o'clock tomorrow." Is this ultimatum appropriate? Should the principal be concerned that if he does not provide Mr. Coulter with some kind of answer by that time that he may act on his references to physical conflict with the coach? Or, does Mr. Coulter, understandably, simply want immediate action?

11. At 1:22:00 Principal Jones suggests the two end their conversation so he can begin investigating. Should he have continued the conversation or does bringing closure demonstrate that he is taking the situation seriously and will immediately begin investigating?

12. Construct a specific, step-by-step plan and rationale for what Principal Jones should do as soon as Mr. Coulter leaves the office.

13. The allegations in this case are certainly serious. How can Principal Jones approach them seriously while still respecting the basketball coach's reputation and due process rights?

14. Identify areas in which you believe the principal acted effectively.

15. Identify areas in which you believe the principal could have acted more effectively.

REFLECTION AND DISCUSSION QUESTIONS

Balcony View

Generally speaking, how did the principal perform in this scenario? What would you have done differently?

Standards in Action

Which standards do you see as relevant in the scenario? Does the principal effectively meet them? Are there standards and/or criteria left unmet by the principal's actions?

Peel the Onion

Like an onion, leadership challenges have multiple layers. The presenting issue may be singular or appear simple in nature. Often, however, it represents one part of an underlying, more complex issue. The best leaders address concerns in the moment, while not losing sight of root causes. What is/are the presenting issue(s)? Do you see potential nuanced factors that should be explored?

Self-Check

We all come to our roles with unique experiences, perspectives, and biases that influence our perceptions and actions. Picturing yourself in the principal's chair, describe your emotions.

Switch It Up

How might your thinking or approach change if the gender, ethnicity, language, age, sexual orientation, socioeconomic status, disability, or other descriptors of the players involved were different?

Equity Lens

Equity-driven leaders understand that diversity takes many forms. What equity- or diversity-related issues could be present in this scenario?

Power and Presence

In televised presidential debates, "looking presidential" is an important measure of a candidate's performance. The same is true for principals. Halpern and Lubar (2003, p. 3) define leadership presence as being more than "commanding attention" to include "the ability to connect authentically with the thoughts and feelings of others." Does the principal exert an effective presence? Describe the power balance between the principal and the visitor. Does positional or personal power between the principal and visitor seem uneven or problematic? What does body language say that words do not?

Principal's Priority

How *serious* is the situation?
How *soon* should the principal address this situation?
Should the principal inform a supervisor of this issue and get them involved?

Reach Out?

Should the principal involve other individuals, professionals, resources, or organizations?

In a Word

Capture the principal's performance in the scenario using one word.

Collaborate

Collaborate with a classmate or colleague to rewrite or alter the case with a different set of circumstances. Share your new case with other colleagues to ascertain how they would approach it.

Extension and Internship Experiences

- Ask the administrator in charge of personnel at your school or district to review the step-by-step plan and rationale you constructed in #12 above. Note any areas that you missed or neglected. Ask the administrator to share the relevant district policy for alleged abuse by school employees with you.

- Examine the laws in your state concerning relationships between school employees and students. Access records for educators who have lost their licenses and/or been imprisoned for inappropriate relationships.
- Conduct a search of records of alleged inappropriate relationships between educators and students that were later shown to be false.
- Discuss suggested steps a new principal should take in a case such as this with your school district attorney.

REFERENCES AND RESOURCES

Blad, E. (2019). Will new federal data quantify teachers' sexual misconduct? This researcher is skeptical. *Education Week.* Retrieved from https://www.edweek.org/leadership/will-new-federal-data-quantify-teachers-sexual-misconduct-this-researcher-is-skeptical/2019/09.

Children's Center for Psychiatry, Psychology and other Related Services. (July 11, 2018). *Sexual abuse by teachers is on the rise.* https://childrenstreatmentcenter.com/sexual-abuse-teachers/.

Fauske, J. R., Mullen, C. A., & Sutton, L. C. (November 2006r). *Educator sexual misconduct in schools: Implications for leadership preparation.* Paper presented at the 2006 University Council for Education Administration Convention, San Antonio TX. Retrieved from http://www.ucea.org/storage/convention/convention2006/proceedings/FauskeUCEA2006.pdf.

Grant, B. J., Wilkerson, S. B., Pelton, D., Cosby, A., & Henschel, M. (2017). *A case study of K-12 school employee sexual misconduct: Lessons learned from Title IX policy implementation.* National Criminal Justice Reference Service. Retrieved from https://www.ojp.gov/pdffiles1/nij/grants/252484.pdf.

Halpern, B. L., & Lubar, K. (2003). *Leadership presence: Dramatic techniques to reach out, motivate, and inspire.* Penguin Group.

National Education Association. (2006). *Teach but don't touch.* Retrieved from https://nea-nm.org/wp-content/uploads/2018/05/TeachDontTouchColor.pdf.

Shakeshaft, C. (2004). *Educator sexual misconduct: A synthesis of existing literature.* Prepared for the US Department of Education Office of the Under Secretary Policy and Program Studies Service Doc#2004–09. Retrieved from http://www.ed.gov.

Shakeshaft, C. (2013). Know the warning signs of educator sexual misconduct. *Phi Delta Kappan* 94(5): 8–13. https://doi-org.libproxy.unl.edu/10.1177/003172171309400503.

Stop Educator Sexual Abuse Misconduct and Exploitation (SESAME). (2021, August). https://www.sesamenet.org/.

The Training Isn't
Taking (Elementary)

With five children enrolled in elementary school, John and Sara Skretta are immersed in their kids' education. Sara leads the school's parent-teacher organization, and the couple counts two school board members as good friends. John, who runs a contracting company, says he represents a growing number of families who are increasingly upset about a lack of cultural responsivity from school staff and frequent microaggressions that fail to honor the "dignity of the children." He comes to the principal's office with pointed questions about cultural responsiveness training, microaggressions, and disparities, wanting action.

Multicultural education draws its roots from the civil rights movement of the 1960s and has become a focal point of education as racial, ethnic, cultural, religious, and other forms of diversity have grown in the United States. Demographic trends suggest declines in non-Hispanic white population coupled with significant population growth among people of color will continue, with ethnic minorities accounting for more than half of the U.S. population in 2060 (Banks & Banks, 2020). Accordingly, schools will continue to seek ways to respond to the accompanying challenges and opportunities (Sleeter, 2018).

Growing diversity has promoted innumerable research opportunities for scholars aiming to inform schools' efforts to meet the needs of an increasingly diverse student body, such as responding to student trauma (Blitz et al., 2016) and supporting white teachers' efforts around cultural responsiveness with Black students (Matias, 2013). Others (Darvin, 2018) have explored teacher recognition and reduction of microaggressions as a key to improving school and student outcomes, while Gay (2010) argued that school environments need transformation for broad-based cultural responsivity. In a large synthesis of literature, Khalifa et al. (2016) identified culturally responsive school leadership (CRSL) as having "tremendous promise for children of color as well as other minoritized children" (p. 1296).

Sue et al. (2007) characterized racial microaggressions as "brief and commonplace daily verbal, behavioral, and emotional indignities, whether intentional or unintentional, that communicate hostile, derogatory, or negative racial slights and insults to the target person or group" (p. 273). Beyond the educational, social, and psychological impacts of microaggressions, Gates (2015) estimated that microaggressions may cost the United States up to $500 billion in lost workplace productivity. Sue and colleagues offered descriptions of other deleterious layers of microaggressions:

> Mircoassault: "explicit racial derogation characterized primarily by a verbal or nonverbal attack meant to hurt the intended victim through name-calling, avoidant behavior, or purposeful discriminatory actions" (p. 273). Examples include referring to a person as "colored" or "Oriental" or displaying racist symbols or images.

> Microinsult: messages "that convey rudeness or insensitivity and demean a person's racial heritage or identity" (p. 274). Examples include statements or questions about job qualifications or avoiding eye contact or interaction with persons of color in meetings or social settings.

> Microinvalidation: messages that "exclude, negate, or nullify . . . thoughts, feelings, or experiential reality of a person of color" (p. 274), such as expressing surprise that an Asian American born in the United States speaks clear English or asserting that one does not see color and that all people are the same, thereby ignoring the lived experiences of people of color (Helms, 1992).

While definitions offered by Sue et al. (2007) provide tools for identifying microaggressions, many are unwilling or unable to see them. Edwards (2017, p. 11) noted that "the subtle nature of each individual microaggression often leads to a dismissal of microaggressions as nonexistent or the resignation of microaggressions to cases of miscommunication and overreaction." Weiner et al. (2021) built on work by Sue et al. (2007) to examine the presence of microaggressions in administrator preparation programs in work that is particularly salient for aspiring school leaders.

Increasing attention to multicultural approaches and cultural responsivity in education is not without controversy, however. A quick review of popular media, political speeches, and conversation at coffee shops, grocery stores, and gas stations demonstrates that not everyone views microaggressions as legitimate. Campbell and Manning (2014) describe an emerging culture of victimhood. Thomas (2008, p. 274) dismissed the aforementioned definitions offered by Sue et al. (2007) as "pure nonsense." Lillenfield (2017, p. 138) argued that while progress against racism and prejudice has been made, it "remains an inescapable and deeply troubling reality of modern life," also noting that the concept of microaggressions "has been the target of withering attacks from social critics, especially—although not exclusively—on the right side of the political spectrum" (p. 140). Lillenfield argued for a distinction between social critics' criticism of microaggressions and a need to question the science behind the concept's core assumptions and consideration of a different term.

As is always the case, school leaders find themselves at the epicenter of complicated educational, social, and political issues and questions. As former Speaker of the House, Tip O'Neal once said, "all politics is local," and John Skretta has brought a national issue to Principal Machal's office.

THE TRANSCRIPT

Principal: Hi. Hi. How are you?

Dad: Hi, good morning, McKenna. I'm doing well, thanks. Nice to meet you.

Principal: Yes, it's nice to meet you as well. Come right in, take a seat.

Dad: I'm a little amped up this morning. I just wanna reassure you though, it's not the caffeine.

Principal: Okay! What's going on?

Dad: Well, first of all, do you mind if we record this meeting?

Principal: Um, sure.

Dad: I'm just kidding, McKenna! We don't need to do that. There's a level of trust here between you, a school leader, and me, one of your constituents and a parent.

Principal: Okay.

Dad: Yeah, well. Let me just tell you a little about myself. So, we haven't had the privilege of meeting before, regrettably. That's because I'm very busy. I'm consumed with my work, but we have five children who attend your school and they're in grades one through five. I'm sure you've met my wife, Sara. She's the president of your PTO. . . .

Principal: Yes, yes, uh huh.

Dad: And helps lead the annual carnival. Yes, wonderful, wonderful, incredible woman . . .

Principal: Oh, so sweet.

Dad: Thank you, and together we are raising our five children. And, you know, previously I would have said I was proud to have them enrolled here at your elementary school. . . . You know my wife and I, we've approached our parenting with a sense of moral purpose and inclusivity. Not sure if you know our children and how frequently even you're able to get out of your office and actually interact with kids in your role. But, two of our children are our biological children, three were initially placed with us as foster children and we've subsequently adopted them.

Principal: Oh, that's awesome, yes.

Dad: Yes, and they're our children and they are all God's children, as all children are, wouldn't you agree?

Principal: Mm hmm.

Dad: Well, what I wanted to express to you today are the concerns that my wife and I have, and unfortunately share with many parents that there are some unaddressed issues here that are not dignifying the personhood, the individuality, and the dignity of the children who attend this school. And I'm gonna share with you some examples from our own experience that we've found very troubling.

Principal: Is it okay if I take some notes on this so I can keep track of everything and go back?

Dad: McKenna, you're gonna wanna take some notes and I can assure you I've documented a few things myself here to ensure we have appropriate follow up afterwards.

Principal: All right.

Dad: So, my first question for you would be to what extent has your staff had any training in understanding cultural proficiency and addressing microaggressions in the classroom?

Principal: Cultural proficiency is something that every year, staff get trained on. That's something very important to our district as a whole, and then especially at the school level, I think that's so very important.

Dad: Well, let me just interject here that the training is not taking with some of your staff.

Principal: Can you give me some examples?

Dad: I am gonna give you some examples, because we've heard countless situations over the years and I'm tired of what our children have been enduring and these slights need to stop.

Principal: Okay, yes. Let me, let me hear some of those examples.

Dad: So, our child, Roberto, of Hispanic descent, being told his English is very good, for a Mexican.

Principal: Okay.

Dad: Or, how about this one? Our daughter, Grace, who is Asian American, being told that she writes surprisingly well, but the same teacher saying, "We knew you'd be good at mathematics." What's that about?

Principal: Okay.

Dad: Or, our son, Fabian. Sudanese. On the playground being told by a playground supervisor, "We're not in a refugee camp. We take turns in America."

Principal: Okay.

Dad: I could go on and on. And believe me, we're not the only parents who've experienced this.

Principal: Okay.

Dad: But I'm someone who's got the moral courage to come in here and confront you about the complacency that exists on your faculty.

Principal: Okay.

Dad: Are you familiar with the CRDC?

Principal: I am not, can you tell me a little bit more about it?

Dad: Well, it's a required annual federal report. I'm a little bit staggered that you're not aware of it. How about AQuESTT, have you heard of that?

Principal: I have heard of AQuESTT, yes.

Dad: Uh huh. Have you done an analysis of the achievement gaps that exist in this school?

Principal: Yes, we look at those achievement gaps every year, especially right away, starting in the summer. We look back at those report card data and really dive into the discrepancies.

Dad: Well one thing that shows a number of discrepancies that you might want to make yourself aware of and avail yourself of the information that's publicly available, McKenna, would be the Civil Rights Data Collection.

Principal: Hmm, okay.

Dad: Are you aware of the rate of office referrals, suspensions, and student discipline incidents that are disparate based on the treatment of students of color in this school?

Principal: I know that that is a problem in general and it's something we have been working on . . . to really address.

Dad: It's a big problem.

Principal: So, I'm, I'm really glad, first off, and I want to commend you for coming in here and talking to me about this, 'cause this is important stuff that we need to address.

Dad: Well, McKenna, let me help you out, here, okay?

Principal: Okay.

Dad: Out of my respect for protocol, I came in to address this with you today. Now, Lanny and Don, on the district's board of education, are good friends of ours. I haven't shared this concern with them yet out of a sense of protocol and an understanding that it's your role as the leader of learning to address this, right? Now, I run a company, we're a contracting company, and I can tell you some of what I shared with you, if those behaviors were demonstrated by employees in my organization, there would be swift and immediate consequences.

Principal: I take this very seriously. I'm really glad that you brought this to me because I didn't know that these comments were being made. So, it's very important to me and I'm very happy that you brought this to me, 'causecause this is something we do want to address. Uhm, I'm really sorry that this, that these things have been said to your family and you're correct, it's not okay.

Dad: Rest assured, our children will be fine. They're perseverant. They're resilient. And they know they're loved unconditionally by their parents. But it's time for you to fix this mess. I'm gonna leave you with my business card and I expect a follow-up within about two weeks to inform me of what the staff training plan will be to support the end of these microaggressions being allowed to continue.

Principal: Yeah, okay. I will definitely be following up with you. Can I ask you one more, a couple more clarifying questions because I want to make sure I'm looking into this with the fidelity and the, ah, perseverance that it needs? So, you said that some of these, these were happening, did this happen this year or are these things that happened throughout the past?

Dad: McKenna, I'm not gonna do your job for you and conduct the investigation. But what I'm gonna tell you is that we've spoken with other parents who have children in this elementary school, and they'll share with you very similar concerns. But they've been afraid or reluctant to come forward for fear of retribution against their children.

Principal: That makes me, I'm very sad to hear that. I just wanna make sure that I'm addressing this with the teachers or the staff that it needs to be addressed with, which is why I just wanna ask some of those clarifying questions so I know exactly where to go to to start to fix the problem.

Dad: Oh, well, you could start with Mr. Anderson in the kindergarten. Okay. And then let's go with Mr. Shanahan in the first grade. . . .

DISCUSSION AND REFLECTION QUESTIONS

1. Identify the primary and secondary issue(s).
2. Identify areas in which you believe the principal acted effectively.
3. Identify areas in which you believe the principal could have acted more effectively.
4. John seems intent on putting Principal Machal on the defensive at the start of the meeting when he asks (:16) if he can record the meeting, only to say he is kidding. What message might this send Principal Machal? How would you respond to the question?
5. John shares (:52) that his wife, Sara, serves as president of the school's parent-teacher organization. Some might interpret this as small talk or perhaps positioning himself as a supporter of education and the school. Others might interpret it as entitlement or being a kind of "insider." What is your impression early in the conversation?
6. At 3:23 Principal Machal asks about specific comments made by teachers and John shares several. Evaluate Principal Machal's response to the incidents described.
7. After the principal agrees disparate student discipline referrals and achievement gaps are problematic and thanks John for sharing his concerns, John references his friendship with two members of the board of education. How should principals respond when stakeholders reference or emphasize their relationships with powerful individuals in the school and/or community?
8. At 6:42, John says, "it's time for you to fix this mess" and that he will leave his business card so Principal Machal can follow up within two weeks to describe the training plan for building staff. Is it appropriate for him to dictate to Principal Machal when she will follow up? Evaluate Principal Machal's response at 7:01.
9. At 7:27 John says that the microaggressions and staff statements he has described are an ongoing problem and that he and Sara have spoken with other parents with the same concern. He says other families have not raised the issue because they fear "retribution against their children." Given the power teachers hold over students, how should Principal Machal respond to John's assertion? Should the principal share this reluctance with teachers and staff? If true, what could be done to improve trust between families and school staff? Have you known teachers or leaders prone to retribution if criticized?
10. At 7:45 Principal Machal asks for specifics about the alleged statements by teachers and staff, and John shares some names. Should she speak only to the staff members mentioned or is it an issue for the

entire building? Should the investigation and follow-up involve students? Outline the specific steps the principal should take following the meeting.

11. Depending on the outcome of Principal Machal's investigation, we might anticipate John's reactions. How should she prepare for the follow-up meeting and communicating what she has found? Should she have another staff member present in the meeting? Why or why not? To whom would you go for guidance in preparing for such a meeting?

REFLECTION AND DISCUSSION QUESTIONS

Balcony View

Generally speaking, how did the principal perform in this scenario? What would you have done differently?

Standards in Action

Which standards do you see as relevant in the scenario? Does the principal effectively meet them? Are there standards and/or criteria left unmet by the principal's actions?

Peel the Onion

Like an onion, leadership challenges have multiple layers. The presenting issue may be singular or appear simple in nature. Often, however, it represents one part of an underlying, more complex issue. The best leaders address concerns in the moment, while not losing sight of root causes. What is/are the presenting issue(s)? Do you see potential nuanced factors that should be explored?

Self-Check

We all come to our roles with unique experiences, perspectives, and biases that influence our perceptions and actions. Picturing yourself in the principal's chair, describe your emotions.

Switch It Up

How might your thinking or approach change if the gender, ethnicity, language, age, sexual orientation, socioeconomic status, disability, or other descriptors of the players involved were different?

Equity Lens

Equity-driven leaders understand that diversity takes many forms. What equity- or diversity-related issues could be present in this scenario?

Power and Presence

In televised presidential debates, "looking presidential" is an important measure of a candidate's performance. The same is true for principals. Halpern and Lubar (2003, p. 3) define leadership presence as being more than "commanding attention" to include "the ability to connect authentically with the thoughts and feelings of others." Does the principal exert an effective presence? Describe the power balance between the principal and the visitor. Does positional or personal power between the principal and visitor seem uneven or problematic? What does body language say that words do not?

Principal's Priority

How *serious* is the situation? Are de-escalation techniques needed?
How *soon* should the principal address this situation?
Should the principal inform a supervisor of this issue and get them involved?

Reach Out?

Should the principal involve other individuals, professionals, resources, or organizations?

In a Word

Capture the principal's performance in the scenario using one word.

Collaborate

Collaborate with a classmate or colleague to rewrite or alter the case with a different set of circumstances. Share your new case with other colleagues to ascertain how they would approach it.

Extension and Internship Experiences

- What are the laws in your state regarding consent and recording of face-to-face meetings and phone calls? Does your district or mentor have policies or recommendations?
- Interview the leader responsible for determining professional development offerings in your school or district. How are topics determined, presenters selected, and quality and effectiveness evaluated?
- Review demographic changes in your building or district in recent years, along with changes in technology, curricula, school/community demographics, and local/societal issues, etc. Do professional development offerings align with these changes? Are noncertified staff members included in professional development opportunities, such as cultural responsivity training?
- What goals can you articulate related to CRSL? Describe your position and plans related to professional development and microaggressions in schools.

REFERENCES AND RESOURCES

Banks, J. A. (1996). *Multicultural education, transformative knowledge, and action.* Teachers College Press.

Banks, J. A., & Banks, C. A. (Eds.). (2020). *Multicultural education: Issues and perspectives* (10th ed.). John Wiley & Sons.

Blitz, L. V., Anderson, E. M., & Saastamonien, M. (2016). Assessing perceptions of culture and trauma in an elementary school: Informing a model for culturally responsive trauma-informed schools. *Urban Review* 48(4): 520–542.

Campbell, B., & Manning, J. (2014). Microaggression and moral cultures. *Comparative Sociology* 13(6): 672–726.

Darvin, J. (2018). Becoming a more culturally responsive teacher by identifying and reducing microaggressions in classrooms and school communities. *Journal for Multicultural Education* 12(1): 2–9. https://doi.org/10.1108/JME-03-2017-0020.

Edwards, J. F. (2017). Color-blind racial attitudes: Microaggressions in the context of racism and white privilege. *Administrative Issues Journal* 7(1): 4–18.

Essien, I., & Wood, J. L. (2021). I love my hair: The weaponizing of black girls' hair by educators in early childhood education. *Journal of Early Childhood* 49: 401–412. https://doi.org/10.1007/s10643-020-01081-1.

Gates, J. F. (August 31, 2015). Microaggression: The new workplace bigotry. *Huffington Post*. Retrieved from http:// www.huffingtonpost.com/john-fitzgerald-gates-phd/microaggression-the-new-w_b_5544663.html.

Gay, G. (2010). *Culturally responsive teaching: Theory, research, and practice* (2nd ed.). Teachers College Press.

Halpern, B. L., & Lubar, K. (2003). *Leadership presence: Dramatic techniques to reach out, motivate, and inspire*. Penguin Group.

Helms, J. E. (1992*). A race is a nice thing to have: A guide to being a white person or understanding the white persons in your life*. Content Communications.

Khalifa, M. A., Gooden, M. A., & Davis, J. E. (2016). Culturally responsive school leadership: A synthesis of the literature. *Review of Educational Research* 86(15): 1272–1311.

Lillenfield, S. (2017). Microaggressions: Strong claims, inadequate evidence. *Perspectives on Psychological Science* 12(1): 138–169.

Matias, C. E. (2013). Check yo'self before you wreck yo'self and our kids: Counterstories from culturally responsive white teachers? . . . to culturally responsive white teachers. *Interdisciplinary Journal of Teaching and Learning* 3(2): 68–81.

Sleeter, C. (2018). Multicultural education past, present, and future: Struggles for dialog and power-sharing. *International Journal of Multicultural Education* 20(1): 5–20.

Sue, D. W., Capodilupo, C. M., Torino, G. C., Bucceri, J. M., Holder, A. M. B., Nadal, K. L., & Esquilin, M. (2007). Racial microaggressions in everyday life: Implications for clinical practice. *American Sociologist* 62(4): 271–286.

Thomas, K. R. (2008). Macrononsense in Multiculturalism. *The American Psychologist* 63(4): 274–275. https://doi.org/10.1037/0003-066X.63.4.274.

Weiner, J. M., Cyr, D., & Burton, L. J. (2021). Microaggressions in administrator preparation programs: How Black female participants experienced discussions of identity, discrimination, and leadership. *Journal of Research on Leadership Education* 16(1): 3–29.

Hot Seat #13

My Son Is a Good Boy!
(Elementary School)

No two days in the lives of building principals are ever the same. One never knows what issues might arise, who might visit, the needs of someone or what might happen during lunch duty or in the bleachers. Many times, the need to "think on your toes" and take quick action brings joy and fulfillment to building leaders. However, on rare occasions, even experienced leaders who are drawn to the variety of the principalship encounter unfamiliar situations with the potential to knock them off balance.

Ms. Logan, the hardworking mother of an elementary boy, stops in for a visit with the principal in between shifts at her two jobs. As she enters, Principal Harvey greets her warmly and Ms. Logan responds in Spanish, "¡Buenos días!" They begin communicating, with Ms. Logan using both English and Spanish. While Principal Harvey seeks an interpreter to assist, Ms. Logan appears to nod off. As the exchange continues, Principal Harvey works to understand Ms. Logan's complaint that her son's teacher is mean, as well as what may be causing her sudden periods of apparent sleep.

Not knowing exactly why Ms. Logan continues to nod off generates concern on multiple levels. She mentioned that she works two jobs and is perhaps exhausted. Recent research points to excessive sleepiness being a significant problem. The Sleep in America Poll for 2020 by the National Sleep Foundation found that nearly half of Americans report feeling sleepy between three and seven days per week. Forty percent of adults said that their drowsiness interferes with daily activities at least occasionally (National Sleep Foundation, 2020).

Research also suggests that a lack of sleep is not the only potential cause of excessive drowsiness. She could also be suffering from a medical condition or she could be under the influence. Medications, especially sedatives, can make a person drowsy and disoriented during the day. Antidepressants, pain medications, and over-the-counter antihistamines and other medications can cause sleepiness. In addition, withdrawal from some drugs may provoke drowsiness (Murray, 2016). According to Schwab (2020), mental health disorders can frequently cause drowsiness. For example, it is believed that nearly 80% of people with major depression have excessive daytime drowsiness. Bipolar disorder, post-traumatic stress disorder, and general anxiety disorder are associated with sleeping problems that may give rise to bouts of excessive sleepiness (Suni, 2020). Also, according to the Sleep Foundation (Suni, 2020), several brain conditions can cause excessive daytime sleepiness. In addition, narcolepsy is a prominent example as it is a neurological condition in which the brain cannot properly regulate the sleep-wake cycle. Narcolepsy affects around one in every 2,000 people and makes them prone to falling asleep rapidly, including at inopportune times.

As the scenario unfolds, Principal Harvey navigates a cloudy maze of communication, growing health and safety concerns, culture, and assumptions.

THE TRANSCRIPT

Principal: Hello Ms. Logan.

Ms. Logan: Buenos días.

Principal: Hola.

Ms. Logan: Como estás?

Principal: Bien, y tú?

Ms. Logan: [Spanish]

Principal: Oh, that's really all the Spanish I know. Do you understand English?

Ms. Logan: You don't speak Spanish?

Principal: I don't speak Spanish. I speak a tiny bit.

Ms. Logan: [silence, sighs]

Principal: Would you like me to have somebody join us that speaks Spanish?

Ms. Logan: [nods off]

Principal: Ms. Logan? Ms. Logan?

Ms. Logan: Oh, sí, sí, sí.

Principal: Hey, are you feeling okay today?

Ms. Logan: Está bien, necesito cigarillo.

Principal: Ma'am, we can't smoke in the school building.

Ms. Logan: ¿Qué?

Principal: We can't smoke in the school building. Can I have you put that out, please.?

Ms. Logan: ¿No puedo fumar?

Principal: We'll just set it over here. Okay, how can I help you today?

Ms. Logan: [silence, nods off]

Principal: Ms. Logan?

Ms. Logan: Oh, oh, okay, okay, okay, okay, I'm gonna try English.

Principal: Okay.

Ms. Logan: My son is not doing very well. His teacher is really mean.

Principal: You mind if I take a few notes while you're talking?

Ms. Logan: ¿Qué?

Principal: Can I write?

Ms. Logan: Oh sí, yes.

Principal: Thank you.

Ms. Logan: His teacher is really mean.

Principal: Ms. Logan? Ms. Logan. Did you drive here today, Ms. Logan? I see you have keys.

Ms. Logan: Yes, I drive, yes.

Principal: Maybe we should get a ride for you to go home, because I'm worried that you might not be safe.

Ms. Logan: My son's teacher is really mean.

Principal: I did hear you say that. Tell me more.

Ms. Logan: He is a very good boy. He loves school.

Principal: Good.

Ms. Logan: His teacher is very mean.

Principal: What kind of things is his teacher do, that you know about.

Ms. Logan: She's, she doesn't help him. She is really mean. She's really mean, she says very bad things to him.

Principal: What kind of things does she say?

Ms. Logan: She says, he needs to read more. She says, he needs to do his homework. I know he does his homework.

Principal: Okay. Ms. Logan? Ms. Logan?

Ms. Logan: [appears to nod off]

Principal: May I have a moment. Is there a medic, a nurse, an SRO?

Office Staff: I'll call the nurse.

Principal: Thank you.

[Ms. Logan comes to]

Principal: Ms. Logan, Ms. Logan, I'm concerned about your safety.

Ms. Logan: I'm okay.

Principal: Does this happen often? The nurse is going to come in.

Ms. Logan: My son's teacher is very mean.

Principal: Yes, I heard you say that, and I took some notes about it. We'll take care of that. Right now, I'm most concerned about your safety.

Ms. Logan: He does his homework. He's a good boy.

Principal: Very good.

Ms. Logan: Do you know my son?

Principal: I have met your son, but I'm going to talk to you.

Ms. Logan: Is he a good boy here in school?

Principal: He is a good boy, but sometimes we just need to have a little extra help.

Ms. Logan: I'm his mother. Yes, I help him at school.

Principal: Ms. Logan? Tell me about, about you a little bit what is your job?

Ms. Logan: My job? I have two jobs.

Principal: Okay.

Ms. Logan: I work very hard. My son is a good boy.

Principal: Yes, he is.

Ms. Logan: The teacher is very mean. I help him with his homework.

Principal: Ms. Logan?

[Ms. Logan appears to nod off or pass out]

Principal: Nurse!

DISCUSSION AND REFLECTION QUESTIONS

1. Identify the primary and secondary issue(s).
2. Identify areas in which you believe the principal acted effectively.
3. Identify areas in which you believe the principal could have acted more effectively.
4. Believing that Ms. Logan may not speak fluent English, Principal Harvey asks if Ms. Logan would like to have an interpreter join them (:30). How might the presence of an interpreter change the scenario?
5. At 2:19, Principal Harvey expresses concern about Ms. Logan's ability to drive safely and takes hold of her keys. While the safety concern is clear, might reaching for the visitor's keys escalate the situation? Do you believe the identity of the visitor or context of the scenario dictates whether reaching for the keys is advisable? Explain.
6. Ms. Logan mentions several times that her son is a good boy and that his teacher is mean. What would be the appropriate follow up with the son's teacher regarding this situation?
7. Principal Harvey is obviously concerned about Ms. Logan's health and safety. She eventually calls for a nurse or SRO at 3:33. Do you think the principal made this decision in a timely manner? What, if anything, would you have done differently?
8. At 3:45 Principal Harvey moves to support Ms. Logan in her chair, eventually kneeling in front of her. On one hand, this body language shows empathy and concern. Does it also put Principal Harvey at risk?
9. Discuss the significance of Principal Harvey asking Ms. Logan about her jobs (4:30)? Do you believe Ms. Logan's identity influenced the principal's question? How might Principal Harvey respond if Ms. Logan asked, "Are you asking me about my jobs because I'm Latina?"
10. Knowing what has just transpired in the office, how would you follow up regarding Ms. Logan's son? What steps would you take to make sure he will be safe going home? Should other authorities (police, child protective services) be involved? Should Ms. Logan be allowed to drive?

REFLECTION AND DISCUSSION QUESTIONS

Balcony View

Generally speaking, how did the principal perform in this scenario? What would you have done differently?

Standards in Action

Which standards do you see as relevant in the scenario? Does the principal effectively meet them? Are there standards and/or criteria left unmet by the principal's actions?

Peel the Onion

Like an onion, leadership challenges have multiple layers. The presenting issue may be singular or appear simple in nature. Often, however, it represents one part of an underlying, more complex issue. The best leaders address concerns in the moment, while not losing sight of root causes. What is/are the presenting issue(s)? Do you see potential nuanced factors that should be explored?

Self-Check

We all come to our roles with unique experiences, perspectives, and biases that influence our perceptions and actions. Picturing yourself in the principal's chair, describe your emotions.

Switch It Up

How might your thinking or approach change if the gender, ethnicity, language, age, sexual orientation, socioeconomic status, disability, or other descriptors of the players involved were different?

Equity Lens

Equity-driven leaders understand that diversity takes many forms. What equity- or diversity-related issues could be present in this scenario?

Power and Presence

In televised presidential debates, "looking presidential" is an important measure of a candidate's performance. The same is true for principals. Halpern and Lubar (2003, p. 3) define leadership presence as being more than "commanding attention" to include "the ability to connect authentically with the thoughts and feelings of others." Does the principal exert an effective presence? Describe the power balance between the principal and the visitor. Does positional or personal power between the principal and visitor seem uneven or problematic? What does body language say that words do not?

Principal's Priority

How *serious* is the situation?

How *soon* should the principal address this situation?

Should the principal inform a supervisor of this issue and get them involved?

Reach Out?

Should the principal involve other individuals, professionals, resources, or organizations?

In a Word

Capture the principal's performance in the scenario using one word.

Collaborate

Collaborate with a classmate or colleague to rewrite or alter the case with a different set of circumstances. Share your new case with other colleagues to ascertain how they would approach it.

Extension and Internship Experiences

- Interview an experienced principal about Ms. Logan's visit to school. What guidelines does your school or district have in similar situations?
- Access to building-level resources varies widely. What resources or professionals are close at hand in your building? How does your mentor suggest handling a situation like this if your school lacks immediate access to a nurse, SRO, etc.?
- Because the nature of Ms. Logan's difficulties is unclear, compile a list of resources that could be of use to help identify her needs (medical, employment, parenting, addiction, mental health, etc.).

REFERENCES AND RESOURCES

Halpern, B. L., & Lubar, K. (2003). *Leadership presence: Dramatic techniques to reach out, motivate, and inspire*. Penguin Group.

Murray B. J. (2016). A practical approach to excessive daytime sleepiness: A focused review. *Canadian Respiratory Journal*. doi.org/10.1155/2016/4215938.

National Sleep Foundation. (2020). *Sleep in America poll*. Retrieved from https://www.sleepfoundation.org/wp-content/uploads/2020/03/SIA-2020-Q1-Report.pdf.

Schwab, R. J. (June 2020). *Insomnia and excessive daytime sleepiness (EDS)*. Retrieved from https://www.msdmanuals.com/professional/neurologic-disorders/sleep-and-wakefulness-disorders/insomnia-and-excessive-daytime-sleepiness-eds.

Suni, E. (July 2020). *Medical and brain conditions that cause excessive sleepiness*. Sleep Foundation. Retrieved from https://www.sleepfoundation.org/physical-health/medical-and-brain-conditions-cause-excessive-sleepiness.

Hot Seat #14

I'm a Really Good
Mom (Elementary School)

Brenda, the mother of a fifth grade girl (Taylor), has a busy work schedule and stops by Principal Blaha's office unannounced. She says she's concerned that her daughter has not been herself after coming home from a church youth group meeting Sunday night. Mom describes Taylor as a "popular kid" who spends a lot of time on her phone but says Taylor won't come out of her room and has missed school for the last two days. She wonders if something happened at the youth group and seeks help.

Hymel and Swearer (2015) note that bullying is "as old as anyone can remember," and it "permeates popular culture in the form of reality TV and violent video games, and in our free-market, capitalist society" (p. 293). While bullying is as old as humanity itself, it is now typically categorized as either "traditional" or "cyber" (Bauman & Bellmore, 2015). Cyberbullying is distinct from traditional bullying as it uses digital technologies as a means to inflict repeated psychological harm to another individual (Hinduja & Patchin, 2014). Understanding cyberbullying is critically important as it can have lasting impacts on students' emotional well-being (Chun et al., 2020). Cyberbullying is especially complex and problematic, as it transcends the school building (Lee et al., 2018).

From an educational perspective, managing these behaviors is critical (Macaulay et al., 2018). The initial teacher training an educator receives, plus their own attitudes and beliefs towards cyberbullying, significantly impact how students interact with their teachers (Macaulay et al., 2018). When students feel as though their teacher will overreact or become upset with them, they are less likely to reach out for help (Baas et al., 2013). Though many teachers feel as though educating students on cyberbullying might be beneficial, the majority of teachers did not feel confident in their ability to identify cyberbullying and then manage it (Pelfrey & Weber, 2015). The Bullying Research Network (2021) offers an up-to-date clearinghouse of the most recent research related to bullying. In addition, the U.S. government maintains an extensive list of resources, training opportunities, and policies through StopBullying.gov (2021).

As Brenda asks for help in dealing with Taylor, Principal Blaha must determine what happened, when, and whether it is the school's issue to address.

THE TRANSCRIPT

Principal: Hi, it's so good to see you.

Parent: It's good to see you. Thanks for meeting with me.

Principal: Yes, yes. Have a seat.

Parent: I was just I was just passing through town; you know my schedule is just crazy. And so, you know, I'm not here as many times as some of the other parents might be to be able to make appointments with you so, thanks for seeing me.

Principal: No, no absolutely.

Parent: So, I am interested in helping you start a PTO, but I got to tell you there's another thing that happened that I really need your help on and that is with my daughter. She's in fifth grade.

Principal: Do you mind if write down some things here? To take some notes.

Parent: No, no, that's fine. Okay. So, my daughter, Taylor, I mean, she's like, she's super social, she's really, she's got this great friend group. She's, she's kind of one of those popular kids, she's into a lot of things. I mean, you probably know her, I'm sure you do. Anyway, she goes to church group, youth group, and she was at youth group on Sunday night and on Sunday night, she came home from youth group, and she was just not herself. I mean, just, like, really quiet and went straight to her room, and I haven't been able to get her come to school, the last two days. I mean, you know, I travel a lot and I am gone so much, so I really have to rely on her dad, to do a lot of this work, but you know, it's just, he's just not as good getting her to do things. And so, he's letting her stay home. And I don't, I don't know what's going on. All I can think is that something happened at youth group. She's got her phone. She just hangs onto her phone. She won't let me see it. I hear it buzzing, I hear things, you know, it makes noises, but I don't know who it is or what's going on. I mean, she's just sitting there not doing anything.

Parent: *[phone vibrates] O*h excuse me, I have to take this. Yes, sure, sure, I can, you know I'm in a meeting right now, and actually I could come, I could come in, maybe half an hour. Yeah, yeah. Mani and pedi, both. Yeah, okay. Okay, I'll see you then. Thanks. Sorry. . . .

Principal: Mani and pedi. . . .

Parent: Yeah, with my schedule, it's just hard to fit those in, so they've got a cancellation—

Principal: Is Taylor at school today?

Parent: No, Taylor is at home. I mean, she's with her dad, supposedly. But, I mean she's just, she's just in her room, not talking to us. I don't know who she's talking to.

Principal: Are you able to get into her room? Because we really want her here in school.

Parent: She's . . ., well, what do you do?

Principal: Have you ever thought about maybe taking her to that mani and pedi with you? That you just scheduled?

Parent: I mean really, she's, I just want you to find out what's going on, can you just go over to the house and talk to her and try to get her come out of her room.

Principal: You know that will be a good thing, if you and her to have some bonding time, daughter/mother bonding time. That could be a real good thing and maybe then she could open up to you, because maybe she just wants some of that time with you. Well, I mean, you mentioned that you are really busy—

Parent: I'm a good mom. I'm a really good mom.

Principal: Oh no, absolutely, absolutely. Yeah, and I know you want to start that PTA with us.

Parent: Yeah, exactly, I mean that shows how committed I am to this.

Principal: Why don't you do that? I would suggest going home and taking her to that mani and pedi. You know girls, fifth grade girls, they love to have those good nails and those toes done, especially if she's that popular girl. That's something, that's a bonding time. And that gives you time to have some time with her, just you and her and maybe she will open up to you, and then we can really get to the bottom of what's going on. Maybe something did happen at the youth church group. Then you can handle that maybe with the youth church group, or if it's something different you can always come back to school here, and we can handle it over here. Or maybe she needs friends counseling. It just depends on that conversation with you have.

Parent: Just because of the way it all happened, I feel like she's being bullied. I mean, I really feel like this is, because this is so different from what she normally does, and she, she has lots of friends, she rolls with things. But, I think something happened. I don't know, maybe sexting, maybe, I mean I really want you guys to get to the bottom of this.

Principal: We can't really jump to conclusions and quite honestly, when she has her cell phone, that's out of our school area, so that really becomes that parenting issue, we really got to find out what's happening at home. So, like I said, right now I heard that mani and pedi, that would be a perfect, perfect time for you to take some time to talk with her and figure it out. And let us know if it does become a school issue, then by all means, please, please, please, I know you have a busy schedule but please come back, call me, let me know. And then I'd be more than happy if we can, we can go from there.

Parent: So, you think that me taking her to that appointment and have her nails done.

Principal: It's worth a try. Oh yeah, mani and pedi, maybe by each other. She really needs that time. I know you've been really busy, so just some time with your daughter.

Parent: Well, I could try it. I could try it, she's not at school today anyway. Okay, so if I can't get her to come to school tomorrow, can I call you?

Principal: Absolutely, absolutely. Give us a call. You know, I'm here to support you and I am here to support Taylor, too. I want her in school because if she's not in school, she's not learning.

Parent: Well, I know you have policies against bullying, so if that's what's going on, I want you to be sure to take action.

Principal: Absolutely, we will cross that bridge when it comes, but for now, I think the best option would be for you to see, talk with her and see what's going on, because we don't know what's going on right now. As her mother, you need to find out what's going on.

Parent: That's kind of her dad's responsibility, too.

Principal: Both of you, but you're here today. Yes, the parents' responsibility.

Parent: All right, well, I will get, I'll get to my appointment. I'll pick her up, I have just enough time.

Principal: Okay, I appreciate you coming in. Let me know and then we'll keep in contact about that PTA, as well, okay?

Parent: Okay, that sounds great. Thank you.

Principal: Thank you so much for coming in.

Parent: Bye.

DISCUSSION AND REFLECTION QUESTIONS

1. Identify the primary and secondary issues.
2. Identify areas in which you believe the principal acted effectively.
3. Identify areas in which you believe the principal could have acted more effectively.
4. At :31, Brenda begins describing a somewhat hazy picture of how Taylor been withdrawn and missed the last two days of school after coming home from Sunday's church youth group. She also indicates that Taylor's dad isn't good at getting Taylor to do things and that the girl is "supposedly" with him, and that the child is always on her phone. Not long into this explanation, Brenda takes a phone call herself. Describe your initial reactions and impressions. How should Principal Blaha proceed?
5. Many would find Brenda taking the phone call during the meeting to be inappropriate. Would you address this or is it better to simply proceed with the conversation?
6. Given Brenda's description of Taylor's normal behavior compared to the last few days, evaluate Principal Blaha's suggestion to Brenda at 3:03. Will the suggestion result in a more complete picture of what is happening with Taylor? Is it problematic for the principal to recommend Taylor missing school for a manicure and pedicure with Mom, even if the result is Taylor opening up about why she has missed school the last two days?
7. At 3:13 Brenda asks if Principal Blaha could "just go over to the house and talk to her and try to get her to come out of the room?" Evaluate Principal Blaha's response.
8. At 3:34 Brenda says, "I'm a really good mom." Do you interpret Brenda's statement as an indication that she thinks Principal Blaha is questioning her parenting? Or that she seeks Principal Blaha's affirmation? How should Principal Blaha navigate? How can a principal provide parenting support and resources without judgment? Is parenting assistance within the principal's role?
9. Despite her busy schedule and limited direct communication with her daughter, Brenda seems convinced (4:32) that Taylor has been the victim of bullying or possibly sexting (4:48). Evaluate Principal Blaha's response to this suspicion. Should this raise the principal's level of concern?
10. Principal Blaha suggests (5:00) that if the cause of Taylor's absences began at the church youth group, it is "out of our school area" and refers

to a parenting issue. Do you agree? At what point does Brenda's concern and what may have happened Sunday night become the school's issue?

11. At 6:06 Principal Blaha offers support and says, "I want her in school because if she's not in school, she's not learning." Does this contradict the suggestion that Brenda take Taylor to the manicure and pedicure appointment to try and get her to share what has been bothering her?

12. At 6:21 Principal Blaha identifies Brenda talking with her daughter about what is happening as the best option. Given the difficulty some parents have communicating with their children, do you agree? Do you agree with her comments at 6:37 about parental responsibility?

13. Write a list of what, if anything, Principal Blaha should do following the meeting.

DISCUSSION AND REFLECTION QUESTIONS

Balcony View

Generally speaking, how did the principal perform in this scenario? What would you have done differently?

Standards in Action

Which standards do you see as relevant in the scenario? Does the principal effectively meet them? Are there standards and/or criteria left unmet by the principal's actions?

Peel the Onion

Like an onion, leadership challenges have multiple layers. The presenting issue may be singular or appear simple in nature. Often, however, it represents one part of an underlying, more complex issue. The best leaders address concerns in the moment, while not losing sight of root causes. What is/are the presenting issue(s)? Do you see potential nuanced factors that should be explored?

Self-Check

We all come to our roles with unique experiences, perspectives, and biases that influence our perceptions and actions. Picturing yourself in the principal's chair, describe your emotions.

Switch It Up

How might your thinking or approach change if the gender, ethnicity, language, age, sexual orientation, socioeconomic status, disability, or other descriptors of the players involved were different?

Equity Lens

Equity-driven leaders understand that diversity takes many forms. What equity- or diversity-related issues could be present in this scenario?

Principal's Presence

In televised presidential debates, "looking presidential" is an important measure of a candidate's performance. The same is true for principals. Halpern and Lubar (2003, p. 3) define leadership presence as being more than "commanding attention" to include "the ability to connect authentically with the thoughts and feelings of others." Does the principal exert an effective "Principal's Presence"? Explain.

Principal's Priority

How *serious* is the situation?
How *soon* should the principal address this situation?
Should the principal inform a supervisor of this issue and get them involved?

Reach Out?

Should the principal involve other individuals, professionals, resources, or organizations?

In a Word

Capture the principal's performance in the scenario using one word.

Collaborate

Collaborate with a classmate or colleague to rewrite or alter the case with a different set of circumstances. Share your new case with other colleagues to ascertain how they would approach it.

Extension and Internship Experiences

- Review your school's policy on bullying and harassment. Are there specific protocols for investigating reports? Have teachers and school staff received professional development related to cyberbullying, etc.?
- Many schools have individuals or teams devoted to supporting students in need of particular assistance. Does your school offer something of this type? Are resources such as counselors, school psychologists, and family support workers accessible through the building or district or are they offered through another agency? What is the process for accessing these resources?
- Does your school or district provide resources specifically aimed at supporting parents?
- Interview an experienced principal, counselor, or school psychologist about how professionals can support parents while refraining from judgment of their practices.

REFERENCES AND RESOURCES

Baas, N., De Jong, M. D., & Drossaert, C. H. (2013). Children's perspectives on cyberbullying: insights based on participatory research. *Cyberpsychology, Behavior, and Social Networking* 16(4): 248–253.

Bauman, S., & Bellmore, A. (2015) New directions in cyberbullying research. *Journal of School Violence* 14(1): 1–10.

Bullying Research Network. (August 18, 2021). *Welcome to the Bullying Research Network.* https://cehs.unl.edu/BRNET/.

Chun, J., Lee, J., Kim, J., & Lee, S. (2020). An international systematic review of cyberbullying measurements. *Computers in Human Behavior* 113: 106485.

Halpern, B. L., & Lubar, K. (2003). *Leadership presence: Dramatic techniques to reach out, motivate, and inspire.* Penguin Group.

Hinduja, S., & Patchin, J. W. (2014). *Bullying beyond the schoolyard: Preventing and responding to cyberbullying.* Corwin Press.

Hymel, S., & Swearer, S. M. (2015). Four decades of research on school bullying: An introduction. *American Psychologist* 70(4): 293–299. https://doi.org/10.1037/a0038928.

Lee, J. M., Hong, J. S., Yoon, J., Peguero, A. A., & Seok, H. J. (2018). Correlates of adolescent cyberbullying in South Korea in multiple contexts: A review of the literature and implications for research and school practice. *Deviant Behavior* 39(3): 293–308.

Macaulay, P. J., Betts, L. R., Stiller, J., & Kellezi, B. (2018). Perceptions and responses towards cyberbullying: A systematic review of teachers in the education system. *Aggression and Violent Behavior* 43: 1–12.

Pelfrey Jr, W. V., & Weber, N. L. (2015). Student and school staff strategies to combat cyberbullying in an urban student population. *Preventing School Failure: Alternative Education for Children and Youth* 59(4): 227–236.

StopBullying.gov. (August 2021). *Stop bullying on the spot.* https://www.stopbullying.gov/.

The Ruler and the Walkout
(High School)

Jeremy is not a student who is usually in trouble. Thus, from the moment he shuffles into Principal Weires's office, she knows something is wrong. The sunken shoulders and defeated body language are a dead giveaway. As the upbeat Principal Weires prods him to tell her what has happened, Jeremy says he stood up for another student who was experiencing what is routine treatment in Mr. Jackson's class—being hit on the head with a ruler, little or no feedback on confusing assignments, and a teacher who he says is just "bad, bad, bad."

Jeremy explains that he and his fellow students have had enough poor treatment from Mr. Jackson. He says he came to the aid of a fellow student who, after not paying attention, was getting the familiar tap with the ruler. In confronting Mr. Jackson, Jeremy says he "told him where to stick the ruler." Jeremy claims that students have used Facebook to organize a walkout for tomorrow to assert themselves and demonstrate their objections to the way Mr. Jackson interacts with them.

This scenario reflects the complicated reality in schools, where curriculum, classroom management, generations, personality, and power collide. While students may be unfamiliar with the formal requirements of teacher evaluation, they certainly have their own measures of quality. Ravitch (2004, p. 162) famously labeled many students' school experience as an "Empire of Boredom." In his classic, *A Place Called School* (1984, p. 9), Goodlad noted that many classrooms are places in which "boredom is a disease of epidemic proportion." Sometimes boredom gives way to simple student resistance or lack of effort. Kohl's (1994) *I Won't Learn From You* is a timeless must-read for educators searching for a path forward when resistant students show a "willful rejection of even the most compassionate and well-designed teaching" (p. 2). Work, such as Cushman's (2003) *Fires in the Bathroom* and the subsequent *Fires in the Middle School Bathroom* (Cushman & Rogers, 2008) offered firsthand accounts of what many students seek from their teachers.

Many teachers can remember their first September when a cynical teacher warned rookies not to smile until after Thanksgiving. Regardless of whether we view the statement as sage advice or evidence of a dictatorial atmosphere that is likely to lead to an Empire of Boredom, everyone knows effective classroom management is essential to teaching success. But what is the best way to build rapport and an effective learning environment?

While Taines's (2014) observation that most school flowcharts feature the principal at the top and students at the bottom, scholars have begun devoting new attention to student voice as a way to promote school improvement and support student learning. Connor et al. (2015) urge leaders to view students as *active participants* in the educational process with two key assumptions: "(1) students have valuable contributions to make to educational reform because of their unique vantage point within schools, and (2) students have a fundamental right to participate in shaping decisions that affect their lives" (p. 4). They warn leaders that "protecting the status quo becomes an untenable position for faculty and administrators faced with data that a majority of the students . . . believe that current practices are not helping them learn" (p. 5). Such ignorance likely *invites* a walkout or other pushback from students.

Singer (2019) urged educators to view student activism through social studies standards, noting that while specifics vary across states, most are drawn from national bodies such as the National Council for the Social Studies, among others, and noted that state standards articulate support for student activism in both red and blue states to prepare students for democratic life. Similarly, Anderson and Graham (2016, p. 359) revealed students' understanding of well-being includes "having a say, being listened to, having rights, and being respected."

Whitaker and Whitaker (2006, p. 7) argued that "great teachers focus on expectations, other teachers focus on rules, and the least effective teachers focus on consequences of breaking the rules." In a related tone, Marzano and Marzano (2010, p. 160) concluded "that the quality of teacher-student relationships is the keystone for all other aspects of classroom management" and that "teachers who had high-quality relationships with their students had 31 percent fewer discipline problems, rule violations, and related problems over a year's time than did teachers who did not have high-quality relationships with their students."

Finally, Hassenpflug (2016) reminded principals that appropriate attention to student free speech rights didn't end with *Tinker v. Des Moines Independent Community School District* (1969), *Hazelwood School District v. Kuhlmeier* (1988), and *Morse v. Frederick* (2007) in the aptly titled article, *The Peril of Ignoring Middle School Student Speech Rights.*

With these issues on her mind, Principal Weires starts to listen to Jeremy's account of his (brief) day with Mr. Jackson in algebra and what to do next.

THE TRANSCRIPT

Principal: Jeremy! It is great to see you. How are you doing today? What's up? What's going on?

Student: Mr. Jackson. He's a jerk.

Principal: What happened?

Student: You know how he walks around the room? And I know you know this cause all the kids know you know it. He walks around the room and if you're not paying attention or you didn't turn your homework in, or if you like, whisper something to somebody else, he's got that two-foot ruler and he pops you on the head, you know. And I'm just sick and tired of it, and so Andrew was over on the other side of the room and he was sitting there and he hit him and I stood up and I said, "Mr. Jackson, er, ah, Mr. Jackson, I said, if you have a problem with him why don't you just hit me with the ruler?" And I'm just not gonna take it anymore. I just . . . it's stupid and . . . tomorrow there'll be a walkout of his classroom. I've got him for sixth period. Every period, the students are walking out. We've got it all set up on Facebook and nobody's stopping it and we're just gonna walk out of the building. I mean, it's, we're tired of him . . . I mean just flat-out tired of him.

Principal: So, have you talked to the teacher about the problem?

Student: No! He hits us with a ruler. Why would I talk to him? If I talk to him, he'll probably hit me harder.

Principal: Do you think he's hitting people, like to be mean, like hitting, hitting people or just like. . . .

Student: He's a mean person. He's a bad teacher. He doesn't teach us anything. It's algebra class and he just gets on the board and writes $2x + 1 =$ I don't even know cause I don't learn anything in there.

Principal: How are you doing in that class?

Student: I don't know, he doesn't give us any grades.

Principal: Have you checked your grades online?

Student: Well, I ask him, he says he's working on my homework and he'll get it turned in and I'll have a grade soon. Well, it's like, I don't even know, midterm already and there's nothing posted. He probably doesn't even have his grades turned in.

Principal: So you sound really frustrated with the situation.

Student: Well, I'm not, I mean, he sent me out of the class because I told him where to stick the ruler and he didn't like it, but the other kid, you know, he didn't do anything. All he was doing was just, he's not paying attention. Why would you pay attention? He's a terrible teacher. I don't know, and so we're just gonna, just walk out. Every period, one through seven. Boom. We're all gonna walk out, walk out, walk out and we can . . . we all know we'll get in trouble by our parents but we don't care. We gotta make a point. This guy is bad. . . .

Principal: Okay, Jeremy, let's go back to what happened in class today with you, because I suspect that very soon I'll be getting a write-up. . . .

Student: Oh, yeah.

Principal: Since you came, yeah.

Student: I'll be suspended.

Principal: Did he send you out or did you walk out? What happened there?

Student: No he said . . . he sent me out. I stood up and I told him what I told you about where to put the ruler and he said, "Get out. Go." And, ah . . . that's it.

Principal: Can I ask you what exactly did you say about where to put the ruler?

Student: Ah, I didn't say where to put the ruler. He knows where I want him to put the ruler.

Principal: You didn't say it?

Student: No, I didn't say that, but I said . . . he knows. And I don't ever get in trouble in his class. But I, he wasn't even directing the comment to me. It was Andrew. Andrew was sitting over there. He wasn't even doing anything wrong and. . . . Whatever, I. . . . He's bad. I mean he's been bad. He's been here for twenty years. Go to hatemyteacher.com and boom! Mr. Jackson, right there. It's all up and down.

Principal: Yeah, well, I understand that you're frustrated with the whole situation. Um, is there anything else that I need to hear about what happened in class today from your side? Because I think until I talk to Mr. Jackson about what happened in class today, I can't make a decision about like you're suspended or anything like that and I hope it doesn't come to a situation like that. . . .

Student: Oh, I'm gonna get suspended. He's gonna be pretty explicit in there, I'm pretty sure of it. And I'm gonna get in trouble with my parents, I know all that, but the whole point is . . . I guess it's about my behavior, but we haven't had any conversation about his behavior and what he does as a teacher. I don't know if . . . who evaluates him or who hired him or what, but, I mean, he's just bad. He's just bad, bad, bad.

Principal: When you say, "he's bad," all right, are you talking about the way he's teaching, are you having trouble with the way he's teaching and understanding the algebra?

Student: No, I mean. . . .

Principal: Or is it other things?

Student: No, I honestly think it's the way he treats kids. When you walk around a classroom with a two-foot ruler and tap kids, you know, on there. . . . And then the days when people are like sleeping, he like, tosses a beanbag at you and hits you in the face so you wake up. . . . He doesn't treat people right. And so, if . . . he may be a good teacher but he treats us so poorly that why would you want to learn from somebody that doesn't even care about you? It just doesn't make any sense.

Principal: So, it's like the personal relationship part that we're having trouble with? Not so much the what he's teaching or how he's teaching it?

Student: All seven . . . there's a lot of personal relationships, one through seven, cause everyone I talked to . . . he just . . . doesn't get along with anybody . . . just, you know . . . I don't know anyone who likes him. Maybe you do, I don't know.

Principal: Well, let's again, go back to what happened today, because we do need to sort that out. All right, because, yeah, you know, I'll be making a call to your mom. She needs to know what happened and I'm sure you'll talk to her about it. Actually, we'll call her while you're sitting in here. We'll get her on the phone and get on the speaker. And I can talk to her about it, you can talk to her about it. We'll just kind of clear the air on today's situation. Um, again, I can't make any decisions about what's gonna happen as far as do you need to be suspended or do you need to be out of that classroom for a little while until I hear from Mr. Jackson . . . okay, to get more details.

Student: Okay.

Principal: But you're pretty sure he's not gonna be happy, huh?

Student: No. He's not gonna be happy. And nor will my mother.

Principal: Yeah. You gonna be able to handle that?

Student: Oh, I made a mistake. I know I made a mistake and I'll live with that, but, you know, we'll see what happens.

Principal: So, let's, let's talk about how to get, like, to the root of this. . . .

DISCUSSION AND REFLECTION QUESTIONS

1. Identify the primary and secondary issue(s).
2. Identify areas in which you believe the principal acted effectively.
3. Identify areas in which you believe the principal could have acted more effectively.
4. Jeremy starts his conversation with Principal Weires by noting that Mr. Jackson is "a jerk" (45:26). Given that students are often upset when they're sent to the office for disciplinary reasons, what kind of response should the principal have to Jeremy referring to the teacher as a jerk? What if Jeremy had said Mr. Jackson was "a jackass?" "An asshole?" In other words, how should the principal go about gaining an understanding of what happened in the classroom without potentially piling more disciplinary sanctions on the student for the words he uses in answering her questions? Or should there be consequences for the words students use? If Mr. Jackson is later upset that Principal Weires allowed a student to call him "a jerk" without reprimanding the student, what should she say? Is Principal Weiers on the right track letting the comment slide and trying to get Jeremy talking?
5. At 46:16 Jeremy first mentions a planned walkout of Mr. Jackson's classroom set for tomorrow. Evaluate Principal Weires's handling of the threat of the walkout. If it happens, the walkout would certainly cause a disruption. If you were in Principal Weires's shoes, how would you address the potential walkout?
6. At 46:42 Principal Weires asks Jeremy if Mr. Jackson is hitting students with the ruler to be mean or in some other context, but doesn't complete her question. Does Mr. Jackson's intent matter if he is indeed making contact with students with the ruler? Is he simply asking for trouble? Or is it possible that one of Mr. Jackson's mannerisms is to carry around a ruler and has occasionally touched students with it? Is it likely that Jeremy is exaggerating the story because he is in trouble?
7. Jeremy makes a number of complaints, from Mr. Jackson being mean, to not learning anything, to a lack of feedback on his grade, to Mr. Jackson being a bad teacher. Does Principal Weires effectively address each of these issues? Are there some issues that she should not address with Jeremy because the main concern is that he has been kicked out of class? Or are all of the issues inherently related to his being sent to the office?
8. While a student walkout would certainly be disruptive, many students are sophisticated enough to object to what they see as ineffective teaching or inappropriate treatment from teachers. A walkout or protest

organized online is not hard to envision. Many school mission statements include a desire to create engaged, participatory citizens. Given this and the role of peaceful protests have played in history, do the students have a right to express themselves in this way?

9. At 47:20 Jeremy says he told Mr. Jackson "where to stick the ruler." Does this raise the disciplinary stakes for Jeremy? Explain. In response to Principal Weires's question, Jeremy says most of the problems with Mr. Jackson are related to "the way he treats kids." Evaluate her response to Jeremy. Given his answer, how should she respond with Mr. Jackson? In a larger sense, how can a principal help teachers develop an effective rapport with students? Is this a principal's job?

10. Principal Weires notes that she cannot make any decisions on what will happen to Jeremy until she talks to Mr. Jackson about what happened. Describe the approach and specific questions you would ask Mr. Jackson. If in that conversation, Mr. Jackson says he expects respect from his students and that Jeremy was sent to the office for lack of respect and insubordination, how should Principal Weires respond?

11. Principal Weires indicates that she plans to call Jeremy's mother on the speakerphone with Jeremy present. Is this advisable? Explain. If she makes this call, should it be before or after she has talked with Mr. Jackson?

12. If in the phone conversation Jeremy's mother takes the position that Mr. Jackson caused the situation by "hitting" students with a ruler and that Jeremy should be commended for "standing up to that idiot," how should Principal Weires respond?

13. Given the emphasis that many schools place on character programs, respect, etc., is it possible that Jeremy's actions, while likely to bring some kind of disciplinary action, are warranted, given the way he says Mr. Jackson treats students? If Jeremy's accounts of Mr. Jackson tapping students with the ruler and tossing beanbags at sleeping students are true, is the teacher violating basic tenets of respect in the classroom?

14. Imagine Principal Weires making the following statement to Mr. Jackson: "In this day and age, if you're tapping kids on the head with a ruler, you're inviting one of them to react physically." Do you agree? Should she say this to Mr. Jackson? Imagine that Mr. Jackson responded, "I don't hit anyone. I tap them. And I'm walking around the room to keep them engaged. You don't want me sitting behind the desk, do you?" How should Principal Weires respond?

REFLECTION AND DISCUSSION QUESTIONS

Balcony View

Generally speaking, how did the principal perform in this scenario? What would you have done differently?

Standards in Action

Which standards do you see as relevant in the scenario? Does the principal effectively meet them? Are there standards and/or criteria left unmet by the principal's actions?

Peel the Onion

Like an onion, leadership challenges have multiple layers. The presenting issue may be singular or appear simple in nature. Often, however, it represents one part of an underlying, more complex issue. The best leaders address concerns in the moment, while not losing sight of root causes. What is/are the presenting issue(s)? Do you see potential nuanced factors that should be explored?

Self-Check

We all come to our roles with unique experiences, perspectives, and biases that influence our perceptions and actions. Picturing yourself in the principal's chair, describe your emotions.

Switch It Up

How might your thinking or approach change if the gender, ethnicity, language, age, sexual orientation, socioeconomic status, disability, or other descriptors of the players involved were different?

Equity Lens

Equity-driven leaders understand that diversity takes many forms. What equity- or diversity-related issues could be present in this scenario?

Principal's Presence

In televised presidential debates, "looking presidential" is an important measure of a candidate's performance. The same is true for principals. Halpern and Lubar (2003, p. 3) define leadership presence as being more than "commanding attention" to include "the ability to connect authentically with the thoughts and feelings of others." Does the principal exert an effective "Principal's Presence"? Explain.

Principal's Priority

How *serious* is the situation?
How *soon* should the principal address this situation?
Should the principal inform a supervisor of this issue and get them involved?

Reach Out?

Should the principal involve other individuals, professionals, resources, or organizations?

In a Word

Capture the principal's performance in the scenario using one word.

Collaborate

Collaborate with a classmate or colleague to rewrite or alter the case with a different set of circumstances. Share your new case with other colleagues to ascertain how they would approach it.

Extension and Internship Experiences

- Identify a small number of teachers or leaders in your school or district who are known to have excellent rapport with students. Observe and interview them to learn about what they do to foster these relationships. How is cultivating rapport with students different for teachers and principals?
- Consider developing and administering a survey or focus group discussion with a group of students to learn about teacher qualities they find most important to support learning. Emphasize that you are not merely interested in popularity, but teaching practices that support their learning.

- Convene a group of teachers and/or students to explore the concept of teacher-student rapport and the difference between teachers being liked versus respected. What conclusions can be drawn?
- To what extent is student voice sought, recognized, and valued in the daily functioning of your school? Does student voice come only through formal channels, such as student government? To what extent to students experience key themes from research by Anderson and Graham (2016) (having a say, being listened to, having rights, and being respected)?

REFERENCES AND RESOURCES

Anderson, D. L., & Graham, A. P. (2016). Improving student well-being: Having a say at school. *School Effectiveness & School Improvement* 27(3): 348–366. https://doi-org.libproxy.unl.edu/10.1080/09243453.2015.1084336.

Conner, J. O., Ebby-Rosin, R., & Brown, A. S. (2015). Introduction to student voice in American education policy. *Teachers College Record* 117(13): 1–18. https://www.tcrecord.org/books/pdf.asp?ContentID=18267.

Cushman, K. (2003). *Fires in the bathroom: Advice for teachers from high school students*. The New Press.

Cushman, K., & Rogers, R. (2008). *Fires in the middle school bathroom: Advice for teachers from middle schoolers*. The New Press.

Daniels, M. (2009). The three Fs of classroom management. *Journal of Scholarship and Practice* 6(3): 18–24.

Goodlad, J. (1984). *A place called school: Prospects for the future*. McGraw-Hill.

Halpern, B. L., & Lubar, K. (2003). *Leadership presence: Dramatic techniques to reach out, motivate, and inspire*. Penguin Group.

Hassenpflug, A. (2016). The peril of ignoring middle school student speech rights. *Clearing House* 89(1): 23–27. https://doi-org.libproxy.unl.edu/10.1080/00098655.2015.1122566.

Hazelwood School District v. Kuhlmeier, 484 U.S. 260. (1988).

Kohl, H. (1994). *I won't learn from you and other thoughts on creative maladjustment.* The New Press.

Marzano, R. J., & Marzano, J. S. (2010). The key to classroom management. In K. Ryan & J. M. Cooper (Eds.), *Kaleidoscope: Contemporary and classic readings in education.* Wadsworth.

Morse v. Frederick, 551 U.S. 393. (2007).

Ravitch, D. (2004). *The language police: How pressure groups restrict what students learn.* Vintage Books.

Singer, A. (2019). How schools can and should respond to student activism. *Phi Delta Kappan* 100(7): 62–66.

Taines, C. (2014). Educators and youth activists: A negotiation over enhancing students' role in school life. *Journal of Educational Change* 15(2): 153–178.

Tinker v. Des Moines Independent Community School District, 393 U.S. 503. (1969).
Whitaker, T., & Whitaker, B. (2006). *Study guide: What great teachers do differently: Fifteen things that matter most.* Eye on Education.

Hot Seat #16

Nobody's Boy (High School)

In this scenario, Willie, a star football player and honor student, arrives in the office to complain that a teacher addressed him as "boy." As he complains to Principal Hawkins about the racist slur, Willie shares his frustration with the teacher's personality and the way he interacts with students. When Principal Hawkins learns that Willie has already called his mom and she is on her way to school, she's faced with a delicate situation rife with socially constructed assumptions about race, gender, language, and power, with little time to decide her next step.

For more than a generation, research from national to local levels has demonstrated that students of color are suspended and referred to the office at significantly higher rates than other students (Skiba et al., 2002), a phenomena Cagle (2017, p. 1) referred to as "the elephant in the room," adding, "Overwhelmingly, Black students are 'wounded' permanently when they are suspended over and over for offenses that are overlooked when their white counterparts commit the same infraction." Hotchkins (2016, pp. 16–17) found that Black high school students "were labeled by White teachers as being involved in mischief, involved with problematic behavior, and disengaged with the educational process."

In her classic essay *White Privilege: Unpacking the Invisible Knapsack*, McIntosh (1990) theorized that white people are taught not to recognize white privilege. Howard (2006, p. 79) suggested that "too often, the legacy of privilege and the legacy of ignorance have prevented us from seeing and hearing one another." Delpit (1995) built on the age-old adage of walking in another's shoes in order to fully realize the promise of effective communication and education across all groups.

> When we teach across the boundaries of race, class and gender—indeed when we teach at all—we must recognize and overcome the power differential, the stereotypes and the other barriers which prevent us from seeing each other. (p. 134)

Sue et al. (2007) defined racial microaggressions as "brief and common-place daily verbal, behavioral, and environmental indignities, whether intentional or unintentional, that communicate hostile, derogatory, or negative racial slights and insults to the target person or group" (p. 273). Examples include "old fashioned racism," such as derogatory terms, names, avoidant behavior or racial epithets. Microinsults were defined as demeaning actions that communicate rudeness and "subtle snubs . . . but clearly convey a hidden insulting message to the recipient of color" (p. 273). Microinvalidation includes messages "that exclude, negate, or nullify the psychological thoughts, feelings, or experiential reality of a person of color" (p. 273). Despite the frequency and impact, Edwards (2017) noted how these messages may be ignored, discounted, or attributed to overreaction on the part of the receiving person of color.

In his best-selling book *How to Be an Antiracist,* Kendi stated, "What other people call microaggressions I call racist abuse" (2019, p. 47) and argued that simply not being racist is not sufficient to bring about real equality. Kendi posited that that racism is ultimately structural and influenced mainly by policy that diverts attention away from people impacted by those policies. Kendi offered examples of serious dialogue, steps toward becoming antiracist, and actions to challenge the status quo, including "zero-tolerance policies preventing and punishing these abusers" (p. 47).

As Willie shares his anger and frustration, Principal Hawkins's office becomes an example of how, like student free speech, societal issues don't stop at the schoolhouse gate.

THE TRANSCRIPT

Principal: Hi. How are you, Willie?

Student: Not good.

Principal: You're not good?

Student: Not good at all.

Principal: Well, come on in and let's talk about this. Have a seat. What's going on? You've got a big game coming up. What's going on here?

Student: No, I'm sitting in class and we're working on something. And I can't remember if I was talking or what was going on and then I look over at the teacher and he's sitting there and he said something along the lines of "Boy, you better shut up" or "Boy" something or something along those lines and I don't play that stuff.

Principal: Okay, can you tell me what class this was?

Student: It was in math class.

Principal: Math class. And who's your teacher again?

Student: Mr., ah, Falubell.

Principal: Mr. Falubell, okay, okay. And, so what were you doing prior to this that . . . were you talking to someone. . .?

Student: We were just sitting there talking, we were just sitting there talking.

Principal: You were talking with who?

Student: With Santrise.

Principal: Okay. And you were just . . . was he doing instruction on the board or. . . .

Student: I don't know what he was doing. It doesn't matter what he was doing! He can't call me a boy! That's like calling me a nigger. There ain't no difference.

Principal: Well, I think we. . . .

Student: So, we're all focused on what I was doing. He's the one that's in the wrong, not me! He . . . yeah, I shouldn't have been talking but he can't call me that.

Principal: Okay, so. . . .

Student: He's lucky I didn't knock his ass out.

Principal: Okay, now first of all, you need to relax for a second, okay? We're just gonna talk in a normal tone of voice, and we're gonna get to the bottom of this. Okay? We'll figure out a solution.

Student: What are you gonna do?

Principal: We're gonna get to the bottom of it, and we'll find a solution, but first you have to understand that when you're sitting in a classroom and when the teacher is up in front of the class giving instruction, your job as a student is to be there, 'cause your job is to learn, right? If you have a question, you raise your hand and you ask the teacher the question. You don't ask who's sitting next to you, who's sitting behind you. 'Cause if your conversation. . . .

Student: What does that have to do with him calling me a boy? Tell me. . . . Make the connection for me.

Principal: The problem first of all is that you were not behaving in the way that you should have. Now, as far as what he called you or what he said, that's a situation that we'll talk with him about that. . . .

Student: I was talking and there was nobody . . . everybody talks in that class all the time. So, my talking is no different than anything else going on in there.

Principal: So, when he's up in front giving instruction, everybody in the class is just randomly. . . .

Student: Have you observed him lately?

Principal: When I observed him, I did not see that behavior in the class.

Student: Then you were in the wrong class.

Principal: 'Cause when I was observing, everybody was paying attention, they were doing their math problems and he actually gave a very good, ah, instruction that day. He gave a good lesson. So, I think that. . . .

Student: That day. Okay.

Principal: Well, the days that I've been in there. And granted, I'm not in there every single day like you are, but I do stop in and check on my teachers and see the different things and interactions that are going on in the classroom. How is your relationship with him outside of the math?

Student: Not his boy.

Principal: Okay, so do you have conversations with him. . . .

Student: I'm a student in that class just like everybody else. Not his boy.

Principal: Have you had . . . have you had conflict with him in the past?

Student: Not that I can recall.

Principal: Okay, so today's just kind of an isolated incident. Otherwise, he's been friendly to you . . .

Student: Isolated racist incident, yeah.

Principal: Has he been friendly to you? Do you feel as if, up to this point. . . .

Student: He talks crazy to everybody in there, so I don't. . . .

Principal: Do you think that he . . . he's treated you equally except for this. . . .

Student: I think, yeah, he treats me like everybody else. He talks to me crazy like he talks to everybody else. It's not, that's . . . that's his personality.

Principal: Okay, and what's your current grade in his class?

Student: An A.

Principal: Oh, good. So obviously he's a good teacher and. . . .

Student: Obviously I'm a good student.

Principal: And you are a good student, yeah, just like you're a good football player, too. Right?

Student: So, again, what does this have to do with him calling me a boy and what are you gonna do about it? 'Cause I can tell you what. When I go home and get my mom involved—matter of fact, I ain't even gonna wait for that. When I called her, and matter of fact, she's probably already on her way up here, 'cause when I called. . . .

Principal: You called your mom on your way up here?

Student: Heck yeah.

Principal: That's okay, we'll have your mom come in and I think we'll also go get him. . . .

Student: Oh, and when she comes in, you better make sure there's a security guard between him and her, 'cause I'm telling you, she ain't gonna play that either.

Principal: Yeah, and you know when I look in my files here, it looks like he has a prep period next period. And so, I think what we'll do is we'll keep you in here with me and we'll continue having a conversation and if your mom comes, she can come have a seat. And then the four of us will sit down we'll discuss the situation. . . .

Student: And what are you gonna do about him calling me a boy?

Principal: First of all, we need to find out how this all happened. You know, I need to hear that yes, you know, maybe you misunderstood what he was saying. . . . Maybe if you were talking. . . .

Student: Nah, boy is boy. You know, I'm not a toy, so I guess it could've been that, but boy is boy.

Principal: Well sometimes when you're having a conversation with somebody else, you might have caught the tail end of his conversation and then. . . .

Student: Boy, you need to quit talking, I think is pretty . . . yeah.

Principal: So, and I don't think that he meant it to be anything racial.

Student: What do you think he meant it as, then?

Principal: I think sometimes teachers would say, like I might say, ah, you know if you would come in and I'd see that you had a good game last night I'd say, "Hey, you know, way to go last night," or "Hey, boy, you had a great game," or "Hey, guy," or, ah, that's just conversation. . . .

Student: And I'd make it real clear to you that I wasn't your boy, either.

Principal: And I'm not saying that you are my boy.

Student: Okay.

DISCUSSION AND REFLECTION QUESTIONS

1. Identify the primary and secondary issue(s).
2. Identify areas in which you believe the principal acted effectively.
3. Identify areas in which you believe the principal could have acted more effectively.
4. Does Principal Hawkins establish whether Mr. Falubell sent Willie out of the classroom or whether Willie left on his own? Does it matter? Explain.
5. Evaluate Principal Hawkins's response to Willie's assertion (1:00) that Mr. Falubell is lucky he "didn't knock his ass out." Would you respond in the same way? Should/could she interpret Willie's comment as a threat that should be addressed?
6. At 1:00 Principal Hawkins says she intends to get to the bottom of the situation in "a normal tone of voice," followed by telling Willie that his job as a student is to pay attention, raise his hand, etc. Evaluate.
7. Willie is unmoved by Principal Hawkins's review of his responsibilities as a student. Evaluate her assertion (1:00) that the first problem is that he was misbehaving. How should she respond to Willie's belief that he was singled out because of his race, when students talking is common in the classroom?
8. It may not be surprising that Willie asked Principal Hawkins if she has seen what goes on in Mr. Falubell's classroom, given his claim that students routinely talk during instruction, etc. Evaluate her response to his question about whether she has observed in the classroom. Is it appropriate for Principal Hawkins to discuss what she observed or her judgment of the quality of instruction? Does this part of the conversation merely confuse the issue? Or is it a relevant part of the discussion because she is trying to establish the accuracy of Willie's claim that random student talking is common in Mr. Falubell's classroom?
9. Evaluate Principal Hawkins' decision to bring Mr. Falubell into the office for a conversation next period, possibly with Willie, his mother, and the principal. Would you proceed the same way? Would you be concerned about Willie's suggestion of having a security guard present?
10. If you would not have the meeting next period, describe how you would proceed. Describe the conversation and questions you would have with Mr. Falubell.
11. As Willie presses Principal Hawkins to say what she plans to do about Mr. Falubell's alleged use of the word "boy," she suggests that Willie may have taken it out of context—an argument Willie quickly dismisses. Is it reasonable for a white person to tell a person of color

that the statement in question was taken out of context? If Mr. Falubell indeed used the term, does it fit the description of microaggression offered by Sue et al. (2007)? Explain.

12. At 1:02 Principal Hawkins asks Willie about his grade in the class. She concludes that Mr. Falubell must be a good teacher since Willie has an A. Willie counters that he is a good student. What does it appear that Principal Hawkins is trying to do at this point in the conversation? Is it successful? Advisable? How would you proceed?

13. At 1:03 Principal Hawkins suggests that she does not believe Mr. Falubell intended his statement to "be anything racial." Is this an example of a principal supporting and defending a teacher? Is it an example of Edwards's (2017) assertion that microaggressions are often dismissed or discounted? Is it a case of the principal automatically defending the teacher before collecting enough information? If the comment was indeed made, does Mr. Falubell's *intent* matter, given conclusions from Cagle (2017) and others?

14. How should Principal Hawkins respond if she determines that the situation points to a lack of cultural competency or racism on the part of Mr. Falubell and/or others? How should Principal Hawkins go about making such a determination?

15. As a white woman, can Principal Hawkins adequately understand Willie's position as a person of color? Do Willie's and Principal Hawkins's racial identities complicate the exchange? What principal support is Willie entitled to?

REFLECTION AND DISCUSSION QUESTIONS

Balcony View

Generally speaking, how did the principal perform in this scenario? What would you have done differently?

Standards in Action

Which standards do you see as relevant in the scenario? Does the principal effectively meet them? Are there standards and/or criteria left unmet by the principal's actions?

Peel the Onion

Like an onion, leadership challenges have multiple layers. The presenting issue may be singular or appear simple in nature. Often, however, it represents one part of an underlying, more complex issue. The best leaders address concerns in the moment, while not losing sight of root causes. What is/are the presenting issue(s)? Do you see potential nuanced factors that should be explored?

Self-Check

We all come to our roles with unique experiences, perspectives, and biases that influence our perceptions and actions. Picturing yourself in the principal's chair, describe your emotions.

Switch It Up

How might your thinking or approach change if the gender, ethnicity, language, age, sexual orientation, socioeconomic status, disability, or other descriptors of the players involved were different?

Equity Lens

Equity-driven leaders understand that diversity takes many forms. What equity- or diversity-related issues could be present in this scenario?

Power and Presence

In televised presidential debates, "looking presidential" is an important measure of a candidate's performance. The same is true for principals. Halpern and Lubar (2003, p. 3) define leadership presence as being more than "commanding attention" to include "the ability to connect authentically with the thoughts and feelings of others." Does the principal exert an effective presence? Describe the power balance between the principal and the visitor. Does positional or personal power between the principal and visitor seem uneven or problematic? What does body language say that words do not?

Principal's Priority

How *serious* is the situation? Are de-escalation techniques needed?
How *soon* should the principal address this situation?

Should the principal inform a supervisor of this issue and get them involved?

Reach Out?

Should the principal involve other individuals, professionals, resources, or organizations?

In a Word

Capture the principal's performance in the scenario using one word.

Collaborate

Collaborate with a classmate or colleague to rewrite or alter the case with a different set of circumstances. Share your new case with other colleagues to ascertain how they would approach it.

Extension and Internship Experiences

- The issue of *intent* often surfaces in cases involving perceived harassment. Often, those accused of making offending statements say "I didn't mean anything by it." Many leaders advise that the person making the statement is not the one who gets to determine whether it is offensive. The one who hears it does. Ask the official responsible for initial harassment investigations in your school or district to review procedures and share questioning techniques with you.
- Examine relevant demographic changes in your school or district over the past five, ten, or twenty years. What, if any, changes have taken place? What, if any, professional development opportunities for staff have specifically addressed these changes? If not, investigate how the school or district might provide a relevant and effective experience.
- Hall and Hord (2011) suggest that examining issues that are present in school but seem forbidden for discussion is important for exploring school culture and climate. Conduct an informal survey of students and/or teachers to identify issues they believe are rarely openly discussed.
- Consider developing a teachers' discussion/study group around McIntosh's *White Privilege* essay, DiAngelo's (2018) *White Fragility*, or Kendi's (2019) *How to Be an Antiracist*.

REFERENCES AND RESOURCES

Barrett, D. (February 19, 2009). Holder says Americans afraid to talk about race. *Boston Globe*. Retrieved from http://www.boston.com/news/nation/washington/articles/2009/ 02/19/ holder_says_americans_afraid_to_talk_about_race/?page=full.

Cagle, J. F. (2017). The cost of color in public education: An examination of disproportionate suspensions. *Journal of Organizational and Educational Leadership* 3(1): 1–33.

Delpit, L. (1995). *Other people's children: Cultural conflict in the classroom*. The New Press.

DiAngelo, R. (2018). *White fragility: Why it's so hard for white people to talk about racism*. Beacon Press.

Edwards, J. F. (2017). Color-blind racial attitudes: Microaggressions in the context of racism and White privilege. *Administrative Issues Journal* 7(1): 4–18.

Hall, G. E., & Hord, S. M. (2011). *Implementing change: Patterns, principles, and potholes* (3rd ed.). Pearson.

Halpern, B. L., & Lubar, K. (2003). *Leadership presence: Dramatic techniques to reach out, motivate, and inspire*. Penguin Group.

Hotchkins, B. (2016). African American males navigate racial microaggressions. *Teachers College Record* 118(6). https://doi.org/info:doi/.

Howard, G. R. (2006). *We can't teach what we don't know: White teachers, multiracial schools*. (2nd ed.). Teachers College Press.

Kendi, I. X. (2019). *How to be an antiracist*. One World.

Klotz, M. (2006). Culturally competent schools: Guidelines for secondary school principals. *Principal Leadership (Middle School Ed.)* 6(7): 11–14. Retrieved from Education Full Text database.

Marshall, C., & Oliva, M. (2010). *Leadership for social justice: Making revolutions in education* (2nd ed.). Allyn & Bacon.

McIntosh, P. (1990). White privilege: Unpacking the invisible knapsack. *Independent School* 49(2): 31. Retrieved from EBSCO*host*.

McKenzie, K. B. (2009). Emotional abuse of students of color: The hidden inhumanity in our schools. *International Journal of Qualitative Studies in Education* 22: 129–143.

Singleton, G. E., & Linton, C. (2006). *Courageous conversations about race: A field guide for achieving equity in schools.* Corwin Press.

Skiba, R. J., Michael, R. S., Nardo, A. C., & Peterson, R. (2002). The color of discipline: Sources of racial and gender disproportionality in school punishment. *Urban Review* 34: 317–342.

Smith, L. T., Tuck, E., & Yang, K. W. (Eds.). (2018). *Indigenous and decolonizing studies in education: Mapping the long view*. Routledge.

Sue, D. W., Capodilupo, C. M., Torino, G. C., Bucceri, J. M., Holder, A. M. B., Nadal, K. L., & Esquilin, M. (2007). Racial microaggressions in everyday life: Implications for clinical practice. *American Sociologist* 62(4): 271–286.

Teel, K. M., & Obidah, J. E. (2008). *Building racial and cultural competence in the classroom: Strategies from urban educators.* Teachers College Press.

Hot Seat #17

Pornography or Literature?
(Middle School)

Mr. Jeff Dieken enjoys his reputation around town as a strong family man and a deacon in his church. "Deacon Dieken" stops by Principal Olsen's office on a sunny Friday afternoon to complain that several books assigned in his daughters' English classes are inappropriate.

From the moment he shakes Principal Olsen's hand, we feel an undercurrent of tension in their meeting. Mr. Dieken has brought with him books that are the sources of his objections, complete with highlighted passages and dog-eared pages. He begins making his case by reading aloud a passage from one of the assigned books, *What's Eating Gilbert Grape?* (Hedges, 2005). As the conversation deepens, he also questions Principal Olsen about popular music being played during art class and whether she is blindly supporting her teachers, even to the point of promoting pornography.

Bolman and Deal (2010, p. 133) asserted that "most of the knotty issues in schools involve tough choices between competing values." Often those competing values relate to the way social issues, current events, popular culture, science and religion permeate school walls. Perhaps the most famous case boiled over in Tennessee in 1925 in what is commonly known as the Scopes Monkey Trial, in which a high school teacher was accused of violating the state's ban on the teaching of evolution. A look at the day's top news stories demonstrates the interplay of these issues in schools is far from settled.

Other values-related controversies frequently involve literature and music. From what music should be played at the homecoming dance to whether language in *Huck Finn* (Twain, 1990) should be edited and student access to books like *Heather Has Two Mommies* (Newman & Souza, 2009), principals routinely find themselves drawn into what some call the culture wars. Experienced principals know well the complexity of local definitions and expectations and parental concerns. They also know that issues that have become major sources of controversy in one community may pass without attention in many others.

With schools everywhere going to great lengths to promote student engage-ment, reading, and literacy, what is selected is as important as who is making the decisions. Hartsfield and Kimmel (2019, p. 443) noted the significance of this process. "Selecting books that will enliven literacy instruction and promote adolescents' reading engagement is a significant responsibility for reading teachers, classroom English teachers, librarians, and others who con-nect adolescents to literature." They also advise a thorough and thoughtful consideration of censorship, given the International Literacy Association's Children's Right to Read Initiative (ILA, 2018).

Martinson (1996) offered guidance for school administrators who find themselves responding to these issues. First, administrators should remember that those questioning these materials are often confident that they are doing the right thing on behalf of students. While administrators certainly want to make themselves and the schools look good, Martinson argued for a more productive focus on genuine communication that refrains from portraying the other side as an enemy. Rumberger (2019) also makes the point that as students are more immersed in online texts and media sources "it is impera-tive that they have the critical skills to evaluate content and determine the inherent perspectives and assumptions within each text" (p. 419). Students cannot develop the ability to dissect and evaluate texts if they are not allowed to do it on their own.

The conversation between Principal Olsen and Deacon Dieken demon-strates this is sometimes easier said than done and that decisions about what is appropriate are subject to values, interpretation, and emotion.

THE TRANSCRIPT

Principal: Jeff, Angela Olsen.

Dad: Hi.

Principal: Nice to meet you.

Dad: Nice to meet you. Should we sit?

Principal: If you'd like to sit, that would be great. What can I do for you today? Again, what can I do for you today?

Dad: I have been . . . I have a daughter that's in eighth grade and a daughter that's in eleventh grade and they are doing some things in English class that are kind of bothering me. First let me tell you some things that's outstanding. Your middle school English teacher, Language Arts teacher really knows how to differentiate with students. You know, the kids that are a little lower? She helps them, the kind of average kids that are just going through the typical curriculum, and then the high-end kids, they do get some, you know, higher stuff. Well, my daughter happens to be one of those that's, you know, a little higher. And ah, one of the books that um, that she, ah, is sharing with those higher kids . . . well, here's the book that they're reading in class. *Harry Potter and the Goblet of Fire.* . . . Have you read any of these?

Principal: I have not.

Dad: Okay, well there's about thirty of them. . . .

Principal: Okay.

Dad: and they're all about this long and . . . you know, there's a lot of things like witches and warlocks which is not something that really. . . . You know, I'm a deacon on the . . . "Deacon Dieken" on the Presbyterian service here in town and if the Presbytery heard about this, this would be a huge issue for them.

Principal: Okay.

Dad: So, there's that. Well, she's a little more advanced so they wanted her to read this one, *What's Eating Gilbert Grape?* Have you seen that movie?

Principal: I have not.

Dad: Okay, well, it's a very, it's a great movie but in this, um, but there are some things. . . . Let me just read you a couple things in this book. Now, she's in eighth grade. . . .

Principal: Okay.

Dad: This is, I'll set this up for you. This is Gilbert talking with . . . um, this woman who he's having an affair with, um. . . . "I'm dialing. . . . " He's actually calling her husband while this is happening. I'm dialing, I hope this can wait 'til I'm done. She unzips my pants, kissing my tummy. She licks lower . . . I dialed wrong, I think, so I hung up and she giggles. I dial again, she pulls down my underwear, the phone's ringing . . . I say, ah, but there's no stopping her. She holds me in her hand and puts me in her mouth."

Principal: Okay, so. . . .

Dad: Well, just a second. . . . That's just one thing. I mean, then there's a part . . . I mean this book is full of masturbation and adultery and it's ah, there's another one here where . . . well, let me find it . . . I mean, I've got them marked . . . all over. . . .

Principal: Can I just ask you a couple of questions before you go on?

Dad: Sure, sure.

Principal: Um, so these were both eighth grade . . . am I understanding correctly that these were both books that your eighth grader was given to read as an assignment from the teacher?

Dad: Yeah, but that's not it. My eleventh grader, um, and I know you're just middle school, but my eleventh grader was given these books. Now, um, this one is *The Awakening* by Kate Chopin . . . this one's about, ah, freedom, letting women, you know, giving them a way to escape life. . . . And this is sex and adultery and . . . this, that's horrible. Now, my daughter, my older daughter, went about this the right way and said listen I'm not interested in reading that. And. . . .

Principal: Did she go to the teacher with that comment?

Dad: Yes, absolutely, absolutely. And the teacher said "Okay, let me give you something else," which I think is probably right.

Principal: Okay.

Dad: Uh, but had this one, *The Bridges of Madison County*, now, have you read this one or seen the movie?

Principal: I have seen the movie, yes.

Dad: Okay, well, it's not the same. But this one's filled with, you know, the same thing. Ah, adultery, and you know, the photographer, artistic, artsy fartsy photographer comes to town and the wife is enamored with him . . . and eventually, you know, they end up having sex and, you know, it doesn't work. So, again, she read this book. She read the first book, wasn't, didn't really like it, said that I shouldn't be reading that, so she gave her this book and then she asked for a different one and they gave her, ah, *The Handmaid's Tale*, which I don't have cause she's still reading it but, would you like me to read you some things out of that one?

Principal: No, I think I have enough information from what you have gathered and what you have brought to me.

Dad: Oh, one other thing though, my eighth grader in art class, um, now I know you have an electronic policy, the school's, you know, no cell phones and iPods only in art class because it helps them be more creative and whatnot and I'm okay with that that. Well, the art teacher allows kids to bring in their iPods and she's got a fancy CD player that plays iPods. Well, some of the music that they're playing is a little over the top. For example, are you familiar with Soulja Boy?

Principal: I'm not. Can you just. . . .

Dad: Okay, well there's this song called "Superman That Ass" or something like that. . . .

Principal: Can I ask you, are these songs being played out loud or are these songs being played out loud or on the iPods?

Dad: Oh no, out loud! Yeah, cause they, it's like there's a dock and they plug it in and so my eighth grader is like, I don't know, they wanted to use that song for the talent show and I didn't really know. I can't understand what they're talking about but my eleventh grader, at dinner, we're sitting down and she's talking about Soulja Boy "Superman That Ass" or something like that and my eleventh grader says "What?!" And she explains what "Superman That Ass" is. Are you. . . . Should I tell you . . . it has to do with ejaculation and masturbation and she. . . .

Principal: No, I don't need any more information . . . I think I have the information that I need. Have you as a parent gone in to these teachers and expressed your concern and your frustration and your, ah, lack of wanting your children to read this type of literature?

Dad: Absolutely!

Principal: Have you gotten any, what types of responses have you received from the teachers?

Dad: They said we differentiate and we offer different books. But every book that they offer is something that. . . .

Principal: Did you get any, um, curriculum-type, standard and benchmark reasoning for why they're selecting the books that . . . did you ask for any of that type of information?

Dad: No, I didn't because I just didn't think that adultery and pornography was in any sort of benchmark. I mean, I figured that you know. . . .

Principal: Well, and I don't think it is.

Dad: You know, it might be at the school on the other side of the tracks but this school. . . .

Principal: I guess my point is did you, did you express to them the exact concern you have with the type of material that they are having your daughters read?

Dad: I asked, "Are you giving my kids books that have pornography in them," and they said "That's literature. These are books by authors who are renown around the world and have been for a long time." And I said again, "Are you giving my kids books about pornography?" And neither of them would answer. You know, but my beef is more with the eighth grade teacher. . . .

Principal: That's a situation that I will, that I will need to look into. I will take the concerns; I will take the titles of the book. . . .

Dad: How old are eighth grade students typically?

Principal: Thirteen, fourteen, fifteen.

Dad: Okay, so a thirteen-year-old learning about boys masturbating and . . . and I mean. . . .

Principal: I understand your concern as a parent. I do. I understand your concern as a parent.

Dad: But you're not . . . do you have kids? Because, I mean, I'm sitting here thinking that you understand it, but you should be irate! You should be irate.

Principal: I do have children. Yes. I do have children. I just, I need you to understand that I am going to support my teachers as well, but I need to go find out the. . . .

Dad: Oh! Wait, wait, wait. You're going to support your teachers while. . . .

Principal: You need to let me finish, please.

Dad: You're gonna support your teachers of promoting pornography to my eighth grade. . . .

Principal: Well, until I find. . . . No . . . I did not say I would support everything, I just need to go find out. . . .

Dad: You know what? I'm just thinking that Deacon Dieken . . . should go to the church now and open up a whole firestorm of stuff that's going on.

Principal: Well, and when I said that, I meant that I need to go to them and find out the information from them. . . .

Dad: It's easy to back away . . . typically we say things that we mean first off. You don't . . . you're trying to come back now and say that, you know, I understand. . . .

DISCUSSION AND REFLECTION QUESTIONS

1. Identify the primary and secondary issue(s).
2. Identify areas in which you believe the principal acted effectively.
3. Identify areas in which you believe the principal could have acted more effectively.
4. Mr. Dieken raises a concern about some of the reading materials that his daughters are being asked to read in English classes. He asks Principal Olsen if she has read a number of them. She has not. Is it the principal's responsibility to read or be familiar with instructional materials that may become controversial? Or is that unrealistic?
5. At 53:22 Mr. Dieken reads a passage from *What's Eating Gilbert Grape?* (Hedges, 2005). Describe any *personal* feelings you have about the book or the passage. Do you feel the book is appropriate for the

eighth graders? Do you feel qualified to make that judgment without reading the entire book? Is this decision better made by others, such as the English department, school board, or a committee?

6. Describe your emotions as Mr. Dieken reads the passage from *What's Eating Gilbert Grape?* (Hedges, 2005). How would you respond? Evaluate Principal Olsen's response.

7. Some would say that Mr. Dieken is working hard to exert masculine power in this scenario from the moment he holds Principal Olsen's hand for an unusually long length of time. Do you agree? Given the content of the passage he reads, do you believe he is trying to intimidate Principal Olsen? Is he trying to capitalize on gender role tension that may be present in their interaction? Do you believe Mr. Dieken would choose to read the same passage to a male principal? Is this a situation in which Principal Olsen should be prepared to communicate with a colleague or secretary through a secret signal that she may need assistance or be in a vulnerable position?

8. At 54:18 Mr. Dieken continues with some objections to materials his eleventh grade daughter was given to read, though he acknowledges that Principal Olsen is only in charge of middle school. Should she try to redirect his attention to only the middle school issues or is it better to allow him to express all of his concerns? Explain.

9. At 55:46 Mr. Dieken shifts his attention to some of the music being played in the art room. Evaluate Principal Olsen's questioning and response to this concern. After Mr. Dieken raises the music issue, the conversation returns to the reading materials. Should the principal continue to explore the concern over the music?

10. When Principal Olsen tries to make a connection between the curriculum and teachers' choices of reading material, Mr. Dieken says he didn't think "adultery and pornography were in any sort of benchmark." He then references that perhaps these materials are acceptable at other schools. On the surface, many schools and communities appear to be quite similar. Experienced educators, however, know that culture, climate and context account for some major differences. It is likely the issue Mr. Dieken is raising might never surface in a nearby school. How can a principal gain a sense of local opinions on issues like this and anticipate potential reactions?

11. After establishing that Mr. Dieken raised his concerns with the teachers, Principal Olsen says she will discuss the issue and the books with the teacher and that she understands his concerns (58:10). At 58:42 she indicates that she will support her teachers, to which Mr. Dieken objects further. Evaluate this exchange and the principal's message. Teachers repeatedly identify principal support as being very important, yet Mr.

Dieken seems intent on using this against the principal here. Ultimately, he threatens to create a stir in the community through a church group. How would you have handled this exchange? At this point, the conversation seems more contentious than a few minutes prior. How should Principal Olsen attempt to bring closure to the conversation? What should happen next? Should Principal Olsen be concerned that Mr. Dieken will leave the meeting telling people that the principal said the books were fine and that she intended to support the teachers' efforts to teach what he believes to be inappropriate? On the other hand, should the principal be concerned that the teachers may think she failed to support their curricular and instructional decisions firmly enough when questioned?

12. One district attracted a considerable amount of media attention after a district administrator pulled *What's Eating Gilbert Grape?* (Hedges, 2005) from the library shelves and English curriculum after a parent objected to the book's content. The administrator acknowledged having not read the book. Was this decision appropriate?

13. From *The Ed Sullivan Show*'s restrictions on the Beatles, the Rolling Stones, and the Doors, controversies over song lyrics are nothing new (Knoboch-Westerwick et al., 2009). Practically speaking, how can a principal stay current on songs that might be objectionable or inappropriate in a school setting?

14. Is this a situation in which a principal should have another person present during the conversation? Explain.

REFLECTION AND DISCUSSION QUESTIONS

Balcony View

Generally speaking, how did the principal perform in this scenario? What would you have done differently?

Standards in Action

Which standards do you see as relevant in the scenario? Does the principal effectively meet them? Are there standards and/or criteria left unmet by the principal's actions?

Peel the Onion

Like an onion, leadership challenges have multiple layers. The presenting issue may be singular or appear simple in nature. Often, however, it represents one part of an underlying, more complex issue. The best leaders address concerns in the moment, while not losing sight of root causes. What is/are the presenting issue(s)? Do you see potential nuanced factors that should be explored?

Self-Check

We all come to our roles with unique experiences, perspectives, and biases that influence our perceptions and actions. Picturing yourself in the principal's chair, describe your emotions.

Switch It Up

How might your thinking or approach change if the gender, ethnicity, language, age, sexual orientation, socioeconomic status, disability, or other descriptors of the players involved were different?

Equity Lens

Equity-driven leaders understand that diversity takes many forms. What equity- or diversity-related issues could be present in this scenario?

Power and Presence

In televised presidential debates, "looking presidential" is an important measure of a candidate's performance. The same is true for principals. Halpern and Lubar (2003b, p. 3) define leadership presence as being more than "commanding attention" to include "the ability to connect authentically with the thoughts and feelings of others." Does the principal exert an effective presence? Describe the power balance between the principal and the visitor. Does positional or personal power between the principal and visitor seem uneven or problematic? What does body language say that words do not?

Principal's Priority

How *serious* is the situation?
What de-escalation techniques could/should be used here?
How *soon* should the principal address this situation?

Should the principal inform a supervisor about this issue and get them involved?

Reach Out?

Should the principal involve other individuals, professionals, resources, or organizations?

In a Word

Capture the principal's performance in the scenario using one word.

Collaborate

Collaborate with a classmate or colleague to rewrite or alter the case with a different set of circumstances. Share your new case with other colleagues to ascertain how they would approach it.

Extension and Internship Activities

- Examine your school or district policy on challenges to instructional materials. Is it well-communicated to parents and the community? Speak with a secretary, teacher, or administrator with a long history in the school or district to determine how frequently, if ever, objections have been raised and how/if they were resolved.
- Access the American Library Association's website (www.ala.org) and peruse the information on banned and challenged books, noting if your school or district uses any of the books identified. Does your school utilize or make available books identified by Klass (2017) as "banned books your child should read?" Discuss controversial instructional materials in the district with a longtime administrator. Are there particular local or political issues that might make particular controversies more or less likely?
- Interview an experienced administrator about how s/he stays informed and handles potentially controversial or inappropriate lyrics or music in a school setting. Does the school have an official policy for acceptable song lyrics for dances and what may be played at school? Do administrators use established criteria to determine acceptability or make determinations on a case-by-case basis?
- Interview a female administrator to explore her thoughts on gender and the principalship. Can she recount incidences of harassment, discrimination, or interactions in which male colleagues, parents, or others seemed

intent on intimidation or bullying related to gender? Does she identify with the oft-heard notion that a woman must be twice as good as a man to be seen as effective?

REFERENCES AND RESOURCES

Ah Nee-Benham, M. K. P., & Cooper, J. E. (1998). *Let my spirit soar: Narratives of diverse women in educational leadership.* Corwin Press.

Atwood, M. (1986). *The handmaid's tale.* Houghton-Mifflin.

Bolman, L. G., & Deal, T. E. (2010). *Reframing the path to school leadership: A guide for teachers and principals* (2nd ed.). Corwin Press.

Chopin, K. (2011). *The awakening.* Random House UK Ltd.

Cobb, M. D., & Boettcher III, W. A. (2007). Ambivalent sexism and misogynistic rap music: Does exposure to Eminem increase sexism? *Journal of Applied Psychology* 37(12): 3025–3042.

DeMitchell, T. A., & Carney, J. J. (2005). Harry Potter and the public-school library. *Phi Delta Kappan* 87(2): 159–165. Retrieved from EBSCO*host.*

Gause, C. P. (2005). Navigating the stormy seas: Critical perspectives on the intersection of popular culture and educational leader-"Ship." *Journal of School Leadership* 15(3): 333–342.

Grogan, M., & Shakeshaft, C. (2011). *Women and educational leadership.* Jossey-Bass.

Halpern, B. L., & Lubar, K. (2003a). *Dramatic techniques to reach out, motivate and inspire leadership presence.* Gotham Books.

Halpern, B. L., & Lubar, K. (2003b). *Leadership presence: Dramatic techniques to reach out, motivate, and inspire.* Penguin Group.

Hartsfield, D. E., & Kimmel, C. E. (2019). Exploring educators' figured worlds of controversial literature and adolescent readers. *Journal of Adolescent & Adult Literacy* 63(4): 443–451, doi: 10.1002/jaal.989.

Hedges, P. (2005). *What's eating Gilbert Grape?* Simon & Schuster Paperbacks.

Hess, D. E. (2009). *Controversy in the classroom: The democratic power of discussion.* Routledge.

Hicks, A. T. (1996). *Speak softly and carry your own gym key: A female high school principal's guide to survival.* Corwin Press.

International Literacy Association (2018). *Children's rights to read.* Retrieved from https://www.literacyworldwide.org/get-resources/childrens-rights-to-read.

Klass, P. (January 2017). The banned books your child should read. *New York Times.* Retrieved from https://www.nytimes.com/2017/01/16/well/ family/the-banned-books-your-child-should-read. html.

Knoboch-Westerwick, S., Musto, P., & Shaw, K. (2009). Rebellion in the top music charts: Defiant messages in rap/hip hop and rock music 1993 and 2003. *Journal of Media Psychology* 20(1): 15–23.

Martinson, D. L. (1996). Confront censorship crusades with genuine school-community relations. *Journal of Educational Relations* 12. Retrieved from EBSCO*host.*

Newman, L., & Souza, D. (2009). *Heather has two mommies.* Alyson Wonderland.

Petress, K. (2005). The role of censorship in school. *Journal of Instructional Psychology* 32(3): 248–252.

Ravitch, D. (2004). *The language police: How pressure groups restrict what students learn.* Vintage Books.

Rowling, J. K. (2000). *Harry Potter and the goblet of fire.* Arthur A. Levine Books.

Rumberger, A. (2019). The elementary school library: Tensions between access and censorship. *Contemporary Issues in Early Childhood* 20(4): 409–421.

Shakeshaft, C., Nowell, I., & Perry, A. (2007). *Gender and supervision. In the Jossey-Bass reader on educational leadership* (2nd ed., pp. 339–348). Jossey-Bass.

Soulja Boy Tell 'Em. (Performer). (2007). *Crank that (Soulja Boy).* On souljaboytellem.com [CD]. Interscope.

Twain, M. (1990). *Adventures of Huckleberry Finn.* Chelsea House.

Walker, J. M. (2010). It takes at least two to tangle. *Journal of Cases in Educational Leadership* 13(4): 22–43. doi: 10.1177/1555458910381464.

Waller, R. J. (1992). *The bridges of Madison County.* Warner Books.

I Think They're Immoral Topics! (Elementary School)

Two affluent and highly engaged grandparents stop by the school to share their concerns about proposed new health curriculum standards with Principal Machal. They imply that their long-standing love for the school can be measured by their recent sizable donation to fund the new library. Though the principal is not directly involved in the development and potential adoption of proposed new health and human development curriculum standards, Patrick and Mary Beth have deep concerns about the content, which runs contrary to their beliefs. They'd like to know Principal Machal's feelings on what they see as an immoral and starkly inappropriate curriculum.

While a robust health and physical education program can provide students with knowledge and the skills to be physically and socially healthy and happy (Goh & Connolly, 2020), it often represents a difficult and controversial curricular area for many parents and educators (Robinson et al., 2017). The tension in this topic typically centers on opinions about what content to share at what age, and parental views about the information presented. At what age is it appropriate to teach what for many are sensitive topics, such as human sexuality, gender, substance use, mental health, and more? Many educators believe that an early introduction can be lifesaving, as the Center for Disease Control and Prevention's Youth Risk Behavior Survey shows that 17% of high school students have seriously considered suicide, and 60% of those students identified as lesbian, gay, and bisexual. Others insist these topics are best left to parents.

Sometimes, the dissenting opinions seem to fall along political lines, adding to the intensity of culture wars. However, Kantor and Levitz (2017) found a majority of parents across political parties believed students should be taught about a wide range of topics in sex education including puberty, healthy relationships, abstinence, sexually transmitted diseases, and birth control in high school. In their comprehensive review of three decades of literature, Goldfarb and Lieberman (2020) found significant support for sexual education to begin in elementary school, including LGBTQ-inclusive education across the school curriculum. Dent and Maloney (2017) noted that while a strong majority of Americans favor sex education at school, what is viewed as appropriate content varies greatly. The authors explain that by starting students off early their knowledge can be scaffolded across grades to provide a more comprehensive understanding of sexuality and emotional health.

Principal Machal finds herself challenged to respond to influential community leaders' questions about what the health education curriculum should look like, who gets to decide, and whether (or how) to share her own views.

THE TRANSCRIPT

Principal: Hi, welcome in.

Patrick: Nice to meet you.

Principal: Nice to see you, why don't you take a seat? What can I help you guys with today?

Patrick: Well, as you know, I think you know that we've given quite a bit of money to the school. We know that the new library has been open, has been funded by us. And so, we've just loved this school, our daughter, our granddaughter, Angel, just loves being here. And so, we really appreciate that. One of the things that we're wondering about is, you know they've been discussing new health standards, and we're wondering what your thoughts are about the new health standards?

Principal: Okay. Yes, first off thank you so much for all those donations, I love that Angel loves our school and that you guys really take such an interest in our school as well. We really appreciate you. . . .

Mary Beth: It is just so family focused here.

Principal: Yes, well good that's what I love to hear because I really want our school to feel like that family and so looking at those health standards, um, tell me a little bit more about some of those standards that you're wanting to know more on.

Patrick: Well just wanting to know your thoughts about the health standards, if you looked at them?

Principal: I have, um, so looking at those health standards, I mean health is always the most important thing that we're wanting to look at when we're working with students, especially to make sure that they are safe and feel okay in school. Um, I haven't looked into them in depth quite yet, so I'll be honest with you on that. But I really appreciate you bringing that to the table, um—

Mary Beth: That's very disappointing.

Principal: Yes, I, I apologize, I'm really glad that you are bringing this to me though, and that tells me that I need to make sure I read those more in depth, especially going forward with this new library donation.

Mary Beth: We can help you with a few things.

Principal: Okay, yes, I would always appreciate your help.

Mary Beth: Well, Angel's in first grade. And so, some of the standards that concern Pat and I especially, are just taking away, in our opinion, the focus on family and parents. An example would be, there's all kinds of discussions about mindfulness, and how to work through emotional distress, not one thing about prayer, not one thing about religion, not one thing about a higher power. For example, in kindergarten, now we're supposed to be talking about cohabitating, same-sex parents, and I'm not sure that Angel would even know what "same-sex" even means. And so, we go on to first grade, gender, gender identity, my favorite is assigned identity. God doesn't assign your identity, God creates you, and nowhere in there does it talk about that, and I could go on and on and on. If you'd like me to.

Principal: No, okay so thank you for bringing that up that it helps me to know what your specific concerns are. So, what I'm hearing is—

Mary Beth: There's a lot more but go ahead.

Principal: Yes, yes, no thank you. It's a good starting point. So, what I'm hearing you saying is you're more, you're more concerned with kind of those newer ideas that are being presented to our students so not having that religious focus in schools and then kind of talking about some of those more those newer topics such as gender identity and same-sex parents, is that correct?

Patrick: For kindergartners and first graders. First grade define gender, gender identity, gender role stereotypes.

Principal: Hmm, hmm, so I want to start with I love that you're bringing those concerns and I know this, this is some heavy information that's being presented to kids.

Mary Beth: I want to know if you to think it's even developmentally appropriate.

Principal: That is a great question and so I think, the nice thing about kids, and something we really want to keep in mind is that there are those developmental stages that we go with with students but knowing too that kids have such a great capacity for learning and I think sometimes we underestimate those abilities, and we want to push them to be as creative and powerful learners as we can have them to be. And so, I agree I think these are heavy topics for young students. However, I think—

Mary Beth: I think they are immoral topics for your students. And I want to know as a school leader. What are you going to do? To talk to district officials to, or do you agree with this?

Principal: I think these topics are important. I do, I think that's something that we, this is the world we're living in now, and these are topics that are getting brought up and little kids are hearing these things that are said to them, and we want to make sure we're giving them—

Mary Beth: Not in our house.

Patrick: Angel's not discussing these things.

Principal: You're correct. Not in every household I agree with you on that. It's not in every household. . . .

Mary Beth: Nor it shouldn't be in any household.

Principal: The thing is, you know with media that social media coming up and even with younger kids, maybe they're not on social media and I honestly that's probably good. However, we know that they're in this society in this world where they're going to hear these things, and we want to make sure they're coming in with that most accurate information they can, and we can help present those ideas to them in a more unbiased way. And so, I am working with district officials, you know, we're talking about what the most appropriate way to talk about these concepts with young children are. And I think that—

Mary Beth: Are you pushing back at all?

Principal: Right now, we're just having the conversations, but the nice thing about you guys coming to us is I can say these are what some of the concerns that our parents have regarding these issues. So I'm really glad that you came in to talk to us about this so that I can bring that to those conversations and say this is some of the concerns we're seeing. . . .

Mary Beth: But we're asking what you think?

Patrick: What age do you think it's appropriate to start with those conversations?

Principal: That's a really tough question, I wish I could give you a better answer, I'm trying to, you know, put myself, because I have a young son, too. Who's not—

Patrick: How old is your son?

Principal: He's only two and so you know, when do I think that's appropriate for him—

Mary Beth: Or getting him ready for kindergarten, to talk about transgender stuff.

Principal: Yeah, I, I see how that you know that seems young especially when they're still figuring out who they are as a person too and I get where you're coming from, I really do. And so, you know, I think that's why we have these conversations at the district level say is it's the most appropriate is it not and I completely see you guys decided that that's there's so young and they're still figuring out who they are as their little selves. . . .

DISCUSSION AND REFLECTION QUESTIONS

1. Identify the primary and secondary issue(s).
2. Identify areas in which you believe the principal acted effectively.
3. Identify areas in which you believe the principal could have acted more effectively.
4. At 1:12 Patrick asks if Principal Machal had looked at the new health standards. Principal Machal explains that she has but not in depth, which Mary Beth finds disappointing. What else could the principal have done here? Is it appropriate for a principal to be unfamiliar with content standards, particularly in an area likely to be controversial? Is it possible for the principal to be familiar with all aspects of curriculum across the spectrum?
5. Mary Beth asks Principal Machal at 3:53 if she believes the new health standards are even developmentally appropriate? This is a direct question of the principal's own views. Principal Machal responds that we should not "underestimate" students' abilities. Evaluate her response. Do you interpret it as an attempt to avoid answering directly?
6. Mary Beth continues to press Principal Machal about her opinion on the standards, which she sees as "immoral." She wants to know what Principal Machal, as the school leader, is going to do about this. What could/should she do? Is it appropriate for Principal Machal to share her own beliefs? Or is it a trap?
7. At 5:10 Principal Machal mentions the media and social media and how information is being presented to children. She specifically says "the most accurate information" and "unbiased." What are your thoughts on this? Was this a move that was beneficial? What point or position does Principal Machal appear to be taking?
8. At 5:57 Mary Beth asks, "But we're asking what *you* think," followed by Patrick asking, "What age do you think it's appropriate to start with those conversations?" How should Principal Machal respond? What role do a principal's personal views have in such a case? Would you have advised a different approach?

9. How does the influence this family holds in making sizable donations come into play in the decision-making process of the principal? Should Patrick and Mary Beth's prominence in the community have any bearing on Principal Machal's interaction with them? Is it naïve to say that their standing in the community does not play a factor?

10. How could the principal wrap up this conversation? What would be an appropriate next set of steps?

REFLECTION AND DISCUSSION QUESTIONS

Balcony View

Generally speaking, how did the principal perform in this scenario? What would you have done differently?

Standards in Action

Which standards do you see as relevant in the scenario? Does the principal effectively meet them? Are there standards and/or criteria left unmet by the principal's actions?

Peelthe Onion

Like an onion, leadership challenges have multiple layers. The presenting issue may be singular or appear simple in nature. Often, however, it represents one part of an underlying, more complex issue. The best leaders address concerns in the moment, while not losing sight of root causes. What is/are the presenting issue(s)? Do you see potential nuanced factors that should be explored?

Self-Check

We all come to our roles with unique experiences, perspectives, and biases that influence our perceptions and actions. Picturing yourself in the principal's chair, describe your emotions.

Switch It Up

How might your thinking or approach change if the gender, ethnicity, language, age, sexual orientation, socioeconomic status, disability, or other descriptors of the players involved were different?

Equity Lens

Equity-driven leaders understand that diversity takes many forms. What equity- or diversity-related issues could be present in this scenario?

Power and Presence

In televised presidential debates, "looking presidential" is an important measure of a candidate's performance. The same is true for principals. Halpern and Lubar (2003, p. 3) define leadership presence as being more than "commanding attention" to include "the ability to connect authentically with the thoughts and feelings of others." Does the principal exert an effective presence? Describe the power balance between the principal and the visitor. Does positional or personal power between the principal and visitor seem uneven or problematic? What does body language say that words do not?

Principal's Priority

How *serious* is the situation? Are de-escalation techniques needed?
How *soon* should the principal address this situation?
Should the principal inform a supervisor of this issue and get them involved?

Reach Out?

Should the principal involve other individuals, professionals, resources, or organizations?

In a Word

Capture the principal's performance in the scenario using one word.

Collaborate

Collaborate with a classmate or colleague to rewrite or alter the case with a different set of circumstances. Share your new case with other colleagues to ascertain how they would approach it.

Extension and Internship Experiences

- Does your district have parental involvement in the curricular adoption process? Review the process for addressing questions and concerns from parents and the public.
- What is the local or district role in curricular decisions? For example, are health and human growth and development and other content a local district or state decision? What avenues exist for community and stakeholder involvement?
- What opportunities exist for you to work with your school board on curriculum?
- Ask a mentor how they have navigated curricular controversies with stakeholders and/or their own beliefs.
- Conduct an exercise in which you identify key power brokers or opinion leaders in the community who have influence over particular schools or the entire district. How does their power and influence manifest? Interview an district experienced leader about how all stakeholders can be assured that their voices are heard.

REFERENCES AND RESOURCES

Bentley, D. F., & Souto-Manning, M. (2016). Toward inclusive understandings of marriage in an early childhood classroom: Negotiating (un) readiness, community, and vulnerability through a critical reading of King and King. *Early Years* 36(2): 195–206.

Dent, L., & Maloney, P. (2017). Evangelical Christian parents' attitudes towards abstinence-based sex education: I want my kids to have great sex! *Sex Education* 17(2): 149–164, DOI: 10.1080/14681811.2016.1256281.

Goh, T. L., & Connolly, M. (2020). Efficacy of school-based SEL programs: Aligning with health and physical education standards. *Journal of Physical Education, Recreation & Dance* 91(5): 16–19.

Goldfarb, E. S., & Lieberman, L. D. (2020). Three decades of research: The case for comprehensive sex education. *Journal of Adolescent Health* 68(1): 1–15.

Halpern, B. L., & Lubar, K. (2003). *Leadership presence: Dramatic techniques to reach out, motivate, and inspire*. Penguin Group.

Kantor, L., & Levitz, N. (2017). Parents' views on sex education in schools: How much do Democrats and Republicans agree? *PloS One* 12(7).

Proulx, C. N., Coulter, R. W., Egan, J. E., Matthews, D. D., & Mair, C. (2019). Associations of lesbian, gay, bisexual, transgender, and questioning–inclusive sex education with mental health outcomes and school-based victimization in US high school students. *Journal of Adolescent Health* 64(5): 608–614.

Richard, G., Vallerand, O., Petit, M. P., & Charbonneau, A. (2015). Discussing sexual orientation and gender in classrooms: A testimonial-based approach to fighting homophobia in schools. *The Educational Forum* 79(40): 421–435.

Robinson, K. H., Smith, E., & Davies, C. (2017). Responsibilities, tensions and ways forward: Parents' perspectives on children's sexuality education. *Sex Education* 17(3): 333–347.

Ryan, C. L., Patraw, J. M., & Bednar, M. (2013). Discussing princess boys and pregnant men: Teaching about gender diversity and transgender experiences within an elementary school curriculum. *Journal of LGBT Youth* 10(1–2): 83–105.

Hot Seat #19

Just a Nod (High School)

Principal McBride has a prominent visitor come to her office—Reverend Watson, who leads one of the largest churches in the state. Reverend Watson shares his concern about what he describes as disturbing messages coming out of the social studies department that coincide with the arrival of a new history teacher. Reverend Watson wants her to know that he and his parishioners have begun a petition to have the social studies teacher removed. He's looking for even a subtle sign as to how Principal McBride feels about the issue.

Teachers and all citizens are protected from persecution by several Constitutional amendments. The 1st Amendment protects teachers' right to freedom of expression. The 10th Amendment situates education as a power of states. The 14th Amendment is an extension of the 5th Amendment, providing equal protection that includes state and local laws (Voros, 2017). The Equal Protection Clause is especially important, as it protects teachers from discrimination based on race, sex, freedom of expression, academics, privacy, and religion. Though these protections seem broad, the academic freedom afforded to teachers is limited (Maxwell et al., 2019). For example, the 1st Amendment protections for teachers are quite limited. For speech to be protected it must be relevant to and consistent with the teacher's responsibilities, and cannot promote a personal or political agenda.

While Reverend Watson's concerns focus particular issues at a specific moment, we know controversies endure across time. Null (2016) noted,

> Curriculum is at the center of every controversial issue within teaching and schooling today. Debates rage on with regard to national or state standards, moral education, religious education, state-mandated testing, intelligent design, whole language versus phonics in the teaching of reading, prayer in schools and other hot button topics. (p. 5)

In his seminal work, Paulo Freire espoused that pedagogical decision-making cannot only be held in the hands of those with power. Pedagogy for "the

191

oppressed is a pedagogy which must be forged with, not for the oppressed . . . in the incessant struggle to regain their humanity. This pedagogy makes oppression and its causes objects of reflection by the oppressed, and from that reflection will come liberation" (1982, p. 25). Newberry and Trujillo (2018) described how Western colonialism is viewed through a lens of normalcy, which can be problematic as it discredits types of knowledge that stray from the typical.

At the same time, others have decried what they see as an anti-American bias, an excessive focus on America's failings, or educational approaches that add to divisions in society. Hirsch (2020, p. 5) lamented, "The costs of a broken approach to schooling leave our children underprepared and erode the American Dream. But there's an even deeper cost. Without the schooling that teaches shared knowledge, the spiritual bonds that hold our society together are loosened."

Between these opposing viewpoints, Lintner (2018, p. 14), arguing for robust social studies curricula, advocated embracing controversy, rather than avoiding or squelching it. "If approached with both fidelity and care, controversy can provide a platform for engaged and engaging social studies teaching and learning." In this scenario, Principal McBride feels the reality of the controversies and unanswered questions summarized by Null (2016, p. 5), "What should be taught, to whom, under what circumstances, how, and with what end in mind?"

Reverend Watson awaits her answer.

THE TRANSCRIPT

Principal: Reverend, it's nice to meet you.

Reverend: Nice to meet you.

Principal: How are you today?

Reverend: I'm good, you?

Principal: Good. You enjoying the weather?

Reverend: Forgive me for my laid-back dress, just got back from playing a little golf with one of your superintendents.

Principal: Oh, lovely. Which course did you play?

Reverend: Hidden Valley. It depends on the day, right. Well, before we go, would you mind if I say a prayer for these over this meeting?

Principal: Sure, that's fine.

Reverend: Dear Heavenly Father, we come to you today, just to be servants for you to do your work, Lord, so we can partner with like-minded people. All these things we pray for In Jesus' almighty name. Amen. All right, thanks. So, I want to give you a little background about me. So again, I'm Reverend Watson, I have the second-largest church in the state, right, so think about that. With that, I have a lot of members that are on the school board, they're . . . also the superintendent, you know, again, he's a good friend of mine. Having said that, had a good friend of mine that came in last week or so and he gave a sermon about just the problems with some of the things that are being taught as far as the Black Lives Matter movement, the 1619 Project as far as how some of those things coming off, it can have a different way of thinking. And initially, you know, it's kind of like, you know, this is kind of troubling. But after listening to him, it kind of made sense. So, having said that my son who's a junior here, he came home, and he was telling me some of the things about the social studies teacher some of the things that she was teaching.

Principal: Now is that American History here?

Reverend: Yes sorry, yes, yes, sorry. So, his teachers telling them these things and I am not on social media like the Insta-face or whatever it is. I really don't do it. But so, I took a look at what he had, and she's, she's on here and she's spewing all these things about how America is not great.

Principal: I am sorry, who is she? Is it the teacher?

Reverend: Yes, the teacher sorry. So, but anyway, having said that, looking at all those things, and you know I'm here I'm here for you. Again, I have second-largest church, a lot of a lot of members, we've talked about these things and we're all on the same page and, meaning I think we have the same thought process. I'm here, I'm here to support you. Right. So again, what I'm looking at as I've started a petition to have this teacher removed as well as petitioning is that the 1619 Project. And so, again, I know they're things you're not able to do because of where you are, but I want to be, I want to work for you in the background so we can have, we have the same agenda so we can get everything going in the direction that we need it to go so that our students are taught things, the proper things going forward.

Principal: So, tell me more about how the 1619 Project has been used in the American History class?

Reverend: Well, just the fact that it's being used. All right, that's, you know, I don't, I don't want my son, having any excuses. Right, so something that meant that happened that long ago, I just I want my son. . . . I came up on my own, you know, so I understand. But my son doesn't have to go through the same things I did. I don't want these things going into his head, changing the way he thinks. So, again, I'm here, I'm here to help you so you don't even have to worry about it. I've got this started; I've got 50 names already.

Principal: Sure. So, let's go back to your son for just a moment here, so did he has some specific concerns?

Reverend: No, he doesn't. I do. These are the things that he doesn't know anything about. So now all of a sudden, he's learning these things, he's changing the way he is around the house around his friends. I need my son back. He's a junior, he's got a bright future.

Principal: Absolutely.

Reverend: And we're, you know, we've got colleges coming looking at him. I need him to get back, but it's bigger than my son, you know, again, my congregation we've talked about this. These are things that we're trying to move away from.

Principal: So, you mentioned your son has changed a little bit. Can you tell me a little bit more about that? I just want to make sure that I'm taking care of him first, because students are really important to me and we'll talk about the larger issue here, but I just want to make sure that I'm doing right by your son.

Reverend: Let's take this, take a step back, my son. I will get him under control. If we can get through social studies teacher under control, and again, with this petition here, I've already taken the initial steps that we need to take. All you have to do is just give me, you don't even have to say yes, just a nod, or anything. And it's, it's done.

Principal: So, I do want to get to that, that part but, before that, in order for me to help understand what's going on in the classroom, it would be really helpful to understand what your son is saying and maybe how that things have changed, so that when I go to the teacher, I have a fuller picture of what your concerns are.

Reverend: So, you haven't been in the classroom, so you don't, you haven't seen these things?

Principal: So, I do appraise that teacher, but I have not been in that classroom for that specific lesson. And so, I want to make sure that I understand from your son's perspective and your perspective what your concerns are, before I go to that teacher, so that I'm able to more fully articulate what the position you have is.

Reverend: Are you on this Facebook, Instagram or whatever it is, are you on those things?

Principal: You know, I do have an Instagram, but I'll be honest I mostly post pictures for my grandmother, I don't do a lot more than that with it.

Reverend: Okay 'cause I mean, she's all over it. I mean, she's got the Black Lives Matters banner, she's got it all up. I mean, anything if you've heard the 1619 Project, I mean she's basically just playing it in class and my son, I checked his phone the other day and he's downloaded on his podcast as well.

So, I mean, if you listen to those things you knew exactly what was going on in there.

Principal: So, what about that is concerning to you?

Reverend: The fact that my son is learning things about them that I don't want him exposed to right now, and his friends, as well.

Principal: Sure, sure. So, when you're talking about this concern, have you have you approached the teacher at all?

Reverend: No, because I want to talk to you first, because I've got this petition ready to go. When she knows anything, she'll be out of a job.

DISCUSSION AND REFLECTION QUESTIONS

1. Identify the primary and secondary issue(s).
2. Identify areas in which you believe the principal acted effectively.
3. Identify areas in which you believe the principal could have acted more effectively.
4. After the initial welcome, Reverend Watson asks the principal if he can say a prayer over the meeting (at :23). Given the separation of church and state, what are your thoughts on how the principal handled the request? Would you have allowed, prevented, or welcomed the prayer?
5. At (:46) Reverend Watson describes the influence he holds in the community (i.e., being the pastor of the second-largest church, golfing with the superintendent). How should the principal respond to this?
6. Reverend Watson mentions "being on the same page" and "having the same thought process." It is clear that he is attempting to get Principal McBride to agree with him. At (2:30) he mentions that the goal of the petition is to have the teacher removed. Principal McBride decides not to address this statement. Was this the right decision?
7. As Principal McBride attempts to redirect the conversation away from the teacher and to Reverend Watson's son, he exclaims (4:28), "Let's take this, take a step back, my son. I will get him under control. If we can get through social studies teacher under control, and again, with this petition here, I've already taken the initial steps that we need to take. All you have to do is just give me, you don't even have to say yes, just a nod or anything. And it's, it's done." How should Principal McBride respond to the reverend's developing petition and implied threat?
8. When Reverend Watson asks Principal McBride if she has been in the classroom (5:13), she responds, "I do appraise that teacher, but I

have not been in that classroom for that specific lesson." Evaluate her response. Would you have responded similarly?

9. Near the end of the conversation, Principal McBride asks if Reverend Watson has talked with the teacher at all about his concerns. He replies, "No, because I want to talk to you first, because I've got this petition ready to go. When she knows anything, she'll be out of a job." How would you go about the ending of this conversation? Are there specific talking points to avoid or make sure to include? Should Principal McBride acknowledge his threat?

10. What would be your next steps? How should Principal McBride inform the teacher? Would you bring the teacher, son, and Reverend Watson together? Why or why not?

11. All teachers want the support of their administrator. If the teacher learns of Reverend Watson's visit and complaint and asks Principal McBride about it, what should Principal McBride say? Was the principal sufficiently supportive of the teacher? Appropriately noncommittal in the conversation with Reverend Watson?

REFLECTION AND DISCUSSION QUESTIONS

Balcony View

Generally speaking, how did the principal perform in this scenario? What would you have done differently?

Standards in Action

Which standards do you see as relevant in the scenario? Does the principal effectively meet them? Are there standards and/or criteria left unmet by the principal's actions?

Peel the Onion

Like an onion, leadership challenges have multiple layers. The presenting issue may be singular or appear simple in nature. Often, however, it represents one part of an underlying, more complex issue. The best leaders address concerns in the moment, while not losing sight of root causes. What is/are the presenting issue(s)? Do you see potential nuanced factors that should be explored?

Self-Check

We all come to our roles with unique experiences, perspectives, and biases that influence our perceptions and actions. Picturing yourself in the principal's chair, describe your emotions.

Switch It Up

How might your thinking or approach change if the gender, ethnicity, language, age, sexual orientation, socioeconomic status, disability, or other descriptors of the players involved were different?

Equity Lens

Equity-driven leaders understand that diversity takes many forms. What equity- or diversity-related issues could be present in this scenario?

Power and Presence

In televised presidential debates, "looking presidential" is an important measure of a candidate's performance. The same is true for principals. Halpern and Lubar (2003, p. 3) define leadership presence as being more than "commanding attention" to include "the ability to connect authentically with the thoughts and feelings of others." Does the principal exert an effective presence? Describe the power balance between the principal and the visitor. Does positional or personal power between the principal and visitor seem uneven or problematic? What does body language say that words do not?

Principal's Priority

How *serious* is the situation? Are de-escalation techniques needed?
How *soon* should the principal address this situation?
Should the principal inform a supervisor of this issue and get them involved?

Reach Out?

Should the principal involve other individuals, professionals, resources, or organizations?

In a Word

Capture the principal's performance in the scenario using one word.

Collaborate

Collaborate with a classmate or colleague to rewrite or alter the case with a different set of circumstances. Share your new case with other colleagues to ascertain how they would approach it.

Extension and Internship Experiences

- Who are key leaders or influencers in your school's community that you need to be familiar with? Are there ways to develop positive relationships with them ahead of time? What are their backgrounds (business, faith community, alumni, donors, etc.)? Construct a list yourself and ask a mentor to do the same, then compare.
- When moving to a new setting, what are some of the things you can do to make sure you have a sense of your community? Develop an entry plan that makes this a priority.
- Who are key people in your district with whom you can talk about teachers' rights? What are your district's policies and guidelines regarding established curricula and teachers' academic freedom?
- Does your district or state association offer guidance for teachers' use of social media? Are teachers aware of the policy?
- Interview an experienced teacher, administrator, or board member in your district to learn about prominent curricular controversies and their outcomes. What policy or procedural changes, if any, resulted? What lessons have been learned?

REFERENCES AND RESOURCES

Adams, H. R. (2020). Advocating for intellectual freedom with principals and teachers. *Intellectual Freedom Issues in School Libraries* 23.

Freire, P. (1972). *Pedagogy of the oppressed Harmondsworth.* UK: Penguin, 19721.

Halpern, B. L., & Lubar, K. (2003). *Leadership presence: Dramatic techniques to reach out, motivate, and inspire.* Penguin Group.

Hannah-Jones, N., In Elliott, M., Hughes, J., Silverstein, J., (August 18, 2019). *The 1619 project.* New York Times Magazine. New York Times Company & Smithsonian Institution.

Hess, D. E., & McAvoy, P. (2015). *The political classroom: Evidence and ethics in democratic education.* Routledge.

Hirsch, E. D. (2020). *How to educate a citizen: The power of shared knowledge to unify a nation.* HarperCollins.

Linter, L. (2018). The controversy over controversy in the social studies classroom. *Southeastern Regional Association of Teacher Educators (SRATE) Journal* 27(1): 14–21.

Maxwell, B., Waddington, D. I., & McDonough, K. (2019). Academic freedom in primary and secondary school teaching. *Theory and Research in Education* 17(2): 119–138.

Morel, L. E. (2020). *A review of the 1619 Project Curriculum.* Backgrounder. No. 3570. Heritage Foundation.

Newberry, T., & Trujillo, O. V. (2018). Decolonizing education through transdisciplinary approaches to climate change education. In L. Tuhiwai Smith, E. Tuck, & K. W. Yang (Eds.), *Indigenous and decolonizing studies in education* (pp. 204–214). Routledge.

Null, W. (2016). *Curriculum: From theory to practice* (2nd ed.). Rowman & Littlefield.

Smith, L. T., Tuck, E., & Yang, K. W. (Eds.). (2018). *Indigenous and decolonizing studies in education: Mapping the long view.* Routledge.

Voros, F. (2017). Understanding the 14th Amendment. *Utah Bar Journal* 30(3), 10–15. PEN America.

Appendix: National Educational Leadership Preparation (NELP) Program Standards

BUILDING LEVEL

Standard 1: Mission, Vision, and Improvement

Candidates who successfully complete a building-level educational leadership preparation program understand and demonstrate the capacity to promote the current and future success and well-being of each student and adult by applying the knowledge, skills, and commitments necessary to collaboratively lead, design, and implement a school mission, vision, and process for continuous improvement that reflects a core set of values and priorities that include data use, technology, equity, diversity, digital citizenship, and community.

> Component 1.1: Program completers understand and demonstrate the capacity to collaboratively evaluate, develop, and communicate a school mission and vision designed to reflect a core set of values and priorities that include data use, technology, equity, diversity, digital citizenship, and community.
>
> Component 1.2: Program completers understand and demonstrate the capacity to lead improvement processes that include data use, design, implementation, and evaluation.

Candidates who successfully complete a building-level educational leadership preparation program understand and demonstrate the capacity to promote the current and future success and well-being of each student and adult by applying the knowledge, skills, and commitments necessary to understand and demonstrate the capacity to advocate for ethical decisions and cultivate and enact professional norms.

Standard 2: Ethics and Professional Norms

Component 2.1: Program completers understand and demonstrate the capacity to reflect on, communicate about, cultivate, and model professional dispositions and norms (i.e., fairness, integrity, transparency, trust, digital citizenship, collaboration, perseverance, reflection, lifelong learning) that support the educational success and well-being of each student and adult.

Component 2.2: Program completers understand and demonstrate the capacity to evaluate, communicate about, and advocate for ethical and legal decisions.

Component 2.3: Program completers understand and demonstrate the capacity to model ethical behavior in their personal conduct and relationships and to cultivate ethical behavior in others.

Standard 3: Equity, Inclusiveness, and Cultural Awareness

Candidates who successfully complete a building-level educational leadership preparation program understand and demonstrate the capacity to promote the current and future success and well-being of each student and adult by applying the knowledge, skills, and commitments necessary to develop and maintain a supportive, equitable, culturally responsive, and inclusive school culture.

Component 3.1: Program completers understand and demonstrate the capacity to use data to evaluate, design, cultivate, and advocate for a supportive and inclusive school culture.

Component 3.2: Program completers understand and demonstrate the capacity to evaluate, cultivate, and advocate for equitable access to educational resources, technologies, and opportunities that support the educational success and well-being of each student.

Component 3.3: Program completers understand and demonstrate the capacity to evaluate, cultivate, and advocate for equitable, inclusive, and culturally responsive instruction and behavior support practices among teachers and staff.

Standard 4: Learning and Instruction

Candidates who successfully complete a building-level educational leadership preparation program understand and demonstrate the capacity to promote the current and future success and well-being of each student and adult by applying the knowledge, skills, and commitments necessary to evaluate, develop, and implement coherent systems of curriculum, instruction, data systems, supports, and assessment.

> Component 4.1: Program completers understand and can demonstrate the capacity to evaluate, develop, and implement high-quality, technology-rich curricula programs and other supports for academic and non-academic student programs.
> Component 4.2: Program completers understand and can demonstrate the capacity to evaluate, develop, and implement high-quality and equitable academic and non-academic instructional practices, resources, technologies, and services that support equity, digital literacy, and the school's academic and non-academic systems.
> Component 4.3: Program completers understand and can demonstrate the capacity to evaluate, develop, and implement formal and informal culturally responsive and accessible assessments that support data-informed instructional improvement and student learning and well-being.
> Component 4.4: Program completers understand and demonstrate the capacity to collaboratively evaluate, develop, and implement the school's curriculum, instruction, technology, data systems, and assessment practices in a coherent, equitable, and systematic manner.

Standard 5: Community and External Leadership

Candidates who successfully complete a building-level educational leadership preparation program understand and demonstrate the capacity to promote the current and future success and well-being of each student and adult by applying the knowledge, skills, and commitments necessary to engage families, community, and school personnel in order to strengthen student learning, support school improvement, and advocate for the needs of their school and community.

> Component 5.1: Program completers understand and demonstrate the capacity to collaboratively engage diverse families in strengthening student learning in and out of school.
> Component 5.2: Program completers understand and demonstrate the capacity to collaboratively engage and cultivate relationships with

diverse community members, partners, and other constituencies for the benefit of school improvement and student development.

Component 5.3: Program completers understand and demonstrate the capacity to communicate through oral, written, and digital means within the larger organizational, community, and political contexts when advocating for the needs of their school and community.

Standard 6: Operations and Management

Candidates who successfully complete a building-level educational leadership preparation program understand and demonstrate the capacity to promote the current and future success and well-being of each student and adult by applying the knowledge, skills, and commitments necessary to improve management, communication, technology, school-level governance, and operation systems to develop and improve data-informed and equitable school resource plans and to apply laws, policies, and regulations.

Component 6.1: Program completers understand and demonstrate the capacity to evaluate, develop, and implement management, communication, technology, school-level governance, and operation systems that support each student's learning needs and promote the mission and vision of the school.

Component 6.2: Program completers understand and demonstrate the capacity to evaluate, develop, and advocate for a data-informed and equitable resourcing plan that supports school improvement and student development.

Component 6.3: Program completers understand and demonstrate the capacity to reflectively evaluate, communicate about, and implement laws, rights, policies, and regulations to promote student and adult success and well-being.

Standard 7: Building Professional Capacity

Candidates who successfully complete a building-level educational leadership preparation program understand and demonstrate the capacity to promote the current and future success and well-being of each student and adult by applying the knowledge, skills, and commitments necessary to build the school's professional capacity, engage staff in the development of a collaborative professional culture, and improve systems of staff supervision, evaluation, support, and professional learning.

Component 7.1: Program completers understand and have the capacity to collaboratively develop the school's professional capacity through engagement in recruiting, selecting, and hiring staff.

Component 7.2: Program completers understand and have the capacity to develop and engage staff in a collaborative professional culture designed to promote school improvement, teacher retention, and the success and well-being of each student and adult in the school.

Component 7.3: Program completers understand and have the capacity to personally engage in, as well as collaboratively engage school staff in, professional learning designed to promote reflection, cultural responsiveness, distributed leadership, digital literacy, school improvement, and student success.

Component 7.4: Program completers understand and have the capacity to evaluate, develop, and implement systems of supervision, support, and evaluation designed to promote school improvement and student success.

Standard 8: Internship

Candidates successfully complete an internship under the supervision of knowledgeable, expert practitioners that engages candidates in multiple and diverse school settings and provides candidates with coherent, authentic, and sustained opportunities to synthesize and apply the knowledge and skills identified in NELP standards 1–7 in ways that approximate the full range of responsibilities required of building-level leaders and enable them to promote the current and future success and well-being of each student and adult in their school.

Component 8.1: Candidates are provided a variety of coherent, authentic field and/or clinical internship experiences within multiple school environments that afford opportunities to interact with stakeholders, synthesize and apply the content knowledge, and develop and refine the professional skills articulated in each of the components included in NELP building-level program standards 1–7.

Component 8.2: Candidates are provided a minimum of six months of concentrated (10–15 hours per week) internship or clinical experiences that include authentic leadership activities within a school setting.

Component 8.3: Candidates are provided a mentor who has demonstrated effectiveness as an educational leader within a building setting; is present for a significant portion of the internship; is selected collaboratively by the intern, a representative of the school and/or district, and program faculty; and has received training from the supervising institution.

References

Halpern, B. L., & Lubar, K. (2003). *Leadership presence: Dramatic techniques to reach out, motivate, and inspire.* Penguin Group.

NPBEA. (2018). *National Educational Leadership Preparation (NELP) Program Standards - Building Level.* Retrieved from www.npbea.org.

Pace, N. J. (2009). *The principal's challenge: Learning from gay and lesbian students.* Information Age.

Pace, N. J. (2013). *Reality calling: The story of a principal's first semester.* Rowman & Littlefield Education.

Pace, N. J. (2014). *Seeking balance: The story of a principal's second semester.* Rowman & Littlefield Education.

About the Authors and Contributors

Nicholas J. Pace, former social worker, teacher, coach, and principal, serves as professor and chair of the Department of Educational Administration at the University of Nebraska-Lincoln. His passion and scholarly focus has been on preparing and sustaining school principals. He is author of four books on the principalship, including *Reality Calling* (2013) and *Seeking Balance* (2014), which are fictional accounts of the events in a principal's first year, and *The Principal's Hot Seat* (2011), which features video footage from an intense role play he developed in 2007. Dr. Pace's work has been published in *Educational Leadership Review, American School Board Journal,* and the *Journal of Advanced Academics.* He has maintained professional affiliations with state-level school administrator associations, the National Rural Education Association, and University Council for Educational Administration.

Pace earned his bachelor of arts in sociology and doctor of education in educational leadership from the University of Northern Iowa and master of science in education from Drake University. He was inducted to the Iowa Academy of Education in 2016 and received the UNI College of Education Award for Outstanding Scholarship and Diversity Matters Award, both in 2012. Outreach and dissemination of his research into the school experiences of gay and lesbian high school students (Pace, 2009) led to his receipt of the Iowa Friend of Civil Rights Award in 2010. He describes himself as a husband, father, seeker, leader, lover of satire, and University of Northern Iowa men's basketball.

Shavonna L. Holman is an Assistant Professor of Practice in the Department of Educational Administration at the University of Nebraska–Lincoln (UNL). She brings a multifaceted understanding of education and educational leadership through her many experiences and perspectives from a unique combination of training, practical classroom experience as a public school teacher and administrator, experience in teaching teachers, and service as the president of the board of education for the Omaha (NE) Public Schools. As the M.Ed. program coordinator, she is instrumental in the development and implementation of the P–12 School Leadership program at UNL. In addition, she advises master's students and teaches M.Ed., ELHE, and Ed.D./Ph.D. courses in the College of Education and Human Sciences. As a former public school administrator, she understands the critical value of good leadership within schools, from district administrators, from the school board, and from those leaders at Nebraska Department of Education and that all decisions, from policies to the actual operational level, affect achievement directly and indirectly.

Holman received her bachelor's in elementary education, master's in elementary education, and master's in administration and supervision from the University of Nebraska-Omaha and her doctoral degree in educational administration from the University of Nebraska-Lincoln, with a focus on race, class, access, gender, and equity. She has been recognized for her efforts as an educator and public servant by receiving the University of Nebraska-Omaha College of Public Affairs and Community Service Alumni Award (2021), the University of Nebraska-Lincoln Distinguished Teaching Award (2019) and the UNL College of Education and Human Sciences Outstanding Teaching Award (2018).

Cailen M. O'Shea is a former mentor, interventionist, teacher, athletic and academic coach, and currently serves as an assistant professor of educational and organizational leadership at North Dakota State University. His research interests focus on school transformation and equitable instructional leadership. Specifically, he looks at ways educational leaders can enhance instruction for all students. He utilizes both quantitative and qualitative research methodologies. Dr. O'Shea's work has been published in *The Rural Educator*, *The Journal of School Administration Research and Development*, the *University Council for Educational Administration*, *Journal of School Leadership*, *International Journal of Modern Education Studies*, and *International Journal of Modern Education Studies Open.* He serves as an affiliate faculty/Advisory Board member for the Center for the Advanced Study of Technology Leadership in Education.

O'Shea earned his bachelor of arts in elementary education, a master of educational administration, a master of elementary mathematics, and a doctorate in educational studies (educational leadership and higher education) from the University of Nebraska-Lincoln. He describes himself as a husband, father, educator, and lover of sports and the outdoors.

* * *

Martin Beckner is a lieutenant with the Cedar Falls, Iowa, Police Department and a certified instructor in de-escalation and use of force. He has taught de-escalation for a variety of groups and organizations for more than 15 years. Marty lives in Cedar Falls, Iowa, with his family and enjoys volunteering with community projects.

Emily Borcherding is a PhD candidate at Iowa State University and the Student Success and Learning Coordinator at the University of Northern Iowa. After earning her BA in mathematics and Spanish teaching from the University of Northern Iowa (UNI) and three years of high school math teaching and volleyball and basketball coaching, Emily completed her master's degree in postsecondary education (student affairs) at UNI. Since that time, she has been working in academic support and teaching at UNI. In her spare time, she likes to play and watch sports, bike, and listen to and play music.

Meena Pannirselvam is a graduate student in the Educational Administration Student Affairs master's program and is a graduate assistant at the Office of Academic Success and Intercultural Services at the University of Nebraska-Lincoln (UNL). After transferring from Malaysia, Meena completed her bachelor of science in business administration at UNL where she majored in finance and minored in economics. As an international student, she is passionate about the betterment of international students' college experience which led to cofounding the International Student Advisory Board, where she advocates for international students. Aside from drinking coffee, Meena enjoys reading anything mystery-, crime-, or horror-related and painting.

Ann Marie Pollard is a voice and movement coach based in Lincoln, Nebraska. Through her private studio, Voice: Realized, she supports and empowers people of all professions to come into the fullest expression of their physical and vocal presence. She serves as an assistant professor of practice at the Johnny Carson School of Theatre & Film and as the resident voice, text, and dialect Coach at the Nebraska Repertory Theatre. You can learn more about her at voicerealized.com.

"PRINCIPALS" AND ACTORS

During **Dr. Willie Barney**'s 23 years in education, he has had an impactful experience as the superintendent of one of Iowa's, if not the country's, most unique educational environments. He has been successful in leadership roles in an urban school district central office. He has provided transformative leadership as the principal of one of Iowa's most diverse high schools and served as both an assistant high school principal and a junior high principal in one of Iowa's larger socioeconomically diverse districts. Much of Dr. Barney's spare time is spent with his wife and their six children engaging in a wide range of sports, activities, and service. A guiding question for Dr. Barney is, "What are you doing to make an impact?"

Erin Blaha is in her second year as an assistant principal for the Omaha (NE) Public School (OPS) district. Prior to entering administration, Erin was an instructional facilitator and literacy facilitator for the Omaha Public Schools. Erin started her career in OPS teaching second grade. She holds a bachelor's degree in elementary education from Iowa State University, a master's in educational administration from Concordia University, and a master's in leadership and teaching and learning from Midland University. When not at school, Erin enjoys gardening, crafting, and spending time with her family and taking her two boys to various athletic events.

Todd Coulter is in his fourth year as the education supervisor for the State Training School for Boys in Eldora, Iowa. Prior to joining STS, he spent 13 years an assistant principal and athletic director administrator in the Waterloo (IA) Community School District. Prior to entering administration, Todd taught physical education and health at all levels. When not at school, Todd likes to spend time watching his children in their athletic pursuits and competing in various road and trail races around Northeast Iowa. His wife, Stacey, is also an educator for the Waterloo Schools.

Dan Cox is a lifelong Iowan who has served students, staff, and families in rural and urban settings across the state as a teacher, principal, and superintendent of schools. In 2018, he became chief administrator of Northwest Area Education Agency in Sioux City, Iowa. Cox earned his BA and MA from the University of Northern Iowa and his PhD in education from Iowa State University. He was a corecipient of the Jordan Larson Outstanding Ph.D. Student award at Iowa State. Professionally, Cox served as president of the School Administrators of Iowa and is the president-elect of the Rotary Club of Sioux City. Cox is an avid world traveler; he and his wife, Lisa, have traversed six continents and look forward to finally making it to Africa.

Jonathan Cox coordinates the TRiO/EOP programs at University of Northern Iowa Center for Urban Education. A former college basketball player and coach, Jonathan has also served as a head of school security. He lives with his son in Waterloo, Iowa, where he is active in youth mentoring programs.

Jeff Dieken has been a high school principal since 2007 in the Hudson (IA) Community School District. Prior to receiving his MAE in principalship from the University of Northern Iowa, Jeff taught high school English at Waterloo (IA) West High School. An avid sports fan, Jeff, his wife (a school counselor), and two daughters attend most Northern Iowa football and basketball games. Jeff plans to continue his studies in educational leadership.

Deb Donlea is a first-grade teacher at Center Point-Urbana (IA) Primary School. She completed her master of arts in principalship from the University of Northern Iowa and plans to pursue an administrative position. Deb lives in Winthrop, Iowa, with her husband, Jason, and two daughters.

Anel Garza De Sandoval is the elementary principal for Woodbury Elementary's dual language program in Marshalltown, Iowa. She obtained her master of arts in principalship from the University of Northern Iowa. She continues to work in the area of dual language education in her district, town, and state. Anel lives in Marshalltown with her husband, José, and their two children.

Kyle Green is an assistant men's basketball coach at Iowa State University. He has been a college basketball coach at the Division I, II and III levels for the past 17 years and spent three years as a junior high and high school social studies teacher in Minneapolis, Minnesota. Kyle played collegiate basketball at Hamline University in St. Paul, Minnesota, graduating in 1992. Following his collegiate playing career, he spent one year playing professionally in Denmark. Kyle is married and the father of a 21-year-old son and an 18-year-old daughter.

Tina Harvey is a 1996 alum of Plattsmouth (NE) High School. She went on to graduate from Nebraska Wesleyan University with a bachelor's in music education in 2000. Following graduation, Mrs. Harvey started her career in the Bellevue (NE) Public Schools teaching elementary general music and beginning band. During this time, she earned a master of education in curriculum development from Peru State College followed by a certification in educational administration from the University of Nebraska–Lincoln. Mrs. Harvey served as a lead teacher in Bellevue (NE) Public Schools before joining the Plattsmouth (NE) Community School District in 2014 as the elementary general music teacher. She is currently the Plattsmouth (NE) High School band director.

Amy Hawkins serves as the chief human resource Director for the Dubuque (IA) Community School District. She holds a bachelor's degree in education from Winona State University and a master's degree in principalship from the University of Northern Iowa. She is in her second year of the superintendency program at the University of Northern Iowa. A former college volleyball player, Amy has also coached at the high school and college levels. Amy and her husband Jeremy live in Dubuque, Iowa, with their two daughters, Madelyn and Morgan.

Gwen Hefel-Busch serves as the department chair of special education at Thomas Jefferson Middle School in Dubuque, Iowa. She started her career by earning her bachelor's degree from the University of Dubuque in 1998 and completed her master's in principalship from the University of Northern Iowa in 2010. Her background involves teaching in a self-contained behavior disorder classroom at the middle school level for ten years. Through her dedication and commitment to her students, she earned Walmart's Dubuque Teacher of the Year award in 2005. Now as department chair, she serves as a liaison between classroom teachers, area education agency consultants, and administration. Gwen has also become a certified Crisis Intervention Prevention trainer who works with district staff in the art of classroom management and de-escalation techniques. Another important aspect of her position is to serve as the Medicaid lead teacher. Gwen enjoys spending quality time with her husband and three children.

Megan Hillabrand is the professional development manager for the Nebraska Council of School Administrators (NCSA), where she has worked for seven years. Prior to NCSA, Megan worked in the surgical residency program at Creighton University and began her education career as a high school social studies teacher and coach. When not at work, you'll likely find Megan outside digging in and harvesting her garden, out exploring on her bike, or enjoying the company of her husband, family, and friends on a patio somewhere.

Patrick Hunter-Pirtle, EdD, is in his ninth year as the director of secondary education for the Lincoln (NE) Public Schools (LPS). He appraises and works with all middle school, high school, and focus program principals throughout the district. Prior to this position, Pat was an associate principal for eight years and principal for eleven years at Lincoln (NE) Southeast High School. He began his administrative journey as an assistant principal at Junction City (KS) Middle School. Pat taught English and social studies for thirteen years at LPS Mickle Junior High, Strake Jesuit High School (Houston, TX), Indian Hill Junior High (Omaha, NE), and LPS Southeast High School. Pat has two adult children, a daughter in Lincoln, and a son in Denver, Colorado. Pat's wife of forty years, Rae, is a secretary in the media department at LPS.

Jeremy Jones is the principal at Holmes Junior High School in the Cedar Falls (IA) Community School District. He has also served as an administrator in various roles in the South Tama (IA) Community School District. He currently resides in Cedar Falls with his wife, Michelle, and three children, Blake, Alexandra, and Emmersyn.

Jeremy Langner is the principal at Waverly-Shell Rock (IA) Middle School, which serves approximately 720 students. He earned his undergraduate and MAE in principalship at the University of Northern Iowa. Jeremy's past work has included assistant principal at Waterloo (IA) West High School and assistant principal at Waverly-Shell Rock (IA) High School. Jeremy and his wife Becky, an elementary educator, live in Waverly, Iowa, where they are raising their three kids.

Brenda Leggiadro, PhD, is starting her ninth year in student services in the Lincoln (NE) Public Schools (LPS), where she supervises the school counseling and school social work programs. Prior to her role in student services, Brenda was a high school counselor for 24 years in LPS and Chadron (NE) City Schools. Outside of school, Brenda enjoys spending time with family and friends.

Dr. Mary Beth Lehmanowsky is a retired educator. She worked for many years in the Lincoln (NE) Public Schools (LPS) as a high school teacher, counselor, assistant principal, principal, and human resources supervisor. Upon leaving LPS, she served for several years as a professor of practice at the University of Nebraska-Lincoln Department of Educational Administration.

Dr. Jane Lindaman serves as the superintendent of Waterloo (IA) Schools. She holds a bachelor's degree in middle school education and master's and doctorate degrees in educational leadership from the University of Northern Iowa. After teaching math for six years, she served as a middle school principal for 12 years. She has been in central office administration for the past 15 years, with the last seven as the superintendent in Waterloo. She is passionate about student achievement, closing the achievement gap, and career development for K-12 students. Jane and her husband, Steve, live in Waterloo, Iowa, and their two sons attend Waterloo Schools.

Dr. Cheryl Logan began her position as superintendent of Omaha (NE) Public Schools on July 1, 2018. Logan comes to OPS from the School District of Philadelphia (PA), where she served as Chief Academic Officer, responsible for the academic achievement of more than 135,000 students. Logan has spent her career in education working in school districts with large immigrant populations from around the world, including with students from significant English language learner populations. Fluent in Spanish, she holds a bachelor of science degree from the University of Maryland, a master of education degree from Johns Hopkins University, and a doctor of education degree from the University of Pennsylvania. In addition to other forms of diversity among the communities in which she has served, Dr. Logan believes a superintendent must collaborate with students, teachers, parents, the board of education, the broader community, and business and faith partners in the service of children and families.

McKenna Machal is in her fifth year as a special education teacher specializing in behavior at Pershing Elementary in Lincoln, Nebraska. She has worked with students in grades K-5 in those five years but has specifically been a case manager for students in third through fifthth grades. McKenna attended the University of Nebraska-Lincoln for her undergraduate degree in elementary education & special education (K-6) and then again for her graduate degree in education administration. When not teaching, McKenna enjoys spending time with her two-year-old son, husband, and two very spoiled dogs.

Colleen McBride is an eighth grade English teacher at Moore Middle School in Lincoln (NE), entering her thirteenth year of teaching. She enjoys working with students and empowering them to learn and grow in order to give them what they need to work towards their dreams and improve their communities. She has served in several leadership roles, including team leader, department chair, and MTSS Tier I Team Leader. Colleen recently finished her master's in educational administration and hopes to begin to pursue her EdD within the next few years. Colleen enjoys spending time with her family, including her four-month-old, Charlie, working out, yard work, and long walks with her dog, Robin. Her husband, Andrew is also an educator and works at Irving Middle School in Lincoln.

Heather McDonald is a high school English teacher at Denver (IA) Community School District. She holds a master of arts in English language and literature and an MAE in principalship from the University of Northern Iowa. Heather enjoys traveling and reading and with her husband in Waterloo, Iowa.

Jesse Neugebauer is in his ninth year as a classroom teacher. He currently works in Scottsbluff (NE) Public Schools teaching third grade. Previously, he was employed with Metro Nashville (TN) Public Schools, where he worked in both urban and inner-city settings. His roles have included team leader, single-gender (male) classroom instructor, social-emotional learning and restorative practices committee chairman, third/fourth grade long-distance learning expedition coordinator, and district model teacher/eLearner instruction facilitator for third grade. Jesse also enjoys pursuing personal fitness goals, horticulture, traveling, and getting lost in the latest literature.

Emily O'Donnell is currently an assistant principal at Liberty High School in the Iowa City Community School district in North Liberty, Iowa. She holds a bachelor's degree in mathematics education from the University of Iowa and a master's in middle school mathematics and a principalship advanced studies certificate from the University of Northern Iowa (UNI). Emily lives in North Liberty with her husband and three sons and enjoys spending time with her family watching sports and being outdoors.

Angela Olsen is the business partnerships/STEAM coordinator and district office director in Spirit Lake, Iowa. Her experiences range from eleven years teaching high school math in Algona (IA) and Estherville (IA), to five years of math at Sprit Lake (IA) Middle School before transferring to curriculum, administration, and her current teacher leader role. Angela and her husband, Shawn, live in Spirit Lake, where they enjoy spending time with their two children, Kyler (junior at the University of Northern Iowa) and Karli (a freshman at Dordt University), bicycle riding, and all outdoor activities. Angela's individual interests include running, reading ,and tutoring students in math.

Dr. Heather Olsen is a professor at the University of Northern Iowa's College of Education and provides global leadership for the National Program for Playground Safety. Her research focuses on playground injury prevention and contextual understanding of thermal comfort as it relates to outdoor play targeting children's health and well-being. Her favorite pastime is spending time with her family outdoors and cherishing the stages of raising four children.

Dameon Place is the high school band director in Pella, Iowa. He graduated with his master's degree in educational leadership from the University of Northern Iowa in 2011. Dameon enjoys spending time outdoors, taking camping trips with his family, and canoeing. His wife, Lindsay, is a preschool teacher turned stay-at-home mom with their three children, Henry, Warren, and Greta.

Kyle Poore is in his third year as security coordinator for Lincoln (NE) Public Schools (LPS). Prior to taking on this role, Kyle held many leadership positions as a teacher including summer school principal and eighth grade team leader. Kyle taught for 15 years at Crete (NE) Middle School, before moving to Goodrich Middle School in Lincoln, Nebraska, for a year and a half. Kyle enjoyed officiating basketball for over 22 years, but just recently retired. Kyle and his wife, Shelley, are avid Husker Volleyball fans. Shelley is a sixth grade humanities teacher at LPS Irving Middle School.

Amber N. Robinson serves as principal of the Royal Legacy Christian Academy in Waterloo, Iowa. She holds a bachelor's degree from Wartburg College in American and world history, a master's degree in curriculum and instruction from the University of Northern Iowa, a master's degree in effective teaching: talented and gifted from Drake University, and a doctorate in educational leadership from the University of Northern Iowa, where the focus of her qualitative research was how African American girls experience school in predominantly white environments. She enjoys traveling and speaking on issues of race, privilege, and implicit bias; however, she has the most fun spending time with her husband, Marshaundus, and two daughters, Ava James and Riley James.

Karolyn Roby is a teaching & learning consultant for the Omaha (NE) Public School District (OPS). Prior to entering administration, she spent three years as a summer school principal, four years as an instructional facilitator, twelve years as an educator, one year as a classroom paraprofessional, and eight years as a school secretary, all with OPS. Outside of school, Karolyn likes to travel, read, and spend time with her grandchildren.

Dan Scannell serves as a special education teacher at Peet Junior High School in Cedar Falls, Iowa. In addition to his duties as special education collaborator in English, social studies, science, and behavioral skills development. Dan is a member of the district's crisis intervention and prevention (CPI) training team. Recently, over the last six years, Dan has developed an interest in coaching and works as an assistant coach for eighth grade football, men's sophomore/junior varsity/varsity basketball, and trapshooting. Dan earned his master of arts in principalship from the University of Northern Iowa and continues to pursue leadership and learning experiences. In his leisure time, Dan enjoys live music, travel, and spending time with friends and family. Dan lives in Cedar Falls, Iowa, with his wife, Heather, and his daughter.

Dr. John Skretta is the administrator for Educational Service Unit #6 (ESU) headquartered in Milford, Nebraska, serving 16 public school districts across five counties. As the chief administrator for the ESU, Dr. Skretta provides consultative support to school district superintendents and oversees the provision of core services to school systems, including professional development and technology. Prior to serving in his current role, Dr. Skretta was a superintendent, assistant superintendent, and high school principal. He began his education career as a high school English teacher at Northeast High School in Lincoln, Nebraska.

Dr. Kim Snyder is the director of statewide teacher and principal support at the Nebraska Department of Education (NDE), where she provides leadership for the development and implementation of Nebraska's Educator Effectiveness system, called Supporting Educator Effectiveness through Development. She has also served as the statewide coordinator of the National Assessment of Educational Progress and as an accreditation specialist for the NDE. Prior to joining the NDE, Dr. Snyder served as a Nebraska educator for 27 years. She enjoys traveling with her husband, who serves as a middle school band director with Lincoln Public Schools.

David W. Stamp is a trial lawyer practicing in Waterloo, Iowa. He received his bachelor's degree from the University of Northern Iowa and his law degree from the University of Iowa College of Law. David, his wife Linda, and all three of their sons are active in music and theater. David enjoys any opportunity to be on a stage, whether it is public speaking at a professional seminar, acting in a community theater play, or performing in a local bar band. However, all his sons are more talented than he is at all these things, so you should see them when you can.

James Watson Jr. is in his eighth year as a special education teacher for Lincoln (NE) Public Schools. James started his teaching career at the Don D. Sherrill Education Center, then moved to Lincoln High School, where he taught adjusted English for five years. The past year James taught physical education and Yankee Hill School. James is also currently the head freshman football coach as well as the head shot put coach for the Lincoln High Links. When not at school, James enjoys weight lifting and playing various sports. His wife Kim is also an educator for the Malcolm (NE) Public Schools.

Karen Weires is a high school mathematics teacher and gifted/talented facilitator in Dubuque, Iowa. She completed the principalship program at the University of Northern Iowa and holds a master's degree in the teaching of mathematics from the University of Illinois at Chicago.

VIDEO PRODUCTION

Paige Besler graduated from the University of Northern Iowa with a degree in general communication and a minor in leisure, youth, and human services. She currently works as a development project manager at Spotix.

Daniel Hartig is currently a video producer responsible for leading the video services department for the College of Education and Human Sciences at the University of Nebraska-Lincoln. Dan received a bachelor's degree in broadcast journalism from the University of Nebraska-Lincoln. While in college, he worked various production positions at a local television station. After graduation, he headed west, where he worked several jobs in California and Arizona before starting his own media production company. In his free time, Dan enjoys traveling, outdoor activities, spending time with friends and family.

Gregory LaVern Lilly was born and raised in the dairy hills of Southwest Iowa. He is currently freelancing for several production companies & advertising agencies across the midwest, producing video film projects for TV commercials: including Oscar Mayer hotd ogs, Kool Aid, Taco John's, BoysTown Hospital, Marriott Hotels, etc. In Greg's free time, he enjoys long-distance bike camping and gardening and advocates for multimodal transportation.

Joe Marchesani is currently the audio/video production coordinator for ITS-Educational Technology and an assistant professor of education in the Department of Curriculum and Instruction at the University of Northern Iowa, where he has been since 1972. Joe received a BA in communications from fFordham University and an MS in speech with a television production emphasis from Brooklyn College. He also obtained an MEd in educational media from Temple University . His wife (Joan), son (David), and daughter (Kristina) all received degrees from UNI, and his son and daughter also work there.

Made in the USA
Monee, IL
08 May 2023

33341433R00136